Dispatches From the Sofa:
The Collected Wisdom of Frank Skinner

ALSO BY FRANK SKINNER

Frank Skinner on the Road
Frank Skinner

Dispatches From the Sofa: The Collected Wisdom of Frank Skinner

Frank Skinner

CENTURY · LONDON

Published by Century 2011
2 4 6 8 10 9 7 5 3 1

First published in Great Britain in 2011 by
Century
Random House, 20 Vauxhall Bridge Road,
London SW1V 2SA

www.randomhouse.co.uk

Addresses for companies within The Random House Group Limited can be found at:
www.randomhouse.co.uk

The Random House Group Limited Reg. No. 954009

A CIP catalogue record for this book
is available from the British Library

Hardback ISBN 9781846059872
Trade paperback ISBN 9781846059698

The Random House Group Limited supports The Forest Stewardship Council (FSC®),
the leading international forest certification organisation. Our books carrying the FSC
label are printed on FSC® certified paper. FSC is the only forest certification scheme
endorsed by the leading environmental organisations, including Greenpeace.
Our paper procurement policy can be found at
www.randomhouse.co.uk/environment

Typeset in Sabon by Palimpsest Book Production Limited,
Falkirk, Stirlingshire
Printed and bound in Great Britain by
Clays Ltd, St Ives plc

For Cath.
Hot and cold beneath the coyote.

Contents

Introduction

I tend not to read introductions to books. They're like ramps, designed to gently raise the reader to a level where they're ready to begin the book proper. I'd say most people are happy to take on, unaided, the sudden steep incline of a chapter one. However, with a book like this one – a collection of various writings – it feels polite to meet you at the door with a site map so you can get your bearings.

Of course, introductions aren't always written by the author of the book. Sometimes they're by another writer – a fan of the book – who's keen to whet your appetite and get you to share their enthusiasm for the work. That kind of introduction is much easier to write. You can rave about the book and the author's many qualities until the reader is straining like a police dog on a leash, desperate to get at the main body of the text. It's a bit trickier to whip up that kind of frenzy when you're talking about your own writing. 'Read this and see how brilliant I am' is an approach that could alienate some people. Better I draw you in with a slightly more circumspect rallying call.

The bulk of the book comprises the weekly columns I wrote for *The Times* newspaper from January 2009 till January 2011. Don't panic. I know no one wants yesterday's papers but the columns, though they are often inspired by a specific news story, soon break free from the shackles of topicality and produce what I would unhesitatingly describe, if I was someone else writing an introduction to this book, as timeless wit and wisdom. The initial facts become a springboard to other things. Thus, a column that begins with a description of Cliff Richard's 2011 calendar soon becomes an essay on the dangers of moderation and another, concerning the joys of air-guitar, morphs into a critique of secular society – with jokes, obviously.

I also include an unpublished obituary I wrote for *The Times* in June 2009. It was unpublished because Margaret Thatcher didn't die after all. Any aspiring writers should note that, when it comes to obituaries, the non-death of the subject can severely hamper publication. It's taken me two-and-a-half years to find a way around it.

Considering these columns were written over a period of two years there's only a tiny bit of repetition. A couple of images and the odd brief anecdote reappear but are employed for quite different purposes. See them like the leitmotifs in a Wagnerian epic. Does that sound a little grand? The truth is you can get a bit carried away with a newspaper column. You feel you have the ear of the people. I honestly thought my ideas for a Prime Ministerial speech to get the electorate back onside would be taken up by Gordon Brown and ultimately win Labour the 2011 election. I also thought my scheme for performance-based student tuition fees would radically change the UK's Higher Education system. Perhaps the column on the thrills of daydreaming explains how I managed to get so carried away.

There's also a longer article about the largely uncelebrated joys of staying in at night and a short story that originally appeared in the *Sunday Times* magazine. The latter is something of an oddity. The editor asked me if I'd write a short story based on Shakespeare's Ophelia. I decided to turn the whimpering victim into a tough, calculating survivor but I felt she should still sound like a Shakespearean character. All I had to do was write like Shakespeare. I don't mean with a big feather, I mean I somehow had to recreate his style. I didn't go as far as a 'thee' or 'thou'. I just put in some words that tickled the lips on the way out and deliberately made my sentences a bit bouncier than usual. It's the first short story I ever wrote. I'm currently trying to peddle it as a half-hour monologue for radio. All it needs is a bit of incidental lute music and we're off. The radio version, like this book, would be an inspirational monument to recycling.

In 2005 I started writing what I now like to refer to as my great unfinished novel. Called *Thunderman and Geoff Phillips*, it was a sort of superhero story but while I wanted it to have the same visceral punch as a modern American comic book, I also wanted it to be very British, and funny – a sort of *Carry On The Dark Knight*. I hadn't read a novel for years and I got it into my head that this was a positive advantage. I would be untarnished by influence. It would be a novel by someone who didn't know what novels were supposed to be. I figured that would make it very original and almost certainly prize-winning. Again, the column on daydreaming may be enlightening here. About 50,000 words in, I decided that any gift I had in the prose department was probably more to do with expression than invention and so I gave up on the project. I've included the first two chapters of *Thunderman and Geoff Phillips* to give you a little taster. If I was someone else writing an introduction to this book, I'd say this great unfinished novel has a sort of Baroque richness to it, heavy with strange digressions and internal dialogues – with jokes, obviously. I've thought about trying to redo it but I can't remember the password for the document containing the other chapters. That isn't a joke. It may, however, be an act of God. I must say, I enjoyed revisiting it after so long. It's written with a lottery-winner-like excess but that makes it a nice contrast to the all-lean-meat discipline of the 900-word columns.

If there was an FAQ section, I'm sure 'Is this a toilet book?' would be on the list. Well, by way of celebrating its four-hundredth anniversary, I've been reading the King James Version of the Bible on the toilet of late. It helps me to understand the concept of God truly becoming man. Consequently, I've come to see *every* book as a potential toilet book. However, if you're actually asking me 'Can this book be easily broken down into shite-sized chunks?' the answer is yes. Now shut up about it. Can't you see I'm trying to pass myself off as an intellectual? I'm not saying I don't talk about toilets any more but, when I do, I try and make it sound spiritual.

Anyway, I'll take your hat and coat and leave you to wander around at your own pace. If I was the sort of person who said 'enjoy' I'd say 'enjoy'. However, generally speaking, I find such people to be imbeciles. Then again, I don't find them as idiotic as people who say 'squillions'. Oh, anyway, I don't have time to list all the key words to look out for when assessing people's varying levels of stupidity. As a general rule-of-thumb, if they're reading this book and either laughing out loud or saying 'That's a really good point. I never thought of that' they are bright as a button and ideal for breeding purposes. Now get stuck in and don't come back till you've found at least one quote you'll use for the rest of your life.

Frank Skinner,
June 2011

PART ONE
THE TIMES COLUMNS

Redneck Revelation: or how I learned to see through the ink and discover the sweet soul within

16 JANUARY 2009

Having scratched around for a couple of weeks I seem to have, at last, arrived at my New Year's resolution for 2009. It's a decision I take seriously. I'm extremely keen on the idea of self-improvement and always on the lookout for another piece in the 'perfect me' jigsaw. I make my New Year's resolutions in pairs, mainly because I resolved, in 1986, to learn French and, having failed to do so, have made that my rollover resolution for each succeeding year. My only advances in that area have come through the Michel Thomas language tapes. Thomas, who died a few years back, was something of a legend on the language circuit. One of his claims to fame, according to the official website, is that he taught Doris Day Spanish so she could sing her most famous song, 'Que Sera, Sera'. As I recall, there are only two Spanish words in 'Que Sera, Sera'. They are 'que' and 'sera'. Ms Day's diligence is an inspiration to us all.

Anyway, as learning French has become my default resolution, I like to combine it, for the sake of variety, with a second, slightly higher-minded one. For example, last year I pledged I would 'listen more'. (In an effort to kill two birds with one stone, I actually wrote 'écouter plus' on my calendar.) I wanted to curtail my unfortunate habit of interrupting people. It went well, though I'm sure some friends, once they became aware of my efforts, started to deliberately tempt me with unnecessary pauses.

This New Year, however, I struggled to come up with the second resolution. Then, last weekend, I was on a plane flying from Houston to Miami. In front of me sat a grey-haired lady and a teenager I rightly assumed to be her grandson. I don't want to be unkind but the youth didn't look like someone who'd be your first choice for phone-a-friend. He was one of those teenage lads who seem to regard breathing through the nose as an unnecessary risk. Soon, however, his blank expression switched to one of concern. He beckoned the rest of the family, seated nearby, and they scurried towards him. The first was a long-haired man with tattoos that covered his hands and arms and crept up his neck to the tops of his ears. I guessed his whole body was tattooed. The general theme seemed to be demons and skulls. 'You OK, Mom?' he said to the old lady, in an accent you'd normally expect to hear accompanied by banjo music. The old lady stared at him but did not reply. He was soon joined by two women with similarly wide-ranging tattoos. I imagined the three of them naked, arm in arm, forming some sort of sweaty triptych. Still the old lady just stared. Tears began to moisten the eyes of the long-haired man. I'd become the accidental witness to this family's crisis but, though I hate to admit it, the tragedy was somewhat diffused for me by *The Jerry Springer Show* nature of the dramatis personae.

Soon an announcement asked if there was a doctor on board. A tired-looking woman, probably mid-thirties, in a crumpled T-shirt and tracksuit bottoms, appeared. She had dark hair pulled roughly back and a noticeably bad complexion. She took the old lady's hand and knelt in the aisle beside her. I'd never seen such caring in anyone's eyes. As soon as she fitted her stethoscope, this drab little woman seemed to be transformed by her vocation. She continued to hold the old woman's hand, speaking kindly to her, trying to get through. At the same time, she calmly quizzed the family about the patient's recent health and any medication she may have been on and instructed a stewardess to fit the old lady with an oxygen mask. When she then told the sick woman to breathe through her nose, the grandson took on the expression of someone witnessing an elaborate magic trick. As all this unfolded, the long-haired man stood gently stroking his mother's hair and repeating in a near-whisper, 'Can you hear me, Mom?' Happily, it became apparent that she could.

I felt bad. I had dismissed these people as white trash but they weren't trash, they were a close, loving family. Come to think of it they weren't even that white. They were mainly blue with some red bits. The doctor also was a challenge to my assumptions. As soon as she saw the sick woman, she came to life, became dynamic, heroic even. So here was my New Year's resolution – don't judge a book by its cover. Assume everyone, even the heavily tattooed, have an inner beauty, not necessarily apparent.

The plane made an unscheduled stop at Tampa and four burly medics, all scrubbed and professional, boarded the plane and took the old lady away in a wheelchair, the family following on behind. These medics barely acknowledged the doctor. Once her patient had gone, she shrunk back to ordinariness and shuffled back to her seat. Nevertheless, my resolution was now in place. And it was soon reaping benefits. The next day I got in a cab driven by a grubby woman with badly dyed blonde hair who, on further investigation, turned out to be a former professional ballet dancer and now an enthusiastic cheap-seat regular at the Miami City Ballet. Of course, there will be disappointments, but then you know what Doris Day said.

Why comedians are cleverer than journalists

23 JANUARY 2009

So I've got a column in *The Times*, I'm discussing new films and novels on BBC Two's *Newsnight Review* tonight and, on Monday, I'm presenting *Panorama*. I seem to have become a one-man dumbing-down operation. Understandably, this has wound some people up. Janet Street-Porter, who I must say I've always liked, suggested in her newspaper column that employing me as a presenter proved that *Panorama* was no longer a 'heavyweight programme'. It seems the government's call for more liberal attitudes towards social mobility is falling on deaf ears. If the show was about Gaza or the social services, I'd see Janet's point but, as it is instead about swearing and bad taste on television, getting me in has the same logic as getting Sue Barker in to do the tennis. I've been swearing and making off-colour remarks on television since 1988. I'm calling that credentials.

I remember the same dumbing-down accusations when Jo Brand first did *Question Time*. I think this is just comedianism. Serious TV presenters are saying stuff like 'These comedians, coming over here, taking our jobs.' And then there's the prevalence of comedianist language. What does it say about a society when words like 'comedian', 'joker' and 'clown' are used as insults?

There is definitely a strong feeling that comics should stick to comedy. I honestly sympathise with that. A comedian who wants to be taken seriously is like a politician who wants to show us their human side, best viewed with mistrust. But I don't want to be taken seriously; it's just that occasionally doing serious stuff makes a nice change. And, the truth is, it's much easier than doing comedy. I know I set myself up for a fall by saying that but it's a fact.

Over the last few weeks, I've interviewed several people for *Panorama*. Obviously, you have to read up on them and have a sense of where you want the interview to go but it's a walk in the park compared to the comedy interviews I did when I had a chat show. A serious interview is just asking questions. It's like helping someone to fill in a form. Then you get what's known as the hard-hitting interview. It's still just asking questions except you ask some of them three or four times. A comedy interview, such as you'll see on tonight's *Jonathan Ross* show, is genuine multi-tasking – like doing an interview and a stand-up act at the same time. Questions are only part of the equation. You have to lead the interviewee towards the clip of them falling over in a charity football match or that paparazzi shot of them snogging someone from Girls Aloud and then look genuinely concerned as they talk about their alcoholism while you're trying to decide exactly the right time to whip out the drunkard's liver prop. It's complicated. Maybe that's why the serious lot get angry when comedians have a crack at their job – they don't want them to find out how much easier it is than comedy. It must have struck you that comics keep cropping up on *Newsnight* or *Question Time* but serious presenters never seem to do stand-up tours.

Of course, if I do fall flat on my face on *Panorama*, it will at least prove that the programme is still heavyweight and thus an unsuitable vehicle for a gimmick-presenter. So that'll be nice. Tonight's *Newsnight Review*, which, of course, I'm only doing because David Baddiel wasn't available, is on at the same time as Jonathan Ross's returning chat show so if I'm rubbish on that, at least there won't be too many witnesses. It seems the storm over Manuel-gate, or Sachs-a-phone as I like to call it, has subsided, the sun is shining and it's safe for everyone to come out into the open again. I saw Russell Brand's new stand-up show in Reading on Monday. There's been much talk of how he deals extensively and enthusiastically with the recent furore but I was more taken aback by his outfit. The last time I saw him live, he looked like a gunslinger, all belt-buckle and cowboy boots. On Sunday he wore leggings and a little black dress. Combined with his lustrous black hair and wispy beard, when he first walked out I thought it was Cher. I suppose if you have sex as often as Russell Brand does, buckles and buttons become a time-consuming annoyance. With leggings and a mini-dress, there's only a little bit of elastication between you and instant pleasure.

I know everyone's anticipating Jonathan Ross's return to be less confrontational than Brand's but wouldn't it be strangely wonderful if Ross came back, instead, with all guns blazing. Imagine the spine-tingling exhilaration if he said the same thing to Tom Cruise he said to Gwyneth Paltrow, especially if Tom, caught momentarily off-guard, responded in the affirmative. It would be the perfect chat show moment – a big laugh followed by a major exclusive.

In fact, the story would be so big, it would surely only be a matter of weeks before Michael Sheen was on the set of the new film, *Ross/Cruise*, doing his best Jonathan Ross impression and recreating the interview with Verne Troyer in a Tom Cruise wig. Perhaps when that film outdid *Frost/Nixon* in box-office takings, comedy-interviewing, and indeed comedy in general, would at last be recognised as the superior genre.

The one good thing about seeing your husband shot in the head

30 JANUARY 2009

I always try to be positive, to see the dark cloud's silver lining, even when I have a day like I had on Tuesday. It didn't start well. When I got in at three minutes past midnight, my girlfriend was still up so I asked her what she thought of the *Panorama* I'd hosted on BBC One that evening, my big move into serious television. 'I really liked the music,' she said. I waited to see if there were more compliments to come. There weren't.

On Tuesday night my team, West Bromwich Albion, were at home to Manchester United. Living in London, home games for me represent a 250-mile round journey. I generally get back around midnight. Things were made worse on Tuesday because, after sitting in horrible traffic on the M25, I dumped my car with little heed to parking restrictions and ran all the way to the ground; only to find the kick-off had been delayed by 30 minutes. Thus I spent the match dreading that announcement 'Will the owner of a silver-grey BMW, registration number . . .' to call me from my seat. I say 'dreading' but by the time we were 4–0 down, I was praying for it.

There's something about Manchester United that makes me become abusive and irrational. When the fifth goal went in I told a slightly confused man next to me that Manchester United not only represented what had gone wrong with football but also what had gone wrong with society.

Back at my car it became obvious that I had a flat tyre. It was 10.45 p.m., I was in a dark, desolate street in West Bromwich and I was handicapped by that most debilitating of diseases – celebrity. You see, when you become a bit famous you get yourself a personal assistant, someone to basically run your life, pay your bills, answer your mail and so on. I phoned my PA, Jenny, but there was no answer. I panicked. I suddenly became painfully aware of how mollycoddled I am. I certainly don't know how to change a tyre.

When I finally managed to contact a breakdown service, I realised that there were lots of other things I don't know. The lady on the other end of the phone asked me what model BMW I was driving. I had no idea. I had to get out of the car to find out what the registration number was and, despite her patient instructions, I couldn't find the spare tyre in the boot. By the way, I've been driving this car for five years.

I didn't fancy waiting for the rescue truck for ages and I started to wonder if I should say: 'By the way, I'm Frank Skinner. You may have seen me on *Panorama*' in order to get some special treatment. I couldn't bring myself to do it, partly because it seemed pathetic and partly because I couldn't take any more tactful comments about the sound-track.

However, I was due to turn 52 at midnight so I told her about that in the hope of getting special birthday treatment. I don't know if that made a difference but a man in a truck soon arrived. Upon recognising me, he asked if I had any photos in the car I could sign for him. I explained that I hadn't. 'You bastard,' he said. I was a little affronted but his facial expression suggested that he intended it as a term of affection.

I felt a bit better about myself when he couldn't find the spare tyre either. 'Maybe it's in a cage underneath,' I said, scratching around for any manly knowledge I might have. He had a quick look but then said there was no spare – there had never been one. 'This model of BMW just comes with tyre-mould so you can patch up your flat tyre and get to a safe location,' he explained.

When he said 'tyre-mould' I felt like a stranger in a strange land. 'You're going to need a recovery vehicle,' he said. For some reason the word 'vehicle' made me feel more secure. It had an official ring to it. Like when people in clothes shops say 'garment'. Soon another man arrived in an even bigger truck and my car was loaded on to the back. As it was finally secured, the first man said 'Oh, tell a lie, it has got a spare after all.' It was in a cage underneath.

So, as I sat in the recovery truck, going down the M1 at 60 mph, I had time to consider the positives of this situation. I didn't have to drive home, I was saving on petrol money and best of all, it suddenly struck me that the whole story could go in this week's column. I'm hoping that any bad things in my life will now be sweetened by the knowledge that they are potential column fodder. I wonder if Jackie Kennedy, as the third bullet ripped into the car, thought 'Oh, this'll be good for the column.' I'm guessing she had one in some New York socialite magazine.

I finally got home at 3 a.m., and, in an attempt to find one last positive, I walked past the man on reception with a look that said 'Yes, I'm 52 but I'm still swanning in at three in the morning.' He looked at my West Brom scarf and nodded sympathetically.

How one wave of the hand changed my life forever

6 FEBRUARY 2009

It seemed odd to hear the leader of the Conservative Party condemning a Labour Prime Minister for using the phrase 'British jobs for British workers'. Had the charge been plagiarism, rather than protectionism, I would have understood David Cameron's outrage. As it is, it shows how much the Tories have changed, or seem to have changed, under his leadership. In fact, were it not for Carol Thatcher referring to someone as 'a golliwog' this week, I would have said there was no continuity left in the Conservative Party.

As it was, Cameron's 'British jobs' attack on Gordon Brown was seen as perfectly natural whilst Ms Thatcher's faux pas has been a cause of some shock. Yes, Margaret Thatcher's daughter may possibly have revealed herself to be a little right-wing. Hard to believe, isn't it? Not only that but there's a rumour going round that the Reverend Ian Paisley's son is a Protestant.

Mr Cameron seemed particularly pleased that the wildcat strikers at Lindsey refinery had taken up the 'British jobs' quote as their unofficial slogan. I enjoyed reading about wildcat strikes in all the papers. It took me back to my youth. I think I even spotted a brazier on one of the news reports. Sadly, that 'British jobs' slogan takes me back to my youth too. For many years, my first workplace, the Hughes-Johnson Stampings, had 'Jobs for Britons first' in white paint, on its exterior brick wall. This was pre-aerosol. The brush strokes were neat and unrushed, as if the artist, confident of widespread concurrence, was not afraid of discovery. Seeing Mr Brown's phrase on placards this week was a scary reminder of what dark shadows can fall across a country when recession bites.

As it was, the foreign workers everyone was angry about were Italian and Portuguese so it didn't seem quite so bad. It's hard to see the Italians as victims when they're so much better dressed and better looking than we are and the mere existence of Cristiano Ronaldo seems to suggest the Portuguese deserve everything they get. The odd thing about the dispute was the management's insistence that the foreign workers were not being paid less than the British ones. This was supposed to placate the strikers in some way. Had I been gathered at the brazier I would have taken great umbrage. The clear inference seemed to be 'They're not cheaper – we just like them better than we like you.'

Maybe the idea is that foreign workers are less trouble. You certainly couldn't imagine a bunch of Italians and Portuguese standing defiantly outside the work-gates in six inches of snow. Surely, even if they did call a strike, they'd soon be ensconced in a nearby wine bar, flirting with the local townswomen and composing a mournful fado about protectionism.

I must admit though, I get all romantic when I hear of British workers on the march – all hand-rolled cigarettes and embroidered banners. The first march I ever went on, back in the seventies, was a protest about student cuts. We all got on a specially chartered train and sang 'We Shall Overcome' from Birmingham to London. It was that day I became a lifelong Labour Party supporter. Not because I was moved by a tear-inducing political speech, or won over by the camaraderie amongst my fellow placard-bearers – the truth is I got very drunk and never made the march – it was because Jim Callaghan waved at me. Neatly, I had ended up outside 10 Downing Street after downing about ten pints. In those days you could stand right opposite the famous front door. Suddenly, it opened and the Labour Prime Minister, Callaghan, stepped out. There were only me and a couple of drunken friends standing there and he smiled and then waved. I waved back gleefully. At that stage, I was 20 and had never voted. 'That's it,' I thought, 'it's the Labour Party for me.' I would advise Gordon Brown to get waving, soon and with gusto.

A few years later I actually did make a march but for all the wrong reasons. It was a protest against nuclear weapons and I was only on it because a local theatre had paid me 15 quid, cash-in-hand, to hand out leaflets for a forthcoming stage-production of Raymond Briggs' *When the Wind Blows*. As we marched through Birmingham city centre, a man in a shirt and tie came to an office window and shouted 'Get back to Russia!'

'Get back to f***ing work!' a nearby marcher with a beard and desert-boots shouted in response. He then turned to me. 'Doesn't that idiot know we're marching for his life and for the life of his children?' he asked.

I shook my head. 'Have a leaflet,' I said.

My last political outing was the countryside march, again for all the wrong reasons. I went on it as part of a sketch for a TV show and was made-over to look like Saddam Hussein. Tony Blair had just told us about Iraq's weapons of mass destruction and I carried a banner that said something like 'Don't worry; the whole country will be a field when I'm finished with it.' One very nice lady gave me a tuna sandwich.

In summary, be careful who you march with and be especially careful if that person says 'British jobs for British workers.' It could be Carol Thatcher.

Red stilettos and other significant reminiscences

13 FEBRUARY 2009

I was happy to read that the Advertising Standards Authority has decided not to pursue the 24 complaints it received about the current Virgin Airlines TV ad – the one with a bunch of glamorous stewardesses lighting-up a grim 1980s airport as they march through in their red stilettos. Some viewers, apparently, felt the ad was 'sexist and presented a stereotypical view of gender roles'. My Political Correctness antennae must be malfunctioning because I love the ad. What's more, when it concludes, with two men gazing in awe at the passing stewardesses, the first man saying 'I need to change my job,' and the second 'I need to change my ticket,' I always feel they should be joined by a third man who adds 'I need to change my pants.' To the 24 complainers, I can only apologise for having had that thought. Of course, it's possible that those complainers love the Virgin ad too, and their use of old-fashioned feminist phrases like 'a stereotypical view of gender roles' is just their way of joining in with the eighties theme.

I think the ad offers an interesting lesson in retrospective. It celebrates 25 years of Virgin Airlines so it's set in 1984, but the girls don't just walk through a 1984 airport, they walk through the eighties. New Romantic hairdos, Rubik's cubes, yuppies with massive mobile phones – they're all there. There is a reference to a more serious eighties theme – the Miners' Strike – but that is on a newsstand outside the airport and thus external to the main narrative. Basically, the ad works because it makes you smile as you recall the absurdities of the period. It's the sort of thing you see on programmes like *We Love the Eighties* or *Top of the Pops 2* all the time. It's why people go to School Disco and Guilty Pleasures nights. People like to laugh affectionately at the past. I wonder if it's a sort of therapy. Our past is something we all got through, despite any attendant traumas, and when we look back at it, it's the silly things that dominate the remembrance of it, the Asteroids machines rather than the Miners' Strike. Our priorities change in retrospect. Somehow, with a bit of distance, it's the minutiae that seem to matter, not the global crises. For example, though I'm confident I've spotted every reference in the Virgin ad, I had to turn to Google when I heard political commentators describing this current economic crisis as 'worse than the recession of 1987'. I couldn't remember that recession at all. *Beadle's About*, yes, Black Monday, no. And it's not just me. When my mum talked about the war, she never mentioned fascism or appeasement; it was all George Formby, powdered egg and drawing a line down the back of your legs so you looked like you had stockings on. Thus, when we look back at the current recession, for all its apparent horrors, we might remember it very differently. It might not seem so important. It might just be outside on the newsstand. I think it helps to consider that.

Incidentally, the Virgin ad's soundtrack is 'Relax' by Frankie Goes to Hollywood, a 1984 single which the then Radio One DJ, Mike Read, refused to play on his show because of its sexual content. Mr Read went on to make his own point about the quirkiness of retrospect when his musical about Oscar Wilde closed after just one performance in 2004. In an interview following this setback, conducted, I imagine, amidst piles of redundant souvenir programmes, he suggested that the show might be a hit in a hundred years' time. He argued that Charles Dickens was unappreciated in the nineteenth century but is now so revered we use phrases like 'Dickensian England'. There are two very wrong things here. Firstly, far from being unappreciated, Dickens was a national hero in his day and, secondly, there seems to be a suggestion that some of us are now living in what will come to be known as 'Readian England'. Nevertheless, Read was right on one point, things can look very different looking back.

If someone makes an ad featuring the essential images of the noughties in 25 years' time – if there's a current company that's survived that long – it won't feature bank bail-outs and repossessed houses. It will be chavs and sat navs, *Big Brother* and Simon Cowell. Instead of the brick-like mobile phones, everyone in 2034 will be laughing at the bulky chip and PIN machines we are currently handed in restaurants. These already look 25 years out of date. I especially like the way they say 'Return Handset to Merchant' after you press Enter. 'Merchant', for goodness' sake! I always expect to see some fat, bearded man in robes and a turban, standing next to an array of spices, bejewelled hand reached out in anticipation of the handset's return.

We might even look back nostalgically at this Virgin ad of 2009, a time before air travel was strictly rationed because of its environmental implications. In 25 years' time the ozone layer might be so threadbare that we, tanned by the unrestrained ultraviolet rays, will all be as orange as an air stewardess. An airline ad might seem then like a cigarette ad seems now, an insight into the naivety of a less-enlightened time – a little snapshot of Readian Britain.

How I control the universe

20 FEBRUARY 2009

As I write, I hear only birdsong and the click-click of my laptop keyboard. I'm in a beautiful but isolated 12-bedroom house in Rutland. Actually, I'm not sure there's still a place called Rutland but I can't Google it because there's no Internet here. Nor is there radio, television, newspapers or any contact with the world outside this house. We had to hand in our phones when we arrived. I'm here with the comedians Katy Brand and Miranda Hart. No, it isn't rehab. Nor is it a remake of *Man About the House*, but it is a television show. The idea is that we're kept away from things for three days and then driven to a TV studio where we're shown a series of news reports and asked to identify which is real and which is bogus.

I don't know why they took our phones away. I rarely call people to discuss the news. I do recall once saying to a friend, mid-phone conversation, 'Did you hear that Jimmy Krankie got badly injured falling off a beanstalk in pantomime?' Like a slightly ironic sub-editor, my friend replied 'I don't think you needed the "in pantomime" part of that sentence.'

Anyway, what I'm saying is that this week's column won't be all that topical. But then I'm never sure if topical is what people want. For years, I've prided myself on doing gags about the latest news. I always imagine people will be impressed by comedy that is hot off the press, as it were, as long as it's also funny, obviously. But it rarely works that way. Any topical comic will tell you that most people have no idea what's in the news so you have to tell them the story before you can do jokes about it. For example, on Monday night I did a stand-up gig and opened with some stuff about Alfie Patten, the 12-year-old 'boy father'. I was confident the story was so big; I didn't need to retell it. I talked about how Alfie looked incredibly young to be a father – 'I imagine he's quite reluctant to hand over the rusk.' I spoke about the idea of a 15-year-old girl giving birth – 'At one point the pain got so bad she had to stop texting.' I soon identified a guy in the front row who had no idea what I was talking about. Now, fair enough, sometimes there are people in an audience who aren't all that bright. Once, at a gig in Bournemouth, a guy in the stalls was telling me how much he hated the town. 'Well, why don't you live somewhere else?' I asked.

'My house is here' was his completely serious reply. Anyway, the guy on Monday night seemed intelligent enough; he just hadn't heard the story.

Now I find myself in a similar state of ignorance. The boy father story has probably moved on a bit during the three days I've been in confinement. As I left for Rutland, we'd already had the unusual phenomenon of teenage boys stepping forward to claim fatherhood. By now the DNA tests may have been completed and you will all know the truth. Looking at those teenagers, I suspect it might be the only test they ever pass.

Of course, you shouldn't judge teenagers by what they look like and you shouldn't judge people on whether they're up to speed with the news – but I do. I split with my girlfriend Cath shortly after she admitted she didn't know who George Galloway was. This was before his *Big Brother* appearance but, even so, I thought it was pretty inexcusable. I then had a brief relationship with another woman who, I soon discovered, didn't know that David Cameron was leader of the Conservative Party. Obviously, that was a deal-breaker.

Happily, I'm back with Cath now and I'm more accepting of her non-interest in current affairs. As she herself admitted, she could have done this TV show without having to go to Rutland. Generally speaking, though, I still think ill of people who don't read the papers. Why? Well, our couple-counsellor said Cath and I had very different worldviews. Cath feels that the universe does to her, while I feel that I do to the universe. Maybe that's at the core of it. I'm a bit like the astronomer in Samuel Johnson's *Rasselas, Prince of Abyssinia.* He thinks an extensive knowledge of astronomy means he can dictate the movements of the planets and ultimately control the universe. Maybe an apparent knowledge of the world makes me feel, deep down, that I somehow have a hand on the reins.

Anyway, I'm not just sitting here pining for the news. We are having fun. There is a swimming pool, sauna and quite a lot of singing around the piano. At one stage I left my shoes upstairs and Miranda and I had to each wear one of her trainers and hop along the gravel path that leads to the building where the snooker table is housed. What with the inventiveness of the shoe-share, the rigour of the hop and the subtle challenges of the resulting snooker match, the whole thing felt like the Duke of Edinburgh's Award Scheme. Katy points out that if there's a nuclear holocaust while we're in here, it will be up to me to continue the species. Oh, well, every mushroom-cloud has a silver lining.

The Queen Mother and the space–time continuum

27 FEBRUARY 2009

I wandered down The Mall, on Wednesday morning, to have my first look at the new Queen Mother memorial. On my way I reminisced about some of my previous encounters with the Royal Family. I did the Royal Variety Performance in 1994, in the presence of Prince Charles. My act didn't go well. The crowd laughed like Hitler laughed – not very often and for all the wrong reasons. To make matters worse, I then had to line up to meet the Prince – the most high-profile witness to my humiliation. As I watched him shaking hands with Shirley Bassey and Larry Grayson I wondered how, when we eventually spoke, he'd tactfully avoid the fact that my performance was uninterrupted by laughter. At last, he reached me. 'Where do you normally work?' he asked, adding, in a sympathetic tone 'Is it in the North?' Before I could come up with a face-saving reply, he'd moved on to Tony Bennett.

Twelve years later, I presented some Duke of Edinburgh Awards at St James's Palace, with the Duke himself in attendance. There were about 50 schoolchildren receiving badges and certificates and they listened attentively as the Duke gave a short closing speech. Then, as he was about to leave the room, he suddenly turned and waved. 'Merry Christmas' he called. We all shouted 'Merry Christmas' and waved back enthusiastically. It was mid-October.

Sadly, I never met the Queen Mother but I was looking forward to seeing the bronze version. What a disappointment. As you may have read, behind the memorial, but towering above it, is the statue of her husband, George VI, erected in 1955, three years after he died, aged

56. The artist who created the Queen Mother statue, Philip Jackson, has said that because of the close proximity of her husband's image, he felt he had to portray the Queen Mother in her early fifties. Otherwise, he explained 'she'd look like King George's mother'. He also put her in the formal robes of the Most Noble Order of the Garter because that's what her husband's statue is wearing. Now, not just for me but for millions of others, the Queen Mother was a smiling, little old lady who had tiny grey teeth and wore nice hats. That is the statue I want to see. I've got nothing against the Most Noble Order of the Garter. Indeed, her big cloak and swinging tassels give the rather pleasing impression that, in a fit of aristocratic impatience, she's emerged prematurely into the public eye, getting slightly entangled in the unveiling curtain like a regal Andrex puppy. Nevertheless, I don't see why her age and apparel should be dictated by that of her dead husband. The matching robes give the pair a slightly silly His-and-Hers feel. If, despite the fact they were erected more than 50 years apart, we *must* see the statues as a pair, let's really go for it. Why not install them in a two-door building, based on one of those little weather-houses? The Queen Mother could come out when it's fine weather and her husband when it's raining. Soon we would hear shivering costermongers mutter 'Blimey, it's a bit George VI this morning.' Yes, that's ridiculous but is it any sillier than the idea that the Queen Mother's statue has to look a similar age to her husband's or onlookers will become confused and dismiss George as some sort of toy boy?

Over in Westminster, Sir Winston Churchill looks considerably older than the nearby Boudicca but this, to my knowledge, hasn't caused anyone to have a chronological crisis. Indeed, the real, flesh-and-blood Queen Elizabeth II now looks older than the statue of her grandmother Queen Victoria that stands outside Buckingham Palace. Does this mean our monarch should no longer appear on the palace balcony in case the assembled crowd look from one queen to the other and think 'Hold on a minute – isn't this a bit Benjamin Button'?

People loved the Queen Mother partly because she was a very old lady who just kept on going. She replaced the Energizer bunny as a symbol of staying power. I used to imagine her with her feet up, reading the sports pages and telling the Grim Reaper she didn't care what instructions he'd been given, he'd have to come back after the flat-racing season. It's remarkable that a major public figure like her should have lived to 101 so why immortalise her in her early fifties? I don't want her young and unfamiliar, and I don't want her in formal robes either. She wasn't wearing that lot when she visited the war-torn East End. The new statue has all the dehumanising trappings of power. Don't give us Queen Elizabeth, as the inscription on the memorial calls her; give us the dear old Queen Mum, with her hat and her handbag. Then, even if there was a revolution, there could never be a Saddam Hussein moment. Nobody would pull down a statue of the Queen Mum and hit it with a flip-flop.

If I had the choice I'd have an enormous 101-year-old Queen Mother – just slightly smaller than the recently commissioned Ebbsfleet horse – sitting on the palace roof, hand raised as if waving to passers-by. Of course, come October, she'd have to move over to make a bit of room up there. That's when Prince Philip puts up the giant inflatable Santa.

Get your brains out for the lads

6 MARCH 2009

Where I grew up, in the West Midlands, academic success was not commonplace. If some kid did manage to pass, say, O-level geography, they'd be pictured in the local paper, wearing a mortarboard and holding up a map of the world. The headline would invariably be something like 'Local girl is top of the swots'. It was best not to wear your brain on your sleeve. I myself was loath to raise my hand in class, even when I knew the answer to the teacher's question. I never told my friends I was deliberately hiding my light under a bushel, partly because they would have ostracised me for being a closet-swot and partly because none of them knew what a bushel was. At least, I don't think they did. Maybe they had bushels just as opaque as my own. Studying was for wimps.

A few years after I was expelled from school – my finest anti-wimp achievement – I went to college to try and get those qualifications I now finally realised were something of a boon in the outside world. I started hanging out with a lot of Asian kids. They had a different attitude to study. They thought learning was cool – that it was OK to pass exams and get good essay grades – that brains were sexy.

Thus, even allowing for cinematic exaggeration, when I watched that scene in *Slumdog Millionaire* where the ordinary guy seems to know all the answers and the whole of India is cheering him on, it kind of made sense.

Of course, you might argue that something similar happened in the UK last week when 5.3 million viewers tuned into the final of *University Challenge* mainly to see Gail Trimble, described by some as the show's greatest ever contestant. Personally, I'd guess about five million of those viewers were hoping she'd lose – hoping they'd see the smug expression wiped off her bespectacled know-it-all face. They were hungry for a sign of weakness – desperate to see the brainbox they call the 'human Google' reduced to a something slightly more fallible – maybe a 'human Wikipedia'. I know she's from Surrey rather than shantytown but I doubt that's the source of the antipathy. They just don't like very clever people in this country. I recall a former head of BBC One saying to me 'What people like about you, Frank, is that you're ordinary. The public don't want to admire, they want to recognise.' I suppose that's why there'll never be a heart-warming British movie called *Poshbird University Challenge*.

Anyway, Gail's victory has now been snatched away from her because it turns out one of her teammates was ineligible for the show. He'd already left university well before the final. Surely, this was a handicap. It's a well-known fact that students, about 48 hours after they leave university, forget everything they ever learnt there. Nevertheless, Gail's been dethroned and she's got what many see as her well-deserved comeuppance.

Now far be it from me to disagree with the British Public. OK, I wouldn't trust them with a capital punishment referendum, but generally speaking, there is some evidence of group wisdom in this country. For example, I very much enjoyed the general rage at Sir Fred Goodwin. If only he'd answered his bonus questions as convincingly as Ms Trimble. And, to be fair, the masses are capable of warming to a very clever person. I'm sure I'm not the only one who occasionally shouts 'Oh, shut your big face' at Stephen Fry on *QI* but, generally speaking, he is viewed as a national treasure. We'll put up with a bit of what one might call Fry's smirkish delight because we love him so. Could we ever feel the same about Gail?

Well, I could. For a start off, she's a good Christian girl. I'm also a believer and I get fed up with the way Richard Dawkins and his lot seem to imagine themselves on the leather Chesterfields of a private club with Bertrand Russell and George Bernard Shaw while I'm stuck in Julie's Pantry with Cliff Richard. Gail would definitely be a welcome intellectual addition to our ranks.

Also, famous clever women don't tend to let themselves down by dating shallow but beautiful people the way famous male intellectuals do. Gail has just got engaged to her boyfriend of five years. Not for her the example of Arthur Miller with Marilyn Monroe or indeed our own Lembit Öpik with Gabriela Cheeky. I doubt we'll ever see Gail doing the red carpet on the arm of a Grimes twin.

In short, Gail is a great role model. She mustn't get lost in the mix of the *University Challenge* scandal. It's now widely reported that four of the last nine winning teams should have been disqualified because of non-eligible players. It sounds like all you needed was the right scarf. We often hear of bright young people not fulfilling their potential because of the blunders and bureaucracy of large organisations like schools or, in this case, the BBC. Let's not let that happen to Gail. Obviously there'll have to be a Radio Two-style cull at *University Challenge* now all this skulduggery has come to light. I vote for Gail as the new presenter. The show's over 40 years old – surely a young, female host is well overdue. Perhaps brains could be sexy again.

Stupid children – their role in entertainment

13 MARCH 2009

I've got a bad back at the moment. I know it's not necessarily a sign of ageing – young men have bad backs too – but as I stood tentatively doing stretching exercises, backstage at a variety show I was hosting the other night, the difference between old men's bad backs and young men's bad backs suddenly became all too clear. A concerned comic, half my age, asked me how my injury had occurred. That was when it struck me. Injuries always used to come with an anecdote attached. Now they just come. He looked at me, clearly expecting the story of an over-enthusiastic dive on the boundary or an unavoidable scuffle with a hooded youth. Instead, I just said, with an air of resignation, 'I don't know.' Such was my condition I couldn't even accompany my answer with a decent shrug.

The next day, after hobbling to the newsagent's, I was soon at my breakfast table reading an article which almost literally added insult to injury. New research shows that children conceived by men over 45 do badly in intelligence tests. In short, old dads produce stupid kids. Now, although I'm 52 and, as yet, childless, I for some reason, found this article strangely cheering. Should I finally get round to having kids, it seems they at least, unlike my back-injuries, will be anecdote-heavy. Obviously, the funny stories will all be of a similar 'my stupid kid' variety but this will season them with a frisson of unkindness – always good for an anecdote, I find. Listeners will laugh and wince simultaneously. That's generally the combination of responses I'm after. And the joy of it is that this whole genre is almost completely unexploited.

There must be thousands of fabulous 'my stupid kid' anecdotes left untold because stupid kids tend to be the offspring of stupid parents rather than great raconteurs. Or, at least, I always assumed as much. This new research changes everything. If I'm going to be the first aged dad to get a whole stand-up show out of his knucklehead-children I'd better start the dunce-production-line rolling soon.

All this may sound flippant, but I do suspect that a great many people beget children so they will, often for the first time in their life, have something to talk about. I mean, how many 'the funny things kids say' stories have you been told by friends or read on the letters pages of populist magazines? Of course, children are beautiful and innocent and, as William Wordsworth said, come 'trailing clouds of glory' but parents are still inclined to view them chiefly as yarn-fodder. And let's face it, 'Kieran is captain of the school football team' or 'Jake simply adores *Treasure Island*' will not be in the same league as my ground-breaking 'Bob set fire to the next-door neighbour's shed because he thought it looked cold.'

Of course, some would say it's a bit late for me on the dad-front. The big test of whether a man is too old to be a father always seems to be whether he'll be able, when the time comes, to play football with his children in the park. I take a different view. It is the great sadness of my life that I've combined an enormous passion for watching, reading and talking about football with a complete inability to play it. I've no desire to reveal this humiliating fact to my children. If I instead stand, balanced on two walking-sticks, watching them happily kicking a ball about between themselves they will be none the wiser. Especially, as I'll no doubt tell them I had trials for West Bromwich Albion and could easily have turned pro were it not for World War II. Obviously, they'll be too stupid to question this story or indeed to question the logic of driving past the nearby Chelsea football ground every other weekend as we commence our 250-mile round-trip to watch West Brom.

I think I've avoided being a father all these years because I often don't like the effect fatherhood has on men. For example, when I see kids' photos on the dashboard of a black cab I always think it's less about love and more about the driver saying he's fertile. Similarly, when I see a man walking along with a child sitting on his shoulders it always seems to me as if he's parading a 'My Healthy Sperm' trophy on a macho lap of honour. You'd never catch me doing that. Not with my back.

Anyway, having read that older men have stupid kids I now find myself, after years of avoiding fatherhood, suddenly beginning to consider it. I suppose, previously, I'd arrogantly assumed it was better I didn't have a child because it would be so bright and witty it would be torn apart by the understandably jealous, acne-ridden, baseball-capped dumbos you see on every street-corner – the way cage-birds who escape are often savaged by legions of mundane house-sparrows and starlings angered by their exotic beauty. Now it turns out my age-mutated sperm will produce kids so thick they'll be able to join the herd unnoticed. And that's not the only advantage of the older dad. I get up three or four times in the night now anyway so a crying baby won't make much difference. Of course, they generally cry less as they get older. Not mine. Not once I've got them those season tickets.

Hey, Fatso! How to save lives and get laughs at the same time

20 MARCH 2009

I was in a bar with a few friends the other day. A barmaid, standing behind the counter, caught the attention of the whole group, male and female alike. She was strikingly attractive with ice-blue eyes and a slim torso. We spent some time speculating on how many customers must have fallen for her. About ten minutes later the barmaid emerged to collect some glasses. Our conversation stopped. The wooden counter and surround had framed her like a work of art but now the uncropped picture was revealed. Her lower-half seemed to be that of another woman. She had an enormous behind and thighs that threatened the seams of her too-tight jeans. I think we all felt terribly let down. I suggested that such disappointments must have been common in the mythical worlds. How often must a young Greek woman have admired the glorious upper body of a handsome centaur, partially obscured by an olive grove, only to baulk when the horsey half clip-clopped into view? How many mermaids were thrown back in by disappointed sailors, lured by a pretty face and buoyant breasts?

I recently started doing a radio show and I put it to my friends in the bar that this dame-of-two-halves experience might be interesting to discuss on air. I could replace my classical references with a slightly more tabloid approach and make the subject radio-friendly. I would ask my listeners to imagine the awkward atmosphere when a bloke who'd spent the whole night chatting-up that barmaid had his desires smashed *Titanic*-like by the sudden discovery of her two-thirds below the surface. Some of my friends thought it would make for an interesting phone-in but I felt uneasy about it and eventually rejected the idea. It just seemed unkind and, well, sizeist. However, things I've read this week have now made me question such sensitivity.

At school, I laughed at the fat kids like everyone else. It was safe in those days because there weren't so many of them. We, the army of the thin, called them Fatty or Fatso and shouted 'Single-file, please' whenever we passed them in the corridor. They inherited a traditional comic role previously filled by Falstaff, Billy Bunter, Mr Creosote and many more. They often became part of the gang but we still called them Fatso, still saw them as an endless source of comic material.

Then, like so many oppressed minorities, they started to fight back. Nowadays, there are, it seems, more fatty jokes than ever, but it's the fatties who are doing them. Dawn French, Matt Lucas, James Corden – all repeatedly acknowledge the fact that fat people are intrinsically comic, especially if they're in tight, revealing clothes, but it's made them stars, not stooges. Look at Chris Moyles on *Comic Relief* – he was the roly-poly hero of Kilimanjaro – a completely rehabilitated Piggy from *Lord of the Flies*. Outside the comedy world it's a similar story. There's an enormous billboard at the end of my road advertising a new magazine. It shows the five-feet tall, 15-stone American singer Beth Ditto naked on the cover and describes her as an 'icon of our generation'. This follows a similar *NME* cover that proclaimed her as 'the queen of cool'.

I had accepted all this as progress until I read, this week, that obesity is as hazardous to health as a lifetime of smoking and that it can shorten your life-expectancy by a decade. What's more, 25 per cent of UK adults are now considered obese. No wonder Channel Five's documentaries don't get the ratings they used to. If you want to see a 50-stone man nowadays, all you have to do is look out of the window.

In the light of this new information, it seems we were doing those fat kids at school a favour when we ridiculed them. We were giving them a great incentive to lose weight. It would stop them being the butt of every joke. Being fat needs to get uncool again as soon as possible. It's a matter of life and death. People are quick to ridicule the thin. I've been pretty scrawny for most of my life and am often reminded, sometimes by complete strangers, that my thinness mustn't get out of hand. People will happily say stuff to me like 'Oh, God, you're looking thin. You need to get some food down you.' It's annoying but it's also a helpful check against wasting away. However, they don't keep fat people similarly informed. They would not see an obese friend and say 'You need to start dieting, you fat pig.' Well, from now on, I'm suggesting they do. It's crazy that size-zero models get endlessly criticised while Beth Ditto is described as an icon. I know skinny-is-cool is a dangerous message but let's recognise that obese-is-cool is every bit as bad.

We bullied and nagged at smokers, made adverts that said they smelled so awful they were unkissable and finally, with the smoking ban, we literally turned them into shivering outsiders – all because we knew it was for their own good. You have to be cruel to be kind and pretending that obesity is groovy is not being kind to anybody. The next time I see Beth Ditto naked on a magazine cover I want the headline to be 'Single-file, please'. Let's go back to fatty-baiting – they might get upset but they'll have ten extra years to get over it.

Google Street View and the death of God

27 MARCH 2009

I've spent quite a few hours this week looking at Google Street View, or as burglars call it, Google Online Shopping. To be fair to burglars and other criminals, up to now they have had the thin end of the wedge as far as CCTV and other surveillance systems are concerned so I guess they were due some payback. Despite that, I love Google Street View.

I was so excited when I first saw my flat on there that I screamed for my girlfriend to come and see. 'Look, look,' I blustered excitedly, 'it's our flat.' She stared, over my shoulder, at the computer screen. Even without turning to check her facial expression, I sensed that she was unimpressed. 'You mean the flat we've lived in for 18 months – the exterior view of which we can enjoy at any time, simply by stepping outside?' she said.

'Yeah, but look,' I replied. I clicked to show her the full 360-degree panoramic view of the flat and our street. When I turned for her reaction, she'd gone. I felt a little deflated but consoled myself with a bracing e-walk around my block. I'm hoping, as I become more adept with the Street View controls, e-jogging will become an option.

I don't go with this argument that Street View is pointless because we could just go and look at these streets for ourselves. The familiar becomes very exciting once it appears on a screen. I get really bored watching those natural history programmes with titles like *Where the Panther Walks*, showing places I'll never visit and creatures I'll never see in the wild, but, a few weeks ago, they showed the dry-cleaners at the end of my road on the telly and I was beside myself with excitement.

Come to think of it, it wasn't dissimilar to my first Street View experience except that this time my girlfriend's response to my shrieking and pointing was 'Oh, you mean the dry-cleaners we see about ten times a week?'

'Yeah, but not in HD,' I said indignantly.

Anyway, it seems, as far as Street View is concerned, that I'm in the minority. There have been several complaints and some images have been removed after protests from people unwittingly caught on camera. One man was upset to discover he'd been photographed leaving a sex shop in Soho. Some felt this was a terrible invasion of his privacy while others felt it served him right and that, if one chooses to frequent such places, one should accept the risk of being seen. My own reaction was: 'Why would a man who had the time and technical ability to browse Google Street View need to go to a sex shop? Isn't there enough porn on the Internet?'

Other images that caused consternation were a drunken man being sick on the pavement in Shoreditch, East London, and a man being arrested in Camden, but I like this Hogarthian side to Street View. Besides, being asked to photograph British streets but to avoid people getting arrested or vomiting on the pavement would be quite a tricky assignment.

These offending images were blacked out before I got to view them, which is a great pity because I like the role reversal of someone off the telly, sitting at home, enjoying pictures of non-celebrities being drunk, arrested or involved in sexual shenanigans. It's not just the criminals who are getting their own back thanks to Street View. The extreme sensitivity members of the public have shown just because there are mundane pictures of their houses online suggests a good deal of hypocrisy. People are very happy to look at Britney's genitalia on the Internet but they don't want anyone seeing their wheelie bins.

I think this ever-growing hysteria about the invasion of privacy in Great Britain might be a direct result of the secularisation of our society. As a Roman Catholic, I've spent my whole life believing that my every move is being monitored. God, after all, is the ultimate CCTV. There have been many occasions when this sense of being watched has led me to do the right thing rather than the easier or more pleasurable wrong one. We hate those intermittent yellow boxes on modern roads but they do, generally speaking, cause us to drive more safely.

Maybe, now that God doesn't feature in most people's lives, society needs things like Street View and surveillance cameras to make people behave better. I don't suppose the citizens whose sins were exposed by Google fear they'll end up sizzling on Satan's griddle as a result but all this fuss about images of drunkenness, crime and lust does suggest a certain sense of shame.

Another picture that got removed was a naked toddler playing in the park. A few years back such an image would have been seen as a symbol of joyous innocence. Now it just reminds us of another social evil we'd rather not think about. Maybe Street View is the mirror that society doesn't want to look into.

Sorry, I've gone a bit voice-in-the-wilderness. I'm halfway through Lent and the fasting is starting to take its toll. Anyway, perhaps the strangest Street View story of the week was the enforced removal of images of the House of Commons. Since I read that, every time I reach for the brown sauce bottle I feel like a master of espionage.

Obamarama. My political messiah relay team

3 APRIL 2009

Three years ago my bank manager told me I was financially secure for the rest of my life. Six months ago he told me I couldn't have access to my money – the same money he'd advised me to put into a 'low-risk' AIG account – and that it was possible I'd lost the whole lot. My current situation is that I've got half my money back and I can't lay my hands on the other half till July 2012. If, in the meantime, the British company that now holds the account goes bust, my cash will probably go with it. There was a time when, if you thought someone was arrogant and unpleasant but you didn't wish to swear, you turned to rhyming slang and called them a 'merchant banker'. Now that's a much worse insult than the word it replaced. Nevertheless, despite my recent experiences with bankers, I've resisted joining in with the general hate campaign. Recession often throws up scapegoats and when people start hanging effigies from lamp posts it's usually a good time to take stock. Public opinion is apt to be changeable. Football fans hanged David Beckham in effigy after the 1998 World Cup, and Indians did the same with Jade Goody after Shilpagate. I doubt bankers will overcome their effigy status and emerge as national heroes but we should keep an eye on who's fanning the flames. Scapegoats are very handy when you're trying to avoid blame yourself. When Gordon Brown, Chancellor during the long run-up to this crisis, lays into bankers for their irresponsibility, it does seem a bit like Fagin, when finally caught, reprimanding his gang for their criminal behaviour.

However, when I read reports this week of grinning City workers waving wads of cash at protesters in the street below, I suddenly felt nostalgia for the guillotine. My bank is an arm of the Royal Bank of Scotland so I didn't feel too distressed, either, when I watched the RBS windows going through on Sky News. I heard that some RBS officials were angry that the police hadn't acted quicker to prevent the attack on their building. I'm sure those officials would agree that the only way to deal with such incompetence is to give the policemen responsible an enormous bonus. Mind you, I wasn't sure about some of the protesters either. I like the peace flags and macrobiotic cake stalls but when I hear people chanting 'Who are you?' and charging the police it just reminds me of every frightening away game I've ever been to.

It seems like 90 per cent of the country is scared of being starved and the other 10 per cent is scared of being lynched. So, who will save us from this economic apocalypse? I know G20 sounds like a guess at Battleships but if they can't fix things who you gonna call? Maybe, in time, we'll come to see this week's wrangling as the dawning of a new more responsible financial age and the beginning of the end of the recession. One thing's for sure, it's been an odd week for me. I hate to follow the herd – to join in with fashionable sentiments – but on Wednesday, after much resistance, I finally gave in. I fell in love with Barack Obama. It happened at his official press conference with Gordon Brown. Mr Brown is, of course, the high priest of uneasiness. He wears a smile like I wear a tuxedo – obviously uncomfortable but determined to make an effort. His smile looks like it was photoshopped from a much happier person. It barely interferes with the rest of his face. Even his top lip seems reluctant to join in, thus leaving the lower lip to bear most of the burden. President Obama's lips are slightly purple – causing my girlfriend to say 'heart-trouble' every time he appears on TV – but those lips like to smile. In contrast to the Prime Minister, Obama seemed so relaxed and confident at the press conference that when he said 'global problems require global solutions' I just knew everything was going to be OK. Then something scary happened. I realised that my new love, Obama, was, in my head, all mixed up with an old love – another smiling presence with a reassuring informality and sticky-out ears. Barack Obama is my new Tony Blair. He reminds me of Blair in his early years as PM, when everything seemed possible. And I don't think I was the only one having happy flashbacks. Gordon Brown suddenly seemed much more at home, back in his familiar role of sidekick to a more charismatic leader. Since Mr Brown became Prime Minister nearly two years ago, it's felt like a very long episode of the ITV series, *Lewis*. DI Robbie Lewis is a likeable, well-meaning chap but it just isn't the same without Inspector Morse.

If the apparent success of the G20 doesn't boost Mr Brown's ratings in the UK opinion polls, maybe it's time for Blair to return, messiah-like, and build a new New Labour. Maybe Peter Mandelson's comeback was just a paving of the way. Four protest groups, outside the Bank of England this week, called themselves the Four Horsemen of the Apocalypse. Maybe they were unwittingly heralding the Second Coming of Tony Blair. Admittedly, this seemed like an outrageous idea when it came to me on Wednesday morning. Then Alan Shearer took the manager's job at Newcastle.

Brown girls in the spring – no, n-no, no, no

10 APRIL 2009

Previously, in this column, I suggested a return to fatty-jokes in a cruel-to-be-kind campaign to discourage obesity. My fatty-bashing initiative was based purely on health, not aesthetics. In truth, I'm no fan of conventional beauty. People generally regarded as very attractive, like Brad Pitt and Angelina Jolie, seem to me like dull identikit pictures of what beautiful people are supposed to be. I'd always choose the rotting elegance of Venice over the ordered neatness of Bath. However, this penchant for imperfection can be a tricky thing to explain to a partner. I seem to recall a certain awkwardness after I told my girlfriend I fancied her because she was 'a director's cut of a beautiful woman'.

Not everyone shares my love of rough edges. I once came third in a Worst Celebrity Teeth poll, behind Pogues frontman, Shane MacGowan and comedian Ken Dodd, so when the BBC sports presenter, Clare Balding, made fun of Grand National winner, Liam Treadwell's crooked teeth last Saturday, I identified it as a further example of teethism in the media. The jockey would've been well within his rights to say, 'Well, what about you and your big man-jaw?' but he wisely chose not to get caught up in a slanging match.

I once interviewed the much-adored Jon Bon Jovi. His teeth were so perfect they ceased to be teeth. There were no grooves or irregular edges and they were so white one could imagine him reading in bed by the light of them. They were the Platonic ideal of teeth, too good for any human mouth. My own pegs are so ramshackle I've developed a condition known as 'tramp-teeth'. This is when the various gaps and cracks hold so much food that one seems to be permanently wearing a sort of bread-based gumshield. Here is an example of a physical imperfection that is actually an aid to good health. My tramp-teeth help keep me slim because I end up flossing away more food than I actually swallow.

In contrast, the quest for physical perfection can be downright dangerous. Several years ago, an old Irish friend said to me 'Never start a relationship in the summertime because everybody looks good with a tan.' It was sound advice for anyone who included Caucasians in their dating Venn diagram. In autumn, when the leaves turned brown and the skin cells turned white, the switch from bronzed to blotchy dampened many a summer love but we accepted this cycle of desire and disappointment just as we accepted things like seasonal availability. In those days, there were no Brussels sprouts in April, no blackcurrants in June and no suntans in November – these were Nature's simple rules. But just as the I-want-it-and-I-want-it-now brattishness of Thatcher's Britain resulted in frozen fruit and veg arriving every day from all corners of the globe, so the pale and patchy became impatient for perpetual tans. Now, in modern Britain, people choose their skin tone like they choose the strength of their tea, and too many are opting for builder's rather than milky. This new generation, particularly females in their twenties, have slowly become addicted to imperfection-masking brownness and disturbing statistics released this week reveal just how many of them have flown, Icarus-like, too close to the sun bed. Malignant melanoma has replaced cervical cancer as the most common cancer amongst British women under 30 and the tanning salon culture is getting most of the blame.

A make-up lady on a TV series once persuaded me to have 'a couple of sun beds'. She was used to working on celebrities with orange skin and white teeth, not the other way round. I didn't actually lie on a sun bed, as I expected, but instead stood in a sealed cubicle, bombarded by loud Europop and ultra-violet light. All I wore were two shiny gold-foil cones that I'd been told to wedge into each eye-socket so I didn't burn my retina. Thus, blind, naked and slightly scorched, I stood, dancing badly to Ace of Base, like an extra in a low-rent musical version of Dante's *Inferno*. I had never sunbathed naked so I ended up burning parts of me not previously exposed. Such was the redness of one particularly sensitive area that, when I went back for my second session a week later, I asked for not two but three gold cones. When I'd slotted them all into place I looked like a nude version of C-3PO. I never went back.

Why does a generation that loves ripped jeans and distressed leather jackets not apply this taste for the lived-in look to their own bodies? I saw pictures of Madonna without make-up this week. I thought she looked fantastic. Her over-exercised arms still looked like she got them from a William Blake illustration but her pale, unpainted face looked beautiful. This gave me an idea – a sort of year-zero approach to natural beauty. I propose a National No Make-Up Weekend during which women go about their normal lives – working, shopping or clubbing – without any make-up whatsoever. I suggest this not to enable amorous young men to avoid the usual pig-in-a-poke lottery of dating slap-enhanced females but rather to help women realise that they really don't need the mask, just like they don't need the bleached teeth and the carcinogenic tan. Love yourself. It's time to stop hiding your special little details. The future is not orange after all.

Pedestrian crossings and their dysfunctional relationship with the animal kingdom

17 APRIL 2009

I was thrilled to hear they're going to build a scramble crossing at London's Oxford Circus. I'm slightly obsessed with pedestrian crossings – I go crazy for the Beatles *Abbey Road* sleeve – and when I visited both Tokyo and Toronto in recent years, I made a special point of trying out their scrambles for myself. The idea is that all four lanes of traffic are stopped at a major crossroads, thus forming, for 30 seconds, a small, impromptu town square that pedestrians can cross any which way they like. Of course, the Japanese and the Canadians are, generally speaking, extremely polite and civilised so both crossings were a delight to use. In England, I spend a good deal of my pedestrian-time bobbing and weaving around people who stubbornly refuse to divert their path or even slightly angle their shoulders for me to pass. They probably think such considerate actions might be interpreted as a sign of weakness. When the scramble begins in London, it'll only need a brushed elbow or a blocked step to spin the whole thing into a whirl of aggressive indignation. By the time the dust has settled the scene might resemble that lingering shot of the Civil War wounded in *Gone with the Wind*.

It's still great news, though. My interest in pedestrian crossings began very early in life. When I was about seven years old I got hit by a car whilst on a zebra crossing. As I lay on the tarmac, the lady who'd been driving the vehicle came over to see how I was. 'Are you all right?' she said. 'I had right of way,' was my icy reply. She grew pale, perhaps fearful that she'd knocked over some sort of boy-lawyer – a legal prodigy who'd drag her through the courts for compensation. In truth, I was embarrassed because, up until then, I'd had complete faith in the zebra crossing. Perhaps its black-and-whiteness suggested the protection it offered was unequivocal but, as I stood picking the gravel from my elbows, I realised the zebra had grey areas. The driver's stopping was largely discretionary. The answer was, of course, to combine a crossing with a traffic lights system. Then the driver really *has* to stop.

This is where the story of the UK's pedestrian crossings gets interesting. No, really. The Department of Transport (or Ministry of Transport as it was then known) developed the new crossing and, obviously deciding they were on to a winner with the black-and-white animal motif, called it the panda crossing. It had stoplights and a sign for pedestrians that said 'CROSS'. However, it didn't have a sign that said 'DON'T CROSS' because, and I love this, that would have contravened the existing right-of-way law. The panda crossing looked a bit like a zebra crossing except the stripes, instead of being oblong, took the form of long thin triangles. Now, I've always been OK with the zebra reference because the essential black-and-white stripiness of that crossing, whilst not accurately mirroring a zebra's markings, gives it a stylised similarity to the living creature. However, there has never been a panda with long thin black-and-white triangles and thank God for that because, if there was, unscrupulous backgammon enthusiasts would stop at nothing to obtain its pelt. Incidentally, there are, for cyclists, tiger crossings – like zebra crossings except in black-and-yellow – but they are rarer than the poor endangered tiger itself.

As with the panda example, the vast majority of pedestrian crossings named after members of the animal kingdom have little or no resemblance to the living creature. Take the pelican crossing, for example. Where, you might ask, is its horrible, wrinkly fish-bag of a throat? Ah, well, the Department for Transport (DfT) switched tactics with this one. Instead of naming the pelican crossing for its supposedly similar appearance to the creature; they sneaked in an acronym. Even the acronym doesn't quite work. It comes from PEdestrian LIght CONtrolled crossing, so actually pelicon not pelican. Then there's the puffin crossing. This is like a pelican crossing except the panel showing the green and red man is just above the user-button. The puffin gets its name from Pedestrian User Friendly INtelligent crossing. Rubbish! Still, you might say, despite the misspellings, there's a common rule that if a *bird's* name is used, it's always an acronym. But no, the toucan crossing, designed so that pedestrians and mounted cyclists can cross together, gets its name because the 'two can' cross at the same time. The DfT's puns are nearly as bad as their acronyms.

Finally, having misused the black-and-white, the stripy and the winged, the DfT went mythical. The Pegasus crossing caters for horses and their riders. Unsurprisingly, there's one outside Buckingham Palace. The Pegasus has a green horse and a red horse instead of the usual little men. I don't know why. It's hardly likely there'll be horses crossing unaccompanied. Does the DfT imagine that a green man would confuse things? Do they think the horse would look back at its rider and say 'This is you, isn't it?'

Anyway, despite the DfT's idiosyncrasies – maybe even because of them – I love pedestrian crossings. They seem to epitomise man's struggle to tame technology – to ensure that even in the pounding, polluting metropolis, there are still safe pathways which fragile humanity need not fear to tread. London's scramble crossing is due to open this November, so I imagine it will be ready just before the Olympics. I know which one I'm most excited about.

Susan Boyle versus Joseph Stalin

24 APRIL 2009

Being a supporter of both West Bromwich Albion and the Labour Party, I keep asking myself how much longer I can deny the inevitability of dual-relegation. I love the idea of winning the last five games, or the pleasing image of thousands of slightly premature David Cameron victory mugs being chucked into a skip, but such fantasies are becoming increasingly difficult to hold on to. In truth, there's probably no hope for the Albion, and for Labour to turn it round they'd have to make two shock announcements – that the election is next Thursday and that the new party leader is Susan Boyle.

I know what you're thinking. Who would replace Ms Boyle in *Britain's Got Talent*? Well, it wouldn't take too much backcombing to turn Gordon Brown into a pretty convincing look-alike and, though I doubt his voice is as good as hers, I imagine it would be extremely poignant to watch him sing 'I Dreamed a Dream'. The thing is I really want Mr Brown to be Susan Boyle – not just in a talent-contest but all the time. I want him to be gauche, unsophisticated and uncool but have a beautiful inner being. That's what I used to think he was like. That's why, when Vince Cable, at the end of last year, became Parliament's king of comedy by suggesting the Prime Minister had transformed from Stalin into Mr Bean, it worried me on two counts. Firstly, the response in the House suggested that those assembled – our elected representatives – felt a change from Stalin, a cruel tyrant responsible for millions of deaths, to Mr Bean, a bumbling, accident-prone buffoon, represented a decline. Secondly, it troubled me that Mr Brown, someone

I thought was an idealistic son of the manse, was, even by way of a joke, comparable to the notorious Soviet leader. I chose to focus on to the nervous-ditherer element of the Prime Minister. For me, Mr Brown was an awkward, self-conscious fellow whose leadership style was reminiscent of a man driving with a police car in his rear-view mirror.

Then the Damian McBride story broke and completely undermined my view of our leader. Suddenly, everyone was saying that smear campaigns were one of Mr Brown's favourite tools to undermine opponents, even within his own party – that he was a ruthless political in-fighter. Clearly McBride was the pit-bull but what sort of person keeps a pit-bull? McBride resigned on 11 April. That same night, I watched Susan Boyle on *Britain's Got Talent* – the Scottish accent, the eyebrows, the audience's derisive sniggers – it seemed to give me back the loveable Gordon I'd just lost. And then, the glorious pay-off – Hagrid does Barbra Streisand. However, the upshot of the comparison with Gordon Brown is that I haven't been able to enjoy Susan Boyle's success as much as other people. Ever since she became a public figure, I've been waiting for her to be exposed – for the nightingale to transform into a Stalin.

First there was the charity CD. Obviously, she was an experienced professional singer with an already successful career. But no, it was ten years ago and was financed by a local council in West Lothian – not exactly big-time. Then there was the man who refuted her claim that she'd never been kissed. I knew it. She's had a string of suitors. Again no, he'd occasionally given her a peck on the cheek and said 'everything's going to be all right' – no burning passion. Lastly, there was the demo tape. She was a fame-obsessed wannabe. The truth is she used the tape to get an audition for Michael Barrymore's *My Kind of People* but he turned her down. Not his last mistake, or indeed his largest, but still quite a howler.

It really looks like Susan Boyle is the real deal. She is decent and sincere and has a cat called Pebbles instead of a pit-bull named Damian. Could she really be, as some have suggested, the antidote to a growing national cynicism? It's a big ask. I find that I'm becoming so cynical now that I search for ever-deeper levels of cynicism I wouldn't previously have considered. For example, I convinced myself that it was Gordon Brown who sent those emails to the right-wing blogger, Guido Fawkes, happy to sacrifice a couple of lieutenants to get the smears themselves maximum coverage. Likewise, when I read allegations that the father of the little girl from *Slumdog Millionaire* tried to sell her to the *News of the World*'s fake sheikh for £200,000, I found myself wondering if the so-called fake sheikh involved was actually Madonna. I also wondered what Gordon Brown would say to the little girl's father. Would he, as I once would have expected, reprimand him for such an immoral plan or would he, as I now fear, tell him that, considering the current recession, it's the worst possible time to sell?

I don't want to be this cynical person. When I watched Jade Goody's funeral it reminded me of when I went to see Agatha Christie's *The Mousetrap*. I eyed everyone with great suspicion and spent the whole time trying to work out their motives.

My only hope – our only hope – is Susan Boyle. And if she does get the Labour leadership job, what happens to the ruthless, sly, underhand, stop-at-nothing, win-at-any-price Gordon Brown? I'd love him to take the West Brom job.

We're all going to die – except Sven-Göran Eriksson

1 MAY 2009

When I first discovered, last Monday morning, that a strain of swine fever, spread between humans, was killing people in Mexico, the news only served to confirm something I'd suspected for a long time – Sven-Göran Eriksson is a jammy bugger. He lost his job as Mexican national coach at the beginning of April and subsequently headed back home to Europe. Knowing his luck, before leaving Mexico he probably used his large pay-off to invest in a company that makes face masks.

Mind you, we're now told that face masks don't actually help. I don't just mean in Mexico – they aren't rendered useless by the proximity of a large, droopy moustache – they don't help anyone. Apparently they need to be changed every few minutes to have any real benefit. This is a pity. A global move towards the wearing of face masks was probably Michael Jackson's last ever chance of blending into a crowd.

Of course, I don't want to make light of a killer illness but there's been so much crying wolf with SARS and bird flu that there is a temptation to not take the threat of a pandemic seriously. They can't even decide on a name. Some prefer the H1N1 virus – the boffin who finds the cure should definitely get that as their car number plate. Maybe we should revert to the original 'swine fever' thus giving the Bee Gees an opportunity to do a 'Candle-in-the Wind'-style rejig of one of their greatest hits. 'Swine fever, swine fe-ver-er. We don't want to catch it.'

So, are we all going to die oinking? Gordon Brown – always searching for a crisis he can be seen to guide us through – says the World Health

Organisation have praised the UK for being one of the countries best-prepared to fight a possible pandemic. That must be a fluke. We'll probably discover Mr Brown, when he was Chancellor in the late nineties, okayed a massive overspend on anti-virals because he thought they'd stop the Millennium Bug.

Anyway, next week we'll all receive a leaflet through the letterbox, telling us how to avoid this potentially lethal illness. When I first heard we'd be getting our swine flu prevention information by leaflet, I wondered if it was just a roundabout way of culling the illiterate. However, it turns out the campaign will also include TV advertising. In the good old days, this would mean we could all look forward to a Public Information Film in which a cartoon pig, sitting at a desk with a stethoscope around its neck, would speak to us in the manner of a very well-informed NHS official. 'Ah, there you are,' the pig would say, in a rather posh voice, 'now we've all heard it said that it would be extremely unusual if pigs flew, but pigs' flu is now very much a reality.' The doctor-pig would then carefully instruct us on stuff like covering our mouths when we cough or sneeze, and washing our hands regularly. We'd almost certainly get a close-up of him blowing his snout or rinsing his trotters as a visual aid. 'And don't let anyone frighten you by saying we're all going to die of swine flu,' the pig would say, in conclusion, 'they're just telling porkies.'

My childhood was full of stuff like this – a cartoon couple called Joe and Petunia watching a man drowning because he'd ignored the coastguard's flags, a cat called Charlie telling us not to talk to strangers, and a fairy-godmother informing an unhappy youth that he'd never keep his girlfriends if he didn't learn to swim. It seems, looking back, like the Public Information Film people had such a massive budget they ended up advising us on things that weren't actually all that imperative. It's my guess that the men at the PIF offices sat around for days, straining to think of ideas they could spend the money on. That's how we ended up with catchy jingles like 'Wear something white at night' and 'Don't overcrowd your car'.

What worries me about the pending swine flu campaign is that we, as a nation, seem to have lost the art of inventing funny cartoons or catchy slogans to spread the word. The government's 'Catch it, bin it, kill it' campaign is pithy but the accompanying diagrams of a tissue on its way into a waste-paper bin and hands being washed are very dull. Having said that, I really hope the swine flu ad makers don't follow the modern tendency to make PIFs that are grim and scary – the dead child who constantly appears to the guilt-ridden driver, the drunken superhero who falls off the scaffolding. This 'scare 'em to spare 'em' approach is also evident in the recent 'condom essential wear' ads but, to be honest, I found frilly knickers with the word 'gonorrhoea' on them strangely enticing – in a sexual-Russian-roulette kind of a way. Anyway, I don't think anyone is going to be helped by an ad set in some steamy nightclub where the writhing dancers all spiral, one by one, to the floor to eventually reveal, in a dark corner, a man in a sombrero, sneezing and not putting his hand in front of his mouth.

No, give me the informative doctor-pig any time. If he can't save us, and swine flu falls upon us like the black death, you know where to find me – as close to Sven-Göran Eriksson as possible.

The one good thing about getting shot in the head by your husband

8 MAY 2009

When I was six years old, I saw a group of kids playing in the street outside my house. They were leaning a small, flat stick against the side of the kerb to form a sort of tiny see-saw. They put a stone on one end and then stamped on the other to fire the stone upward. OK, it's not *Grand Theft Auto* but I couldn't wait to have a go. In my enthusiasm I didn't realise you had to lean back a little to clear the missile's trajectory and, after the mightiest foot-stamp I could muster, I got the stone full in the mouth. This was years before collagen injections but it had a very similar effect on my lips. It also chipped a gap in my two front teeth. Forty-odd years later my dentist offered to finally fix that gap. I was uncertain about the change so he put in a temporary filler to show me how neat my teeth would be without the missing bits. I looked in the mirror and recoiled. The teeth now seemed like two enormous slabs of enamel, dominating my face and turning me into a different person. I got my dentist to put me back to normal immediately.

If that small dental transformation had such a dramatic effect, imagine how this week has been for Connie Culp, America's first face-transplant patient. She looks in the mirror now and sees a completely different face. Psychologists say that face-transplant recipients come to see their identity as a mix between theirs and their donor's. That is quite a concept. I'm still struggling with Norwich Union becoming

Aviva. Clint Hallam, the man who had the first hand transplant, ended up having it amputated because he said it felt like having a dead man's hand attached to his body. There's a reason for that. I don't know if the hand was used again for transplant. If so, it can't be too far away from having its own logbook. There now, I did the Clint Hallam story and stubbornly resisted a pun involving the term 'second-hand'. It's these little acts of willpower that build a comic's strength. Anyway, surely a new face requires a much greater psychological adjustment than a new hand – and not just for the patient. Apparently, families of face donors seem to feel their loved one has gained a second life from the transplant. It's a bit like giving your grandad's suit to a charity shop. I wonder how the relatives of Connie Culp's donor felt when they saw the face doing a press conference. Are they sitting at home saying stuff like 'I'm surprised they stuck with that dimple'? With all this emotional upheaval, a donor's family is likely to be a bit hit-and-miss when it comes to letting friends of the deceased know about the transplant. It could be quite dangerous if you were driving down a main road and saw your dead mate's face smiling at you from a passing car.

Despite these complications, face transplants are a miraculous thing and give the victims of horrible events a second chance. The first ever recipient, a French woman called Isabelle Dinoire, took an overdose of sleeping tablets and went into a coma. Her dog, in an attempt to wake her up, ate her face. I assume this was essentially licking that got out of hand. Mme Dinoire did eventually wake up but by then her face was almost completely gone. Ironically, the dog then began barking because he didn't recognise her. One wonders why barking hadn't been his first port-of-call when he was coming up with a method for waking her up. Dinoire then made two amazing decisions. She decided she wanted to live and she also decided to forgive the dog and ask that he might be allowed to live too.

Imagine being so weighed-down with care you take an overdose. Then, having woken up with those same unbearable problems plus the further downer of having had your face eaten by a pet, you decide, actually, things aren't so bad after all and you want to live. Furthermore, I'm not totally convinced by her generous interpretation of the dog's behaviour. Was he really trying to wake her up or did he just think 'She's in a coma, the doors are locked and I can't use a tin-opener – best tuck-in while she's still edible.' Anyway, the dog was put down and Dinoire had a face-transplant which, three years later, looks very good indeed.

In Connie Culp's case, her husband shot her in the face with a shotgun and then, as they say in news reports, turned the gun on himself. The fact that both are still alive suggests a level of marksmanship that would make Nicholas Bendtner blush.

Many are against face transplants. People say the psychological upheaval is too risky and also that the operation will eventually be misused to give criminals new identities. Judging by Isabelle Dinoire's experience, I think face transplants are brilliant. In fact, I'd be happy to be a donor. My hair-clippings recently sold for £1,000 on eBay. I wonder what I'd get for my face. Before making your offer, ask yourself if you really want to spend the rest of your life having abusive things about West Bromwich Albion shouted at you. Celebrity face donors could be a whole new avenue of enterprise – though I reckon Gary Glitter's could be a long time on the shelf. Of course, everything that happens in the entire world nowadays is, somehow, bad news for Gordon Brown. All these face and hand transplants are going to play Hell with ID cards.

Cleanliness is next to Godliness, but not when it comes to moats

15 MAY 2009

I once saw a very respectable-looking middle-aged woman stopped by a security guard on her way out of a shop in Oxford Street. The woman became extremely indignant when questioned. As the guard grabbed a fistful of CDs from her bag, she shouted, in a hoity-toity voice, 'How dare you go in my bag?' clearly feeling this to be a much worse crime than stealing the CDs. I've relived that scene a few times this week as I've watched MPs, on TV, getting uppity because their expenses claims have been scrutinised.

The thing is, I know we're supposed to be outraged because, ultimately, taxes have been misused but – like the spectacle of the posh shoplifter – I wouldn't have missed it for the world. Oh, how they've squirmed. The truth is, it's probably the first time I've ever felt I was getting my money's worth from politicians. If we divvied out the dodgy-expenses total, it would only cost each taxpayer a penny or two – a small price to pay for all that entertainment. Take, for example, the news that Tory MP, Douglas Hogg, spent about £2,000 getting his moat cleaned. Now it may well be, as Hogg maintains, that there was no public money involved in this. I don't care. Just to know that a Tory MP has a moat is enough for me. The news makes me so happy I'm inclined to stump-up the two grand myself, by way of a thank you. You see, I now realise that David Cameron, with his pushbike and his 'Call me Dave' man-of-the-people-ness, had begun to blur my long-held view of what the Tory party was all about. Thank God, Douglas Hogg and his moat have brought me back to my senses. The most damning criticism aimed at MPs nowadays is that they're isolated and out of touch. It's pretty hard to refute that if you've got a moat.

Then again, one must question the wisdom of getting it cleaned out. Obviously, I love the image of Mr Hogg, swathed in Barbour, shouting 'you missed a bit under the drawbridge' at a man in overalls, but I thought the whole idea of a moat was to keep it as slimy and horrible as possible, thus repelling potential trespassers. I assume this particular moat's purpose is to keep out working-class people so Mr Hogg should beware lest his now crystal-clear moat become an impromptu lido for the local peasantry. I loved the footage of Mr Hogg being pursued through the streets of Westminster by a TV crew. Surprisingly, for a former Cabinet Minister, he seemed unused to such treatment. I suppose door stepping isn't that common when you've got a portcullis.

An 'angry' Mr Cameron was interviewed in the street, on Tuesday morning, wearing, I noticed, an open-necked shirt. I imagine he was about to leave the house, despairing that his cosmetic reinvention of the party had been ruined, when he suddenly had a thought. 'I know. I'll take my tie off. That should re-establish my ordinary-bloke credentials.' Lucky for him it wasn't a chillier morning or he might have absent-mindedly knotted a pastel-shade sweater around his shoulders and handed Gordon Brown the next election on a plate.

Many of the MPs caught making claims that were not within the rules or the spirit of the rules have agreed to pay back the cash, as if that will wipe the slate clean. I'm afraid the horse has already bolted, although not before leaving £389 worth of manure in Tory MP David Heathcoat-Amory's garden. I don't think bank-robbers get let-off if they give the money back, do they? If the posh shoplifter had offered to give back the CDs I wouldn't have thought any better of her. I wouldn't have thought she'd acknowledged her sins and sought to right her wrong. No, I'd have thought she was giving back the booty for one reason only – because she'd been caught. If those expenses hadn't been leaked would any of the party leaders have made a stand to clean up a corrupt system? Not that we should draw moral solace from the leak itself. It wasn't, it seems, a virtuous act. Rumour has it these details of how greed corrupts people were, ironically, sold to the highest bidder – the righteous revelations trafficked like a pole-dancer's kiss-and-tell. No light-amidst-the-darkness there.

So, what next? Well, we have to be careful. A lot of these claims were within the rules and not massively outside the spirit of the rules. Most MPs, it seems, have just dipped their toe in the refurbished swimming pool water. I reckon the Kelly Committee should do a thorough investigation – uncontaminated by media outrage – and isolate the MPs who were properly shafting the taxpayers. Then, before the next election, those MPs should be officially named and shamed. Furthermore, any electoral literature or merchandise they use in their election campaign should include a sort of 'health warning' identifying them as expenses cheats. Even their rosettes and badges should bear this mark of Cain. I thought maybe a stylised image of a bath-plug would be apt. It would remind us of the one Jacqui Smith claimed 88p for. (A pay-per-view porn film is much harder to represent as a logo.) This way the scandal-scarred MPs' constituents get to choose who survives the cull. If they've been excellent MPs in other respects the voters may decide to forgive them. If not, they're out. Thus, we end up with a purged Parliament – cleaner than Hogg's moat – and some good will have come from all this squalor.

If you eat too many prawn sandwiches it lowers your IQ

22 MAY 2009

I was very interested in comments made by Andy Anson, a major figure in England's bid to stage the 2018 World Cup, at the official launch presentation this week. Anson claimed the miserable failure of our bid to host the 2006 World Cup was largely down to the official slogan – Football's Coming Home. 'It was an arrogant slogan,' he said, with clear disdain. Now then, I have great affection for the phrase Football's Coming Home and I wasn't too happy to hear some suit from the FA slagging it off. One reason the phrase has a special place in my heart is because it features heavily in a song I wrote with David Baddiel and Ian Broudie, but that's not the full story. I remember seeing Euro '96 banners bearing the original form, Football Comes Home, several weeks before the idea of us writing a song was suggested. The banners made me proud and slightly dewy-eyed. Maybe the Chinese were kicking a ball about before we were but the modern game of Association Football was born and raised in England. Any objections to that fact always turn out to be quibbling footnotes. The rules of football were drawn up in England, the FA Cup is the world's oldest football competition, and we formed the first football league. 'We've been all over the world,' said Mr Anson, 'and there are many countries that love football and believe they are its home.' They may be its foster-home but we all know what's on the birth certificate. I'd love England to host the World Cup in 2018 – probably not for the same merchandise, sponsorship and corporate-package-sales reasons that Andy Anson would – but I don't think we should deny our footballing heritage in order to get it. The slogan for the 2004 Olympics in Athens was Welcome Home – perfectly reasonable given the city's history. I don't recall anyone dismissing that as arrogant, or any countries who'd won more medals than Greece claiming the Olympic birth right was now theirs.

For all this talk of suicidal slogans, the story I heard – and it may not be true – is that a gentleman's agreement was made in which Germany promised not to challenge England for Euro '96 and we, in turn, promised not to challenge them for the 2006 World Cup. However, Euro '96 went so well, we broke our word and lost a lot of friends in the process. It might just be gossip but it does seem a little odd that FIFA, in their determination to avoid footballing arrogance, gave the World Cup to Germany.

When we wrote 'Three Lions', with the slightly modified Euro '96 slogan at its heart, the song was far from arrogant. It was all about pain, disappointment and that tiny glimmer of hope that keeps football fans going back for more. The fact the FA, during their 2006 bid, flew about in an aeroplane with Football's Coming Home on the fuselage might, I suppose, have seemed arrogant in that it lacked the nuances and qualifications of the complete lyric. Either way, blaming the slogan sounds a bit like trying to excuse a not very good and possibly dishonourable bid.

England's new slogan is 'England United; the world invited'. Generally speaking, any punctuation that appears in a slogan is an endangered species. That poor semi-colon is in for a very hard time between now and the bid's conclusion. Besides, for many football fans, the word United means only one thing, especially when one considers that Anson is a former Commercial Director at Old Trafford, the bid committee includes Manchester United Chief Executive, David Gill, and that the bid presentation featured United legends, David Beckham and Wayne Rooney.

But these latter pair, I hear you say, were a great choice because they are two of England's most famous players. If I wanted to be picky, I'd reply that, though I love them both, were it not for their violent conduct, and resulting red cards in two World Cup quarter-finals, the present England shirt might feature not only three lions but also three stars. Still, condemning Football's Coming Home as nationalistic but inviting a representative of the BNP to the launch is, as cock-ups go, quite hard to beat. Maybe Mr Anson should have topped off the event by introducing a video of the G20 riots as an example of how we'll deal with foreign fans should our bid be successful.

If the bid committee really want to win friends they should stop apologising for being the home of football and start courting FIFA president, Sepp Blatter. The best way to his heart is to back his so-called 6+5 scheme which, if it got past the European Union, would restrict Premiership teams to a maximum of five overseas players. If we supported that plan, or a modified-by-European-law version of it, we would almost certainly win extra votes, but I really can't see Manchester United's Chief Executive going for that. Nor will the FA, of course, because it would upset bosses of the multi-national Premiership clubs, especially the so-called 'big four'. The irony is that backing 6+5 might not only increase our chances of staging the 2018 World Cup, but also our chances of winning it. Incidentally, when Blatter was asked about a possible England 2018 bid back in September 2005, he said 'They should bid – it is the homeland of football.' He should tell Andy Anson.

Why most people shouldn't vote

29 MAY 2009

I read recently that, during the French Presidential election of 1981, a group of French students, backpacking in Thailand, put up pictures of the two candidates, Valéry Giscard d'Estaing and Francois Mitterand, in a small Thai village. They asked the villagers, none of whom had heard of these politicians, to vote in a mock election based solely on the two pictures. They gave everyone a bit of paper and the votes were cast. The Thai village voting mirrored almost exactly the results of the actual election in France. This story teaches us much about the arbitrariness of political democracy and has led me to re-evaluate my voting habits in political elections over the last 30-odd years.

The votes cast, this week, for contestants in the *Britain's Got Talent* semi-finals, are, I would maintain, far more valid than the average vote cast in an election. People watch the performances on *BGT*, often discussing them with their friends and family as they do so. They listen to the judges' analysis, weigh-up all this information and then vote because they genuinely care about the result – not because they feel some social obligation to take part. Admittedly, it's less time-consuming to attain a balanced and well-informed opinion of Susan Boyle than it is of David Cameron, but Ms Boyle is a good example of a candidate who would do much better in the actual contest than she would in the Thai village. We know more about her overall merit than the villagers so our assessment is more valid. Apart from a few political analysts amongst us, when it comes to Cameron, or any other politician, we follow a similarly arbitrary gut instinct to the villagers. Could you, dear reader, give a well-informed summing-up of the differences between the main parties' policies? No, neither could I. I could proffer the odd detail but no grand overview, no deep understanding. My highly sophisticated theory says Labour is working class, the Tories are posh and the Lib Dems will never get in. However, I could talk with some authority about the various merits and failings of the *BGT* semi-finalists – and have done so at length. The irony is, of course, that voting for Susan Boyle, as opposed to Diversity or Stavros Flatley, doesn't really change anyone's life except theirs. Voting for one political party instead of another could be a matter of life or death.

The notion that we all have a moral obligation to vote is extremely counter-productive. Surely people who don't know much about politics should stay out of it and leave voting to the well informed. I mean, it would kill *BGT* if loads of people who didn't watch the show started casting votes based on hearsay, brief clips on trailers or just because they quite liked someone's face. The value of the well-informed viewer's vote would be much diminished as it got lost in the ill-informed swirl of random voting. Likewise, what's the point of one voter, at election time, studying the manifestos and devouring the views of the various political experts if there are a thousand other voters basing the entire contest on eyebrow thickness? Let this latter group opt-out so that the studied vote has the weight it deserves.

Following the MPs' expenses scandal, I've heard loads of people say they'll never vote again. It seems to me they were just waiting for a moral get-out clause. They were only voting because they felt they ought rather than because of any passionate determination that the best candidate should succeed. We are better off without them. They are the sort of people who vote for Stavros Flatley because they once had a nice holiday in Greece. I hereby launch a new campaign called 'If you don't know – don't vote'. This gives everyone the opportunity to decide whether or not they're prepared to do the research necessary to produce a worthwhile vote. Those that aren't can walk away with their heads held high. They don't know enough to vote wisely, they don't want to do the homework and, respect to them, they don't want their random vote to contribute to an erratic result. Those of us who remain – and I've decided to go for the long haul – probably have about a year to swot-up on the various issues and thus make an intelligent contribution in the next General Election.

Of course, the European Elections are upon us but we'll never get our heads around that one in the short time remaining so let's ignore it and opt for the long-term goal of putting the right party in power next summer. If any readers are well versed in the European Election issues – I'm guessing about seven of you – then of course go forth and, after much astute deliberation, vote. You know better than I so I'm happy to trust your judgement. As part of this new campaign, I will relax my long-held affection for the Labour party and create my own political year-zero. Thus I'll approach the knowledge I'm about to consume, with a clear and objective head. Those of you with an urge to learn more, come with me on this voyage of discovery. To the rest of you, adieu, and please never touch another ballot paper. I honestly think we'll all be better off with a low turnout that's high on information. Let's have quality of votes not quantity of votes. If you don't know – don't vote.

Burkas are cosy.
I should tell Sarkozy

26 JUNE 2009

I was once asked if I'd like to be the mascot at a West Bromwich Albion football match. It involved me having to wear a large thrush costume. I mean, of course, the bird. It wasn't some tasteless promotional event where I was dressed as an irritating rash and then seized upon by a man dressed as a tube of Canesten. I agreed to be the thrush but only if no one knew it was me inside. I'm world famous in West Bromwich so I thought it would be novel to stroll around in front of 20 thousand-odd people and not be recognised.

The outfit was quite heavy and hot with just a small slit at eye-level to stop me walking into things. Before the game, I wandered around, waving to the crowd and having my photo taken with small children. Such is the role of the mascot. For these photos, I adopted my regulation warm-hearted grin but, after I'd posed for about 20 such shots, it occurred to me that this was completely unnecessary because I couldn't be seen. I was getting a bit bored and hot by now and it was a real treat to not have to look happy and enthusiastic. Come photograph number 50 I was actually scowling but no one could tell. This was a truly liberating experience and it suddenly made me realise why many Muslim women are reluctant to give up the veil. It can be truly joyous to pass unseen through the outside world with no obligation to smile or look interested – hidden in your own secret place.

The French president, Nicolas Sarkozy, took a much more negative view of the burka issue this week when he said 'we cannot accept that women be prisoners behind a screen, cut off from all social life, deprived of all identity.' I assume he wasn't a big fan of *Blind Date*. He seems to assume that Muslim women are always forced by others to wear the veil. I don't doubt that is sometimes the case but it doesn't seem to be the whole story. One often hears Muslim women in interviews saying they like wearing the burka, not just for religious but also practical reasons. These views tend to be disregarded and seen as the product of indoctrination. Such a dismissive response seems to make these women and their opinions every bit as invisible as the burka does.

The much-demonised garb is seen as a symbol of oppression but oppression comes in many forms. Lots of British women have said to me that they resent being gawped at just because they're wearing a miniskirt or a low-cut top. I always apologise and say I didn't mean any harm. Alternatively, a friend said to me recently that she was saddened to notice that, as she grew older, men had stopped staring at her. She felt she was no longer desirable, no longer receiving approval. These are two very different problems, both by-products of our western cult of physical attractiveness and both solved by the burka.

I don't believe that any man should force his wife to wear a burka but I'm not sure that Sarkozy, the extremely proud owner of a trophy-wife, is the best man to speak on the matter. Add to this the fact that he was once seen to be checking his text messages during a private audience with the Pope and one might also ask whether religious sensitivity is one of his strengths. Either way, his call to actually ban the burka on French streets cannot be the answer.

In the late-nineties, I went to Africa with Comic Relief. A group of us, mainly white middle-class liberals, sat in a village in Burkina Faso and spoke to the village elders. We asked about the distinctive scars many of the men had on their faces and it turned out to be the result of some sort of initiation ceremony. Someone asked if we could see the ceremonial knife. I think we were just trying to sound interested. Eventually a rather disappointing little penknife with a dirty wooden handle turned up and we all passed it around as if it were a beautiful artefact. One of the women from the production team asked if it was used for any other purpose. 'Female circumcision' was the reply. We all went silent and handed the knife back. None of us had the guts to register our disgust. I sat in a disused army barracks afterwards imagining what I should have said. 'I'm sorry. It's one thing having respect for other people's cultures but some things are just objectively wrong.' Only the mosquitoes heard my indignation. Consequently, I do respect Sarkozy for having the courage to speak out on the sensitive issue of cultural difference but on this occasion I think he's being too simplistic. It's not as clear-cut as he suggests. I'm not sure the burka is objectively wrong. Some Muslim women clearly feel oppressed by it but then some clearly don't. To ban it is to remove women's choice, using oppression to combat oppression. Rigid rules that make no allowance for personal choice are more suited to the Taliban than to one of Europe's great democracies. So that's my take on the burka issue – all based on 55 minutes in a thrush suit. Next week: Silvio Berlusconi on why stockings and suspenders should be compulsory.

My breakfast with the Crown Prince of Serbia

3 JULY 2009

I was messing around on the Internet the other day when I noticed a Saver shop in Glasgow was selling inflatable crocodile riders for just 69p. They're called crocodile 'riders', I discovered, because they're sturdy enough for children to ride them across the swimming pool. Of course, I wasn't able to check the quality of the product first-hand but nevertheless it did seem to be a bargain. When I considered this image of something that costs just 69p and still manages to stay afloat, no matter how foolishly the children behave, I immediately thought of the Queen. 69p, I learned this week, is how much she cost each of us last year. Speaking as someone who doesn't have a swimming pool, children, or any interest in making a very low-budget Tarzan movie, Her Majesty would seem to be the better buy. Admittedly, a breakdown of her spending is slightly alarming. For example, she spent £14,000 on a train journey from London to Liverpool. Still, that's what happens when an old-age pensioner tries to operate the self-service ticket machine. Personally, I take a more liberal attitude to the Queen's expenses than I do to those racked-up by our MPs. It stands to reason that she's going to be heavy on the moat-maintenance bills and a floating duck island – or 'target practice', as the Royal Family calls it – would seem, to me, equally acceptable. No, I'm happy to pay 69p a year for the Queen but, of course, it's not just her I'm paying for, is it? It's all those hanger-on relatives.

What does this country gain from spending £150,000 on flying the Duke and Duchess of Gloucester to the King of Tonga's coronation?

What's more, who gets the air miles? And then there's the £250,000 we spent on improvements to Princess Beatrice's student flat. Unless things have changed a lot since my student days, I can only imagine this money was spent on a sterling silver Pot Noodle dispenser and a deluxe display case for traffic cones. No, all that's got to stop. We need to introduce a sort of stamp duty – if you've never been on a stamp, you're off the payroll.

Also, I think the Queen's own case would be helped considerably if she showed some evidence of having noticed there's a recession going on. 'One is so strapped for cash one had to withdraw six million quid from one's personal account' is probably not the way forward. I'm also not sure it's wise to complain that Buckingham Palace has become so dilapidated a large piece of masonry fell off an archway and narrowly missed the Princess Royal. That just puts the idea in the public's mind that if we wait long enough the problem might end up solving itself.

I recently had breakfast with the Queen's godson Crown Prince Alexander of Serbia and his wife Crown Princess Katherine, at their palace in Belgrade – fresh fruit, bacon with scrambled eggs, and then chocolates in the shape of a crown. I asked the Prince if the latter ever caused him to exclaim 'Well, I'll eat my hat'. He smiled politely. As Serbian Royal breakfast banter goes, it was one of the highlights. I have to say, I think our Royal Family could learn a lot from their Serbian counterparts. As we walked through one beautiful room I noticed signs of staining on the floor. 'The roof leaks,' explained the Crown Prince, 'but these are hard times for our country. We must be patient.' We were making a documentary but I'm pretty sure we weren't being filmed at that point. The Prince wasn't playing to the camera. He was just a Royal, amidst a world financial crisis, being realistic. He pointed out several other parts of the two royal palaces that were in need of renovation but he also celebrated the beauty of the buildings and grounds and explained how happy he was to be living there. I'm sure Alexander's positive attitude owes much to the fact he was born in exile – actually in Room 212 at Claridge's. Winston Churchill allowed the room to become Yugoslavian territory for the period surrounding the birth so the Prince could be born on his home soil. That's how to cut travel expenses. I'm sure Gordon Brown, if asked, would have let a few square feet of the Gloucesters' back garden become Tonga for a weekend.

At one point we passed the graves of General Tito's horse, dog and girlfriend in the palace grounds. The General had lived there during his time in power. I asked if Mrs Tito knew about the girlfriend. 'A wise wife never knows,' said Princess Katherine – again, a much more practical attitude than our own Royals with their 'three people in this marriage' whingeing.

Clearly, there's nothing like a bit of exile to make a Royal Family appreciate its privileged position. Our lot have had it pretty easy since 1660. When Buckingham Palace was bombed during the war, the Queen Mother famously said she was glad because it meant she could 'look the East End in the face'. If the Queen wants to be able to look her subjects in the face, she must lead by example and be seen to be tightening her belt like the rest of us. I'm happy to sing 'God Save the Queen' as long as she agrees to make a few savings herself.

Why no loud-mouthed kid is going to stop me liking the emperor's new clothes

10 JULY 2009

The Trafalgar Square fourth plinth project didn't start that well. It got hijacked before it began – by an anti-smoking campaigner, of all things. That's a bit retro, isn't it? Who's next? The suffragettes? I guess they'd instinctively head for the plinth next door, to throw themselves in front of King George V's horse.

I like the idea of Antony Gormley's *One and Other* – 2,400 people representing a living portrait of modern Britain, each getting an hour on the plinth. Many, however, are hostile to the project. I heard it described as 'PC claptrap' (wasn't he in Noddy?). I'm already starting to think you can judge someone's entire inner-being by the way they respond to *One and Other*. Some wear a sweeping dismissal of all forms of modern art as a badge of honour. It's their way of defining themselves as no-nonsense people, not susceptible to hype. They seem to be emperor's-clothes-phobic. 'Is it art?' they ask. For these people, the way to find out is to compare the new thing to something they are absolutely sure *is* art, say Frans Hals' *The Laughing Cavalier*, and then see how similar it is. This seems a restrictive rule-of-thumb to me. One of the worst things that can strike down a human being is the slam-shut closing of the mind – the idea that one's opinion on something has been finally formulated and is now set in stone. I think opinions should be like plasticine – always open to reshaping, always having the potential to become something new.

Many will judge Gormley's project without even going down to the Square to take a look. Determined not to be one of them, I headed off to the plinth on Monday evening, eight hours into the first day. About 15 people were watching a man in a grey suit and a turban who stood on the plinth texting. I assumed this was some hiatus in his performance but it became apparent that this *was* his performance. Maybe he was making some comment about how we allow modern technology to put us somewhere else – with someone else – stunting our response to what is actually going on around us. Or maybe he couldn't think of anything else to do. As I gazed at this spectacle, about 20 feet away from the plinth, a young woman approached me and said, 'Do you know where I can find the Antony Gormley installation?' I pointed at the texting man. It's not the *most* disappointment I've ever seen in a woman's eyes but I could tell this wasn't quite what she expected. Then an elderly tourist came up to me, clearly wondering what was going on. He pointed at the plinth. Rather cryptically, he asked 'Is that man an engineer?' I tried to explain he was actually art. 'Shouldn't he be very still, like him?' he said, pointing at Nelson. I understood his confusion. People pretending to be statues are a commonplace in nearby Covent Garden. They stand totally still and people give them money. It's like working for the council. If one of them was booked for the plinth they could go on as a Saddam Hussein statue and then, over the course of the hour, be gradually pulled over by ropes until, as a grand finale, a little old man ran over and hit them with a flip-flop. I didn't put this idea to the tourist.

I've visited the plinth a few times and keep a regular check on the Sky Arts webcam but, so far, everything I've seen has been absolute rubbish. When Andy Warhol said everyone would be famous for 15 minutes, he was predicting a reality TV world but also making a point about attention span. An hour, in this context, is a bloody long time. Probably, amidst the mix of those 2,400 plinth-people there will be magical moments but, you know what, I don't think that's the point.

One and Other makes me proud to be British. It says more about

Britishness than George V and his horse – maybe even more than Nelson. The fact that a corner of one of our most famous landmarks has been given over to a group of ordinary citizens, to do with what they will, is a fabulous symbol of freedom and free speech. You can go up there and slag off the government, rail about the environment, or just do nothing. It's the art of being free. Imagine trying to get this project off the ground in Iran. It doesn't really matter if they're dull. If you cleared the other three plinths and gave Simon Cowell, Amanda Holden and Piers Morgan one each – with buzzers – it would be a completely different event. This isn't *Britain's Got Talent*, it's *Britain's Got Freedom.*

However, as much as I admired the man who spent half-an-hour driving golf balls at David Blaine when he hung from a crane near Tower Bridge, I hope the plinth-people are protected from that part of being British that it's harder to be proud of – aggressive, drunken young men. If there's one thing these lot don't like it's that which is different. If there's someone up there ballet dancing to whale-calls they'll see it as a provocation. Think of that scenario when you are casually condemning *One and Other*. You must decide whether you're with the ballet dancer or the bullies, the closed minds or the open. Where's my tutu?

War is like sooo 1940s

17 JULY 2009

It's not just about helicopters and the right kind of armoured car, is it? The problem is we, as a nation, can't really do war any more. Our view of it has become too nuanced and complicated. The reasons for war always required a good edit in order to be persuasive – the dark motivations snipped-out to give the public a focused image of a just and winnable conflict. A war relies on a certain naivety back home in order to be acceptable. I hate to say it but nowadays we know too much. The golden wall behind which the powerful have always hidden their little secrets – their MPs' expenses, their celebrity phone-taps and their waterboarding – has been breached so often of late it's beyond repair. I watched, this week, that video of Iraqi prisoners, hooded and forced to squat in the agonising 'stress position' – a British soldier screaming at them and calling them apes. I'm glad I saw it and I wished I hadn't. It wasn't the image of war I grew up with. It wasn't fearless Tommy Atkins battling the evil Hun with a wink, a whistle and a self-rolled cigarette. It was more like one of those sickening slices of city-centre violence when testosterone's heavy in the air and you just look straight ahead and keep walking. It seemed like yob culture had been institutionalised and put to practical use. But what do I know? What would I do if I was out there – that mysterious 'there' that we don't want to even think about? Maybe when you've been shot at a few times your opinions change. Maybe those people who spent their gap-year 'doing' the Middle East – soaking up its fabulous customs and culture – developed a slightly more affectionate view of the locals than someone who's there to fight the Taliban. Once someone becomes the enemy, plain and simple, it doesn't really matter if they have an interesting cuisine or not. They're just the bad guys. Or are they? Well, back home, it's easy to enjoy the intriguing ambiguities of the good-guy-bad-guy conundrum. Should we be there? Who are the real villains? I suspect such intellectual teasers aren't quite so much fun when your mate is dead in the sand.

Patriotism used to be a great antidote for doubt in these matters but that tends to get lumped with racism and insularity now. I watched Sky Arts' programme about Trafalgar Square's Fourth Plinth last week. Ken Livingstone dropped his avuncular manner for a moment to point out that the other plinths and, indeed, the central column, were occupied by 'war criminals and people involved in the invasion of India'. If Nelson isn't a hero any more, what hope is there for Nathan from Chelmsford? Ken's remarks show that war – and the idea of heroism in war – isn't just unpopular nowadays, it's unfashionable. Political correctness has made a soldier a naff thing to be. They've deheroicised the troops and redrawn them as right wing pawns – short-haired lads in big boots beating up people in turbans. It's as if that 'stress position' video was the whole story. Alternatively, we get the regular glowing references to 'our boys' from the red tops. But even that feels like trying too hard – a conscious reaction to the PC view. It seems to be an attempt to stem the tide. The truth is white van man, with his England flag in the back of the cab, is also unsure about this war. The government's arguments are often designed, with limited success, to win over the broadsheet reader but, meanwhile, they are, as a by-product, driving away the old-fashioned patriots. White van man doesn't want our boys fighting for women's rights and better schooling in some country that's got, it seems, nothing to do with us.

Most of us are anti-war nowadays but we feel we can hate the sin but love the sinner – support the spotty lad with the rifle whilst condemning the horrors of the bigger picture. I'm not sure we can. I watched the Conservatives questioning Secretary of State for Defence, Bob Ainsworth this week. Inevitably, the debate became an opportunity for an attack on the government – they were letting the soldiers down and expecting them to fight with *Dad's Army* equipment – regardless of the effect such talk might have on the morale of both the troops and their relatives. Perhaps equipment isn't our biggest problem. I suspect it's pretty hard to fight in a war that seems to be becoming more and more unpopular – a war that's constantly deconstructed and devalued by a million bits of comment and analyses. When I saw those coffins going through Wootton Bassett, with the townsfolk standing respectfully at the kerbside, it seemed like something from a bygone age. It was as if those mourners had decided to put their knowingness on hold for a while and simply respect the fallen – a sort of simplicity flashback. Even then, within a few moments of the cortège's passing, we had a man from the crowd being interviewed on TV and saying, of the war, 'we shouldn't be there.' We seem to have outgrown war – to be too wise to buy into the propaganda – but war hasn't gone away. Someone is actually out there, in a less-nuanced life-or-death world, and we need to find a middle way between blind belief and undermining condemnation.

Air-guitar and the death of God

24 JULY 2009

I spent last weekend at the Latitude Festival in Suffolk. The experience completely restored my faith in festivals. I went to V a few years back and decided there that my festival-going days were behind me. It wasn't really a festival at all – just an enormous gig. A festival, to me, is not just about which big-name acts are playing. I need some peace and love – a sense that people have left their anxieties and aggression at the gate and bought-into a three-day idyll. That's what Latitude is. The fact that 35,000 people flock to such an event suggests to me that they have an inner yearning, not just to dance, get stoned and have sex in a tent, but also to live in a world where people smile, talk to strangers and wear anything they like – a world that doesn't seem to exist on the other side of the festival fence.

It didn't matter, for example, that I was a man in my fifties. I was accepted for what I was, uncool as that might be – with one interesting exception. On several occasions over the weekend, as I watched bands on the various stages, I spontaneously played air-guitar. These were the only times I felt like a genuine outsider. The looks I got from those around me were less about sniggering and derision and more about genuine confusion. I'm not telling you a tired tale of groovy-uncle-dancing embarrassing the young. No, it went deeper than that. I think it was specifically related to the nature of air-guitar – to why air-guitar is a genuine challenge to modern sensibilities.

The fact that I even noticed how people were reacting to my invisible axe shows that I too was letting self-consciousness restrict my spirit. There is an adage I've long adhered to which states that true happiness has been achieved when one is able to 'dance like there's no one watching' – to be content in one's own skin and untroubled by the opinions of others. The sort of dancing I'm referring to is all about unrestrained joy, not the gruelling discipline of those rictus-grin manne quins on *Strictly Come Dancing*. It is a losing of oneself, not a public performance. I feel the same about air-guitar. There are air-guitar competitions but these seem to directly contravene the spirit of the thing. They are entered and judged ironically, with a knowing look. Air-guitar should never be ironic.

I once asked Eric Clapton if he ever played air-guitar. He looked perplexed. 'Why would I?' he asked. 'I can play real guitar.' He seemed to be missing the point. Air-guitar isn't for people who can't play real guitar. I play real guitar – not as well as Eric Clapton, obviously – but the pleasure it gives me is completely different from the pleasure I get from air-guitar. I'm not sure I even like the phrase 'real guitar' – it seems to champion materialism and commercialism. An air-guitar has no maker's name, no pre-ordained design. It belongs to the player in a more real way than any physical object can belong to anyone. Admittedly, in my early days, I played air-guitar more as a substitute real guitar rather than an instrument in its own right. I would begin by taking an air-plectrum from my jeans-pocket, often stepping on an air wha wha pedal and even gesturing to an air roadie, pointing at my ear and suggesting I needed more volume. I was confined by all this – my air-guitar falsely restricted by the limitations of its wood-and-metal counterpart. For example, I always switched to left-handed for a Hendrix track and held my strumming-hand 18 inches away from my body for the Gipsy Kings. Air-guitar should not acknowledge such restraints.

I think the reason I was stared at by the surrounding youth as I played my mystical instrument last weekend was more to do with our conflicting world-views than my lack of cool. I think, in a society where belief in God – in some supernatural world beyond the physical – has largely disappeared, air-guitar represents a provocative example of belief in the unseen. Music is often a challenge to materialist reductivism. It seems to be more than the sum of its parts – more than the human beings and instruments that generate it. It seems to touch something within us which is of another place. Air-guitar is a celebration of this. It says that our experience of music cannot be broken down into player and listener. We share it equally, as a unified group with no hierarchy separating those who have the technical capability to produce music and those who do not. Air-guitar symbolises this democracy. I know that what I felt on Sunday night, when Magazine played 'Shot by Both Sides', was a liberating, deindividualising experience shared by everyone present but, at the same time, all the various ingredients of our separate personalities meant that we, and I include the members of Magazine, also each had an individual response to the song. Air-guitar makes manifest the slightly ungraspable, invisible nature of all this. It seems a more appropriate instrument, at that moment, than the physical objects from which the sound is actually emanating. When the youth take up air-guitar again they will realise that the spiritually charged, love-infused world they spend the whole summer searching for is right there at their fingertips. Yes, it was a very good festival.

A speech to win Gordon Brown the General Election

31 JULY 2009

If we are to believe Lord Mandelson – a heart-stopping dive into the gullibility deep-end, I must admit – there will be a US presidential-style TV debate between Gordon Brown and David Cameron before the next General Election. Anyone who's ever watched an ox being terrorised by a squirrel – the lumbering beast snorting and wincing as the tiny claws score a million scratch-marks on his surprisingly sensitive hide – will be eagerly eyeing the TV listings in anticipation. But what if Mr Brown, at that eleventh hour, managed to spring a surprise, to turn things around when all seemed lost – a little shimmy, the soft sound of squirrel against soil and, before it can scramble to its feet, a spine-snapping, eye-popping hoof splats it into silence. All it would need would be one killer opening speech, honest and clear, to place Mr Brown, hoof raised, above the terrified rodent. But what could he say that would win us over at that late stage in the game? I offer here a transcript of a speech that would probably persuade me.

Good evening. May I begin by saying that those of you who've tuned-in to see the famous 'Gordon Brown inappropriate smile' will, I'm afraid, be disappointed. I gave it a go but it wasn't me. It looked out of place, like when a vacillating supermarket customer leaves an incongruous jar of strawberry jam on the household detergent shelf. I've always felt that my wife, Sarah, and I get on so well because we share a sense of humour. We have to – I don't have one. It's time to stop pretending I do. Speaking of relationships I feel that my relationship with you, the British people, has gone through a very bad patch.

You may even be thinking of dumping me. This handsome young chap over here (gesturing towards Cameron) has flattered and flirted his way through a charm-offensive with which this loyal, loving but unspectacular fellow on your arm has struggled to compete. In case you're wondering, he smells lovely – of mint leaves and bergamot – whereas I smell like a cross between a lemon curd sandwich and an antiquarian bookshop. I know you've gone off me and like every insecure partner, I've sat with friends, emptying my heart and listening to their extensive advice – try YouTube, wear lighter colours, talk about your private life, say there won't be cuts, smile. I've tried to be something I wasn't. Conscientious, honest, hard-working people are never that sexy. Look at Officer Dibble in *Top Cat*. He was a dedicated officer of the law but that fast-talking, bobbing-and-weaving Top Cat made him look like a flatfooted fool. However, when you've been mugged or burgled, if you're sick or frightened in the night, who you gonna call? Not Top Cat. He'll be out with his fat cat friends playing hands of poker for more than you earn in a year and making jokes about those who aren't part of his smug little in-crowd. Close friends get to call him DC. It's Officer Dibble who's going to care about your plight, who'll work overtime to sort things out, who'll do his very best to help. My predecessor, Tony Blair, used to say to me, 'Gordon, you've got some great stuff in your storeroom but your shopfront scares everyone off.' He was right. Tony was a tough act to follow. He was charismatic, a master of the soundbite. How popular would John the Baptist have been if he'd followed Jesus rather than preceded him? I'm crying out in the wilderness, living on locusts and honey and wearing a filthy animal skin. No wonder I'm lagging in the polls. Tony, like the original messiah, got crucified in the Middle East but seems to have risen again. Yes, he's come back as a bloody eco-friendly, millionaire-next-door, Tory toff on a sodding pushbike. Don't get fooled again. Alesha Dixon has great legs but will she really be a better judge than Arlene Phillips? Or will she just look better? David Cameron looks fabulous hissing-out his smarmy, Flashman-like repartee in the prat's vacuum that is Prime Minister's Questions – politics' answer to speed dating – but that's not the place to pick your next leader. It's more like a panel show than a political debate with straightforward, honest Gordon the butt of every bitchy joke. *Mock the Weak*, it should be called. Yes, I am quite weak and, I'll admit it, intimidated in the face of all that Bullingdon Club, thrash-the-fag aggressiveness. That is why I care about the weak in society, the bullied, the stammering and the slow. I see through all that and judge people by their hearts not their sparkly exteriors. David Cameron, or David Camera-on as I call him, might give you an exciting time at first but, when your calls are going unanswered, when you feel let down and deserted, maybe you'll remember solid, dependable Gordon. I wasn't born to rule like some of my social superiors. I had to learn on the job. I made mistakes. I've learned a lot from those mistakes. Three strikes and you're out sounds great but what about the knowledge and experience accrued during and after the missing of that third strike? Must that always be squandered? As you watch tonight's debate, I ask you to listen closely to what's being said and not be dazzled by the fireworks. Or indeed the smiles.

The menacing poetry of choral abuse

7 AUGUST 2009

If, as you read this, you're sitting at Headingley cricket ground, on a fresh English morning, all set for the Test Match, I'd ask you to do me one favour – ignore all requests to the contrary and boo Ricky Ponting. Boo him so loudly your collected boos form an ominous thunder reverberating in the pit of his stomach. Thus he might come to know that we are indeed, the mighty, mighty, England, and that the days of polite applause, silent suffering and weak-kneed, after-you-Claude defeatism are long behind us. He'll know full well that such treatment is reserved for only the very good or the very annoying. He'll also know that, though he occasionally dabbles in the latter category, he is firmly entrenched in the former. This is a slight worry for me because I once played cricket against the Barmy Army and they ridiculed me all day long, on the pitch and off – I doubt it was because I was 'very good'. Ponting will take each boo as a compliment but he'll also know this crowd have not come to enjoy a nice day out at the cricket. They've come to see England win the Ashes and they will boo and sing and anything else they need to do in order to contribute that maximum-potential 2 or 3 per cent effect a big crowd can have on a game. If sledging's OK for the players, why not for the fans? Not every Australian player is as gritty as Ponting. Some will die inside at every jibe and jeer. All that is tentative will become terrifying. That's Test Cricket and if the crowd don't fulfil their role with determination and gusto – do not fill the sails with noise – they should not be surprised if their team are tragically becalmed.

I was at Edgbaston last week when Ponting became the highest run-scorer in Australian Test Match history. The whole ground, even myself, loudly applauded his achievement. Ponting raised his bat and acknowledged us all. He knows the Edgbaston crowd is the loudest and lippiest in the country and thus he also knows that any ovation from them is not ritual politeness but rather hard-earned respect. I never usually applaud opposing batsmen, even for double-hundreds. I prefer the arms-crossed scowl. My greatest delight at a cricket match, particularly an Ashes game, is English runs coming from overthrows – the joy of their angry and accusing little faces beneath those baggy, green caps. It even beats an inside-edge for four from an English number 11. I'm with the former England skipper Douglas Jardine who said 'I'm not here to win friends – I'm here to win Test Matches.'

So why is there such a fuss about crowd-noise at these games? The Barmy Army is the best thing to happen to English cricket since *Test Match Special*. As a kid I would hear players talk about the fearsome Hill at Sydney Cricket Ground and wonder why our supporters couldn't be similarly intimidating. Now I feel proud that we have such an obviously passionate following wherever we play. I love the singing. I love the trumpet. Wherever I sit at a Test Match, there seems a general approval of the Barmies. Their chanting is almost never sweary and often hilarious. The trumpeter does a fabulous 'Theme from *Home and Away*'.

Dissenters lump together noisy support and drunkenness. The theory is that people drink too much, get loud and eventually boo Ricky Ponting. This is simplistic. I believe that if drink was outlawed at cricket grounds, people would still get loud and boo Ricky Ponting. The solid core of the Barmy Army – people who genuinely love the game – don't sing because they're drunk, they sing because they care.

Personally, I'd love to see drink banned at cricket grounds. I know it would reduce the opponent-battering noise-levels somewhat but we'd be left with quality rather than quantity – more constitutional teasing like 'God save YOUR gracious Queen' and less 'Aaaahblaaableblah!' I've seen horrible examples of drunkenness at big matches, and not just in the stands – in the posh seats and hospitality boxes too. I'm not talking about singing. I'm talking about that slow-blink, brooding drunkenness that makes people, at best, tedious and incomprehensible and, at worst, argumentative and quick to take offence. The last two hours of a Test Match, wherever you're sitting, can be like New Year's Eve on the night bus. Those who drink conservatively at the game – there are a handful – will argue that they shouldn't suffer because of the bad behaviour of others. Well, neither should I. There's a ban to prevent secondary smoking. I'm sure secondary drinking causes much more grief – not just at cricket but in the street, on the roads, and certainly in the family home of the drinker. Still, that's another column. I can't imagine anything changing the current policy, which seems to be 'We are happy to sell you vast amounts of alcohol as long as you don't exhibit any of its effects.'

We need plenty of noise to get us through these last two Tests. The Aussies would kill for fans like ours. I doubt they're moved to do truly great things because someone holds up an inflatable kangaroo. I'd rather be booing Ricky Ponting at Headingley than applauding him as he holds up the urn at the Oval. Actually, I'd rather be booing Ricky Ponting than doing most things.

How I learned to love jewellery thieves

14 AUGUST 2009

I was watching Sky News with my girlfriend, Cath, as they showed CCTV footage of the guys who stole £40 million worth of jewellery from Graff, the Mayfair jeweller's. Then they interviewed DCI Pam Mace, standing in front of that TV-camera-magnet, the New Scotland Yard sign. She felt someone would surely recognise these men and come forward to identify them. I asked Cath whether she'd call up if she knew who they were. 'No,' she said, 'what they did doesn't outrage me.' Her reply was no surprise. The night before, with increasing disbelief, she'd read me a long article about the Baby P case. The next morning it was reassuring to hear about a proper crime again – ordinary baddies doing ordinary baddie things. It felt like a breath of fresh air. We noted with relief the fact that no one was hurt, that a hostage was taken but only for a short scramble to the car and that guns were fired but, we were told, always into the ground. These were criminals with understandable materialistic ends and their target was what the Scottish *Daily Record* called a 'swanky jeweller's in London's West End' – posh people selling posh stuff to other posh people. I'm against romanticising crime but after the Baby P article, seeing these thieves as Raffles-like rogues seemed an acceptable indulgence. The newsreader put in a clause, seemingly aimed at nipping such mythologising in the bud. He said valuable gems were often used 'as collateral in a drugs deal or arms trade'. This felt like a deliberate attempt to remove the folk-hero option – to stop us admiring two handsome guys in suits who strolled into a shop that sells expensive baubles to the kind of people who are impressed by expensive baubles and then stopped the vanity-fuelled merry-go-round long enough to help themselves. Encouraging us to associate them with drugs and arms – businesses that we feel are populated by evil men – seemed a clumsy way of diverting us from the fact that expensive jewellery is hollow frippery and melting it down and selling it off feels a bit like a liberating triumph for common sense. I notice also that what were universally described as 'warning shots' were later redefined. A 'source close to the inquiry' said 'it could not be ruled out that the men intended to harm or kill'. Belated spin to discourage us from glamorising the robbers? If so I think it's an error. We're getting better at recognising spin and more resentful when we do. Of course, the people who worked in the jewellery shop must have been terrified but I'd been so desensitised by that Baby P article that I was not horrified by the image of muddy shoes on the store's lush carpet, harsh, impatient words cutting through the sickly muzak, or of disrespectful hands chucking the hallowed gems into a bag. No time for nonsense – get the stuff and get out. These two men seemed like the criminals of yesteryear – bad but fathomable.

All this from me, a man who'd said Ronnie Biggs should serve his time because the romantically titled Great Train Robbery was, in fact, built around an act of bullying violence. Suddenly, in this new context, I could see the Biggsian appeal too. I looked at the morning newspaper, saying old Ronnie – released from prison because he was near to death – had suddenly rallied and would probably be moved to a rest home by the weekend. Maybe that illness, I thought, had got Ronnie out of prison like the old gun-carved-out-of-wood trick. He'd even written, with a letter board, 'I've got a bit of living to do yet.' I looked forward to seeing tabloid shots of Ronnie on the town with Jordan.

So, after all these years of condemning the mythologising of criminals, this brief insight – I'm not sure I want it to last – has given me an opportunity to study the phenomenon first-hand. I think its allure is to do with the redistribution of wealth. The glorifying of people like Biggs is the closest the British people ever get to communism. They see the ordinary bloke taking money from the government or from a swanky jeweller's and they feel the balance has somehow been slightly redressed. It is a very British kind of revolution, no mass anarchy and guillotines – just the occasional attack on the faceless institutions that represent wealth and power. Let the common man take his bonus too – tax-free and self-regulated. Such criminals become our idealised representatives – Joe Public with an extra helping of chutzpah. People watch these men running rings around the authorities – skipping off to Brazil or zigzagging across London in a string of getaway cars – and they feel that well-heeled connections or expensive technological back-up is no match for the street nous of the artful dodger. The recession – with its tales of bankers' excesses and politicians' greed – makes these jewel thieves seem like the people's revenge. The establishment are embarrassed and irate but the bankers left behind many more victims. Meanwhile, the Baby P story leaves us with nothing good to hold on to – no glamour, no clever plan, no courageous operation. There is just a dull sense of relentless, stale-smelling, domesticated evil – the untenable juxtaposition of an adult's laughter with a child's tears. How bad have things got when I need to seize upon a jewellery heist to restore my faith in human nature?

Why we secretly want education standards to fall

21 AUGUST 2009

I'm at the Edinburgh Festival, hosting a nightly variety show. Earlier this week there was a crowd that, due to the quirks of unreserved seating, featured a large group of over-50s to my right and a similarly sized group of teenagers to my left. This led to much banter of a generation gap nature. The white-hairs seemed happy with jokes about not being able to get the top off a jar of piccalilli and impending death while the teens took an easy-going approach to leg-pulls about sexual inadequacy and bad skin. However, my casual aside about getting A-level maths for knowing your nine-times-table did not go down well with the assembled youth. They seemed properly hurt. I thought about this after the show. I'd accidentally been guilty of inverted ageism – that anti-youth attitude which seems to be becoming the country's favourite brand of bigotry. The anti-youth lobby's sniping sounds unnervingly similar to racism – they're lazy, they rut like wild animals, they don't try to mix with us, they don't dress like us, they speak a different language and, most popular of all, they're so thick they can barely read and write.

As with all bigotry, every criticism of *them* becomes a compliment to *us*. The devalued qualifications attack is a fine example of this. If A levels are not as difficult as they used to be, then *our* A levels take on a renewed importance. They were not only hard won but, due to falling standards, they are now beyond equal. It's like when the old cricketers say, 'I'd like to have seen him bat like that on the pitches we had to play on.' Indeed, a couple of years after I started doing stand-up, a comedian from the early days of Alternative Comedy said to me 'You lot have got it easy. When I was doing the Comedy Store in the late seventies, the crowds were much tougher than they are now.' I explained that, having seen several of his generation of comics on video and TV, I felt that the audiences were only raucous and aggressive back then because the comedians were so crap. It was harsh but I suppose I felt the same sting those teenagers felt at my gig. Don't boost your own achievements by undermining mine.

Teacher friends of mine say the better grades phenomenon is less about exams getting easier and more about teachers spending ever-increasing time on examination technique. The anti-youth league doesn't like that theory. It makes them sound like industrious dullards who could have achieved much more if they'd only had the guile of the modern pupil. No, that's unacceptable. They point at the goofy kid in the baseball cap and trackie bottoms, smoking a cigarette at the bus stop, and say it's obvious to anyone that modern youth has slid a link or two back down the food chain. But the stupid are, and always have been, with us. We notice the mouth-breather youths more because they haunt the street corners while the smart ones are hidden away doing more interesting things. In truth, today's youth are the generation of the written word. I never wrote a note to a friend when I was at school. I'd draw a weeping penis on the cover of their exercise book but there were no written social arrangements, jokes or general thoughts on life. Now, with texting, Twitter, Facebook, emails and all the other various forms of cyber communication, the written word is dominant. The anti-youth lobby, often not as cyber-literate as their fresh-faced enemy, dismiss this written revolution as lowbrow and malformed. They sneer at text-speech and the random commentaries of the Tweeters and explain that this is not proper literacy. But if we turn to old-fashioned book reading, the new generation still impress. When I was growing up in the sixties and seventies, the idea that kids would queue for hours to buy a book being released at midnight – and a big, fat, picture-free book at that – was completely unimaginable. This is not just the cyber generation – it is the Harry Potter generation too.

The anti-youth lot are afraid. I understand that. Words like 'youth' and 'youths' regularly feature in newspaper articles about anarchic behaviour and violent attacks. I am unsurprised when my girlfriend, as I step out of our flat to remonstrate with noisy hoodies, asks me to leave some sperm in the freezer as a safeguard. Youth is scary and chaotic. I went to see a band called Enter Shikari a while back. Being a slightly nervy middle-aged man I sought a balcony viewing spot, above the writhing crowd. I've never seen moshing like it. The bouncing, shrieking, crowd-surfing, stage-diving box of maggots below me looked terrifying – but I saw no trouble. Though half-naked, sweat-soaked teenagers slammed into each other and got intermittently trampled on, there was clearly love in the room. For every surfer who crumpled towards the floor, two or three kids made sure the fall was broken and that the faller came to no harm. It seemed a potent symbol for modern youth – wild, uncoordinated, scary but ever-so-slightly awe-inspiring.

Even if the anti-youth lobby are right and educational standards are dropping, they should be careful where they lay the blame. You can't discredit the contest without discrediting the contestants. Anyone who did well in their A levels this week should be seriously proud. We're just jealous because you're prettier than us.

Bob Dylan guided me through my adolescence, and now he's guiding me through a slightly tricky one-way system

28 AUGUST 2009

Bob Dylan said this week that he'd been talking to a couple of car companies about the possibility of voicing their satellite-navigation systems. This story held great significance for me. I first discovered Dylan when I was a nervy 17-year-old, trying Valium as a substitute for the alcohol I was already much too fond of. I felt, like many struggling adolescents over the years, that he seemed to speak directly to me and his music became a sort of handrail to get me through those difficult years. I soon gave up the Valium but only to concentrate on liquid alternatives. Yet Dylan remained ever on my Walkman, like a poetic commentator adding colour and significance to my grey, industrial West Midlands, ordinary life. However fanciful that may seem in retrospect, when a musician gets so close to your core, it hurts if he then does something that disillusions you. Dylan bleating 'After 300 yards, turn left' sounds, at first, like an embarrassing sell-out. Johnny Rotten's butter ad is mildly disconcerting but, in truth, the Sex Pistols always enjoyed winking at the camera and telling us we were being swindled. Dylan, however, seemed like a mystical outsider figure – an Old Testament-style visionary who could never be bought or sold. In fact, this image of him has got harder and harder to hang on to in recent years.

In 2004 he appeared in an advertisement for Victoria's Secret, the American lingerie company. As his song 'Love Sick' plays, he appears, looking sullen – angry, even. It's a look he used to reserve for masters of war and arrogant rich kids who casually threw things at black wait-resses. In the ad he aims that look at a woman on a plinth who strikes a series of poses in a quite nice bra and knickers. It's like he's turned up for a very expensive nude drawing class and feels outrageously short-changed. I forgave him for this capitalist indiscretion because when asked, at a press conference in 1965, 'If you ever had to sell-out to a commercial interest which one would it be?' he replied 'Women's garments.' Thus the Victoria's Secret advert seemed, somehow, further proof that Dylan was the prophet so many had claimed him to be. Had his answer to that 1965 question been 'the satellite-navigation system' his prophet status would now be magically cemented and his sat-nav contract would seem some sort of holy covenant. But things got worse. In 2005 Dylan released an album to be sold exclusively in Starbucks and this year he allowed his archetypal protest song 'Blowin' in the Wind' to be used in an advertisement for the Co-Op. Maybe I should just shout 'Judas' and walk away. But the sat-nav deal is different. At least, it is for me.

It would not be an over-statement to say that the satellite-navigation system has completely changed my life. I have spent the last 50 years getting lost. I even – and this isn't a joke – get lost in my own flat. I will often, for example, turn in to the toilet expecting it to be the bedroom. I once asked a psychologist about this directional disability and she told me that one develops one's sense of direction during the crawling stage. Some babies, however, just don't crawl. I asked my older sister if she recalled me crawling. She said she did but only when I'd been drinking. By then, the sense-of-direction horse had long since bolted. When I started driving, things got even worse. On most accom-panied journeys, my fretful passenger would eventually ask 'Are we lost?' I'd smile and say we most certainly were and had been for about 20 minutes. I accepted it as part of life – something I would always have to live with. My first sat-nav changed everything. Suddenly I could go anywhere and didn't have to factor getting-lost time into the journey. I even, on one occasion, when I had to park about a mile from a party I was attending, used the sat-nav to find my way from my parked car to the venue. I was delighted to discover that, even as a pedestrian, I could still see myself as a moving arrow on the screen. I started to run faster and faster to see how quickly I could make the arrow move. I seemed to quite scare one couple as I hurtled past them, dressed in a suit and tie, and emanating loud electric-voice commands as I went. Maybe they thought Professor Stephen Hawking had built himself a new body and was exuberantly putting it through its paces. 'After 300 yards turn left – because I can.' I even took my little arrow to the kerb of a main road and started running into the road and then backing out again, each time at a slightly different angle. I was thus able to roughly recreate, on the tiny screen, the opening credits of *Dad's Army*. Anyway, I love the sat-nav. It leads me through the mysteries and horrors of road travel like Bob Dylan, many years before, led me through the mysteries and horrors of growing-up.

Consequently, I'm not seeing Dylan's sat-nav voice-over as a sell-out. I'm seeing it as the two great guiding lights of my youth and middle years finally coming together to lead me on to eternity. With sat-nav technology and Bob's reassuringly familiar, wisdom-soaked tones combined, I feel I can never be truly lost again.

How I climbed a mountain with Eddie Izzard

4 SEPTEMBER 2009

As you've probably heard, the comedian and actor, Eddie Izzard is attempting to run 40 marathons in 47 days, for Sport Relief. He passed through Edinburgh last Sunday. I was up there performing at the Fringe Festival and was invited to join him for part of the route. In truth, I'm thoroughly confused by the whole charity thing. I can't believe, for example, that there's a TV advertisement, asking us all to give a few pounds to stop cruelty to children. When they slice up the taxes cake, does someone actually say 'They need x money to stop cruelty to children but let's just give them y and the public can top up the fund – though, admittedly, probably not to the amount that's actually required'? Are some of the other things on the tax-list fully funded because they're considered more important than preventing cruelty to children and, consequently, we need a whip-round to try and make up the shortfall? Anyway, none of that is the fault of the charities so I put my political questioning on the back burner and joined Eddie on his run.

When I was a kid, the marathon was viewed as some sort of weirdo extreme event that only a few people with freakish slow hearts and high-capacity lungs could possibly take on. Even the top athletes in other disciplines seemed to view the marathon as a race reserved for bizarre super-beings. So how come it's now an event for 80-year-old grannies and blokes in Mother Goose costumes? I suppose somebody who wasn't a super-being decided to just keep putting one foot in front of another and see what happened. That's probably the best approach to taking on the apparently impossible.

Though Eddie's never struck me as much of an athlete, I still wasn't particularly surprised when I heard about his thousand-mile run. It kind of made sense. When we first met, about 20 years ago, he was the regular compère at a London comedy club. He refused to write material – believing that the best and truest stuff is created onstage. He would stride out, week after week, and see what he could conjure up from the ether. Sometimes it was brilliant; sometimes it was rubbish. Eddie never seemed daunted by the sharper end of the experience. He continued to take risks and remained fearless in the face of audience indifference. Eventually the brilliant bits took over and Eddie became an international star. Many comics have their progress impeded by getting tangled up in their own safety nets. Not Eddie. He could walk nonchalantly through the valley of death because his eyes were fixed on the horizon. This epic run just seems like another manifestation of those parts of Eddie's character – his fearlessness and focus on the master plan.

When I joined him in Edinburgh City Centre, I was not quite so fearless. I used to run eight miles a day, every day, but that was over 20 years ago. I haven't done any proper exercise for ages. I was thinking I'd be thrilled if I could complete a mile. I was also thinking it would really spoil Eddie's contribution to Sport Relief if I fell, purple-lipped, clutching my chest, and died in a Scottish gutter. Would he still complete the run? Would the BBC pay lip service to my passing with a brief caption at the end of the Sport Relief programme, showing my dates and a smiling picture of me in an England football shirt? These thoughts went through my mind as I did my warm-up exercises. Suddenly, Eddie appeared, carrying a Scotland flag and waving to well-wishers. I caught up and soon settled into a rhythm. We chatted and laughed as we ran. I explained how I'd been to watch the London Marathon this year and discovered that the runners had their names on their tops so the crowd could cheer them individually as they passed. I shouted 'Come on, Flora' at three different runners before I realised it was the name of the sponsor. Eddie told me his legs were getting so muscular he feared they'd never look good in heels again.

The thing is, acts of human endeavour like this, whilst raising money for the charity, also touch people in less obvious ways. As Eddie ran his twenty-ninth marathon, I was secretly climbing my own little mountain. I was remembering how it felt to be a runner – the elation of it. I didn't tell Eddie how significant my six-and-a-half miles from Edinburgh to Dalkeith felt – it sounded pretty trivial compared to his target – but inside I was punching the air. I'd put one foot in front of another and it was good. I will continue to be a runner now. The experience was, for me, life-changing. After a sweaty hug in Dalkeith, he headed off again. I was a bit-player in it all but bursting with excitement at what I'd discovered about myself. I stepped out onstage that night and proudly declared 'I ran all the way to Dalkeith this afternoon – that's how bad the matinee went.' They want gags, these people, not spiritual journeys. Still, sharing a tiny bit of Eddie's adventure reminded me that human beings are dogged little buggers who have a tendency to endure – to keep going partly because they just like the idea of keeping going. I've been in a pretty splendid mood ever since.

Why alcohol is a bigger threat than terrorism, global warming or a massive meteor careering towards Earth

11 SEPTEMBER 2009

The British Medical Association published a report on the dangers of drink this week, but assured us the organisation is not 'anti-alcohol'. Well, it bloody well should be. Alcohol is directly linked to more than 60 medical conditions and costs the NHS millions of pounds every year. The casualty departments are full of drunks. They also contain the sober victims of alcohol-induced violence, drink driving and various other horrors of secondary drinking. I gave up alcohol on 24 September 1986 but it's still quite possible I will end up in hospital or the morgue because of someone else's drinking. My dad, an enthusiastic patron of public houses, often said, 'If you knocked down all the pubs, you'd have to build a lot of lunatic asylums.' A friend recently said to me if there was a genuine attempt to stop people drinking there'd be rioting in the streets. Clearly, this is a dependency culture. Alcohol is killing people in a variety of ways but a large part of the population can't face life without it so the carnage is allowed to continue.

All our decisions can be roughly broken down into things we do because of love and things we do because of fear. The BMA's reluctance to condemn drink as firmly as it condemns tobacco is not based on the love of those in its care but rather the fear of their outrage if told they should face life head-on, without the soothing softener of alcohol. People need booze to make themselves and their acquaintances seem more exciting. How many parties or nights in the pub have been rescued by booze slowly oiling the social machine? There are pills that do the same job. Would it be OK to use them in the same way? If you turned up at a friend's dinner party and she casually handed out sedatives wouldn't you feel a bit weak and pathetic?

I'm starting to sound like an old-fashioned Temperance League member but it irks me that alcohol is seen as a social necessity, an icebreaker. You get drunk with a new workmate or neighbour in order to bond with them. It loosens people up and makes them more gregarious. Well, what's going on here? Are we saying we need a mind-altering drug to enable us to reach out to another human being or give us the courage to speak in a group? Shouldn't we deal with that? We're back to love and fear again. Why do you drink? Is it because you love the people you're with or because you're slightly afraid of them? Is it because you're unhappy with who you are and so feel the need to change yourself – even if it's just a little bit – with the aid of alcohol? I often sat with friends, the lunchtime after the night before, discussing our drunken exploits. The thing Steve said to the bloke at the chip shop, the way Darren fell off the bus. None of us had the guts to say 'But it wasn't really us, was it? It was us made more colourful by a drug. These things we did – our displays of courage and eccentricity – only happened because they were induced by chemicals. We sit here shining our puny badges of rebellion and celebrating our maverick lifestyle but deep down we know it's all a sham – an alcohol-induced charade. Who are we, when unaided by intoxicants? What stories concerning the real, unaltered us are worth telling? If there are none then we must stop taking the easy option – the short-term fix – and strive to make the real, unaltered us worthy of the tale.' Of course, I never said that or anything like it because I was keen to continue the charade – to tell the stories and enjoy my own part in them.

I was a heavy drinker. I have been known to wake-up in a pool of my own urine in a place I didn't know. So-called social drinkers will read this and say, 'his case is different – he had a problem', but anyone who is reluctant to face social gatherings without the aid of a depressant like alcohol should be asking themselves why. I got drunk, ultimately, I suppose, because I was afraid of being sober. The social drinker is afraid of being sober and of being drunk. He seeks a cosy middle ground where social situations are made that little bit more manageable – that little bit easier to navigate. It is double self-deception – it is neither a real world nor one that is free from dependency.

The government may consider public health less important than alienating voters and rich brewery owners or losing the revenue on alcoholic drinks but the BMA should forget about cosmetic changes like banning advertising and happy hours, drop the niceties, come down at least as hard as it did on tobacco and say what needs to be said: alcohol is a dangerous drug dressed-up as a warm and reassuring companion. It temporarily kills who you really are and replaces it, in varying degrees, with a chemically created persona – that's when it's not literally killing you, making you ill or terrifying those around you who are not similarly benumbed. We can't trust the people to decide for themselves because their dependency – often not readily apparent so easily denied – obviously clouds their judgement. We need the BMA to provide impetus for a great national sobering-up.

Why I hate Sir David Attenborough

2 OCTOBER 2009

I was looking at the new BBC Wildlife Finder website, launched this week. You click on an animal of your choice and you're taken to a selection of short videos featuring that creature. Being curious, I clicked a picture of a wise-looking African bush elephant. Within seconds I was watching 30 lions chasing and tearing to pieces the terrified animal. It was horrible. I used to spend a lot of time looking at hardcore pornography on the Internet, and that could leave one with a slight sense of despair and self-loathing, but this wildly trumpeting elephant, racing at full-pelt with hungry lions hanging off its back, had a much more disturbing effect on me. I wondered, at first, if it was because I'd read one too many political pundits' critiques of Gordon Brown's conference speech, and the glaring analogy was too obvious to bear. But it seemed to go much deeper than that. To my surprise, it felt really wrong to be watching this distressed creature's final moments – I'm back to the elephant now – especially with the whole thing accompanied by lovely classical music and Sir David Attenborough's calm, authoritative voice-over. A lot of compassionate people, nowadays, feel animals have a similar right to dignity and respect as human beings. Medical experimentation on animals is less and less common, as is the use of vivisection and such in educational establishments. There are certainly greater controls on the treatment of animals in the making of films and TV so I'm just beginning to wonder if it's still OK to show them being systematically ripped to bits on natural history programmes.

I know people will say it's the real world – 'nature red in tooth and claw' as Alfred Lord Tennyson put it – but hardcore pornography shows activities from the real world too – though, admittedly, I can't think of a Tennyson quote that sums them up – and people still seem to condemn it. I know lions kill elephants – actually, I didn't till I saw that clip – but is it OK to show the carnage, with classical music accompaniment, as a form of entertainment? And I'm not sure 'it's educational' gets the natural history makers totally off the hook. If I was making a documentary about anti-social behaviour and I acquired a video-clip of a middle-aged man being kicked to death by hoodies, I doubt I'd be allowed to broadcast the whole sorry thing, educational as my intentions might be. I'm not blaming the lions – they have to eat – but that doesn't mean we have the right to turn it into a musical. That lions-on-elephant attack reminded me of recent news stories about people being brutalised and abused by the pack. It's not unimaginable that some kids might end up watching these videos for kicks, whooping and cheering with their mates as the horror unfolds. Could that lead to what would be literally copycat crimes? That's why people are usually worried about kids watching mega-violent movies. Maybe these videos are worse because the butchery is real. Some of the video nasties on BBC Wildlife Finder come with a warning caption though this seems to be a bit ad hoc. The clip of chimpanzees hunting colobus monkeys carries a warning but I didn't find it anywhere near as disturbing as the elephant kill.

I hear you scoffing at all this. You feel there couldn't possibly be anything morally unsound about natural history programmes showing the terrible deaths of animals because Sir David Attenborough says it's 'all right' and he, of course, is a national treasure. Well, not in our house, he isn't. I don't know about you, but if I was in the garden watching my cat about to pounce on, say, a cheerful little robin, I'd make a noise to warn the bird. I know the cat will bother other robins when I'm not around but I'd still feel a moral obligation to save that particular one. However, if instead of warning the cute little seasonal visitor, I reached for my mobile phone and videoed every crunch, flap, whistle and meow, then laid an instrumental version of 'In the Deep Midwinter' all over it and spent the night showing it off to my mates down the pub, I honestly think you'd write me off as a sicko. Sir David, of course, does this sort of thing on a regular basis and what's more he gets handsomely paid for it – blood money, if you ask me. Whenever I watch one of those impala-at-the-watering-hole scenes, with a salivating lion tippy-toeing ever-closer, and hear Sir David saying something like 'the impala has no chance of escape' I'm always shouting at the telly, 'Yes he does and you're it – for goodness' sake, warn him!' But not only does Sir David most definitely not warn him, he seems to be deliberately speaking in hushed tones – like he's making absolutely sure he doesn't lose this chance to get another bloodbath in the can. I imagine him, tucked behind an adjacent fern, becoming ever more spattered with blood and thinking to himself, 'Oh, I say, the lion's ripped the impala's entire head off and is now sucking its brain through its earhole – I'm thinking Barber's *Adagio for Strings*.' Sir David Attenborough is, when the mood's upon him, little more than a glorified happy-slapper. Anyway, that's one national treasure shot down in flames. Next week – Stephen Fry – is he just a smarmy know-all?

Dr Jekyll and Dr Jekyll

9 OCTOBER 2009

What's happened to the Conservative Party? It used to be a dirty little temptress. I've voted Labour my whole life but – I hate to admit this – the Tories have always had a would-but-shouldn't allure. They appealed to my Mr Hyde. Even when I was a slightly lefty student, I'd watch their conferences on TV, with talk of things like a 'short, sharp shock' for young offenders and, while my better self argued that poverty, inner-city housing and mass unemployment caused crime and thus it needed to be dealt with at root, my Mr Hyde would be thinking 'OK, I'm voting Labour but I must admit, if the Tories win, the knowledge that a vicious street-thug will be crying himself to sleep in an icy-cold cell does represent something of a silver lining.' The Conservatives had an animalistic gut-appeal. The good me knew trade unions were admirable institutions that protected the people from exploitation by management but my Mr Hyde was sick of power cuts and bus strikes and could turn a blind eye to a bit of union-bashing and redundancies if it made life more comfortable. Then, when I started earning, it was their juicy tax cuts that enticed me. Conservatism was, I felt, institutionalised selfishness. Yes, the good me wanted to walk back from the pub without getting glassed, and a bit more money in his pocket, and the trains to be running, but he didn't want these things at the expense of higher ideals. My Mr Hyde would have accepted a police state as long as he felt safer, richer and less inconvenienced. Of course, placing this confession in past tense slightly gets me off the hook – I used to be tempted by the Tories' dark delights but not any more. In fact, that's probably more down to them changing than me.

The Conservative Party no longer offers any dark delights. They seem to care about equality, the unemployed, and saving the planet. It's as if that femme fatale at the office – who you've always found sexy but too scary to get close to – has suddenly started talking and dressing like your wife of 30 years. The things that made her so fatale have been discarded and, as you don't quite buy the new image, she now has neither her old animal magnetism nor your wife's warm sincerity. In truth, there are no Tory blues or Labour reds any more – just one big, slightly ungraspable purple party. I know there's always the Liberal Democrats but watching their conference – listening to them talking about what they'd do if they came to power – reminded me of sitting with workmates in the factory canteen, discussing what we'd do if we won the football pools.

The party conference season has, I must admit, shown the Conservatives to be the party of change. They've changed into the Labour Party – who, 15 years earlier, changed into a sort of Conservative Party Lite. Before that, any Shadow Home Secretary would have instinctively known which party would be lining-up a former army chief as a potential minister. He wouldn't have needed to be briefed. David Cameron's Tories aren't even promising Mr Hyde they'll drop the 50-pence tax. When people decide who to vote for in the next election, they can't do it on policies. It's not the old choice of nationalisation versus private enterprise or grammar schools versus comprehensives or even foxhunting versus not foxhunting – it's purple versus purple. There's not much mileage in Gordon Brown saying, 'I'm warning the British people, if the Tories get into power, things will be ever-so-slightly different from the way they are now.' That's not really beware-of-the-bogeyman, is it? The really bad news for Brown is that, in the absence of policies, the election will be decided on personality – Brown versus Cameron – charmless versus harmless.

My highlight of this week was Shadow Chancellor George Osborne taking a punt on a previously untried, eye-catching gimmick – telling the truth. Not the whole truth, obviously, but the truth nevertheless. I imagined Alistair Darling turning to Gordon Brown, as they watched

Osborne's speech on telly, and saying, 'I told you we should have tried telling the truth and you told me not to be ridiculous.' As there are no policy issues in this election, voting in the Conservatives will be like when Rod Stewart gets rid of one leggy blonde and then replaces her with another. The motivation will be quite similar too. Not many people actually think the Conservatives are better – they're just bored with Labour.

Michael Gove, the Shadow Children, Schools and Families Secretary – who looks and sounds like one of those chinless man-from-the-ministry types who used to bully Norman Wisdom – said during his speech this week that 'the whole point of politics is to fight for change'. Makes you wonder why the Conservative Party chose that name. I suspect there'll be a lot more people crying out for change over the next few years – spare change. Gove said he wanted to change exams because they've been dumbed-down. He claimed a GCSE Science paper asked, 'What is nutritionally better for you, a battered sausage or a piece of grilled fish?' Gove thought the answer was way too obvious. I wish he'd asked party chairman, Eric Pickles. The kids sitting that exam were lucky. They had a proper choice. For us it's either grilled fish or grilled fish. I'm not sure that's healthy.

Blah, blah, blah

16 OCTOBER 2009

I like Dannii Minogue. She has good cheekbones. Of course, some cynics might suggest they are the handiwork of a skilled surgeon but, were I to believe such tittle-tattle, it would only make me admire her more. If God gave her such cheekbones she is just plain lucky. If she, having selected them from an online gallery, then commissioned their construction and funded it with her own money, I applaud both her dedication and her artistic eye. Their appearance can only have been further humanised, last weekend, by the trickle of tears that surely graced them. You've probably heard that, on last Saturday's *X Factor*, Dannii said to contestant, Danyl Johnson that, if what she'd read in the papers was true, there was no need for him to change the gender references in the song he'd just performed. A terrible hush gripped the audience, Simon Cowell growled with disapproval and, within a few hours, 82 per cent of the 3,000 people who voted in an online poll said Ms Minogue should be sacked for outing Mr Johnson as bisexual. Twenty-four hours later, one red-top newspaper suggested 'Ten reasons why Dannii Minogue should be sacked'. Interestingly, the same red-top, eight weeks earlier had published a feature on Danyl Johnson which said 'he's a free spirit who dates women AND men' – and I must point out that's their 'can-you-bloody-well-believe-it?' block capitals, not mine.

Now, this might all sound like nonsensical reality TV/ tabloid frippery but I think it's more serious than that. In all areas of public life, any misjudgement or word out of place is greeted by calls for instant dismissal. Politics is particularly volatile in this respect. If you've got a shoelace undone in the House of Commons someone will be calling for your resignation. Take little Alan Duncan MP. He got hoofed out of the Shadow Cabinet for moaning about the injustices of post-expenses-scandal politics, in a secretly recorded private conversation. Surely, an Englishman's right to moan about his job – no matter how prestigious that job might be – must never be called into question. We've seen a similar contravention of a basic human right in the case of Manchester United manager, Sir Alex Ferguson. Sir Alex has been condemned for criticising a referee. What's the point of being involved in football, at any level, if you can't slag off referees? I don't like to see them being terrorised by packs of angry players or being hit on the head by flying pop-bottles, but verbal abuse from the terraces, including the dug-outs, is surely a much-cherished tradition. I've been verbally abusing referees since I was at junior school and I admire Ferguson for sticking two fingers up to the corporate suits at the FA and saying what he actually thinks. I was particularly impressed that he managed to make an original contribution to the field of referee abuse. I've questioned referees' eyesight, intelligence, impartiality, manhood, sanity, parentage and private habits but never once thought to cast doubt on their physical fitness. Psychological warfare is still clearly one of the sharpest arrows in Sir Alex's quiver. Sadly, his resulting written apology lacks all the passion and conviction of the original abuse. While I'm not saying I agree with Ferguson's views on referee, Alan Wiley, I would defend his right, and that of any other football obsessive, to go totally mental when his team receives anything short of forelock-tugging sycophancy from the match referee. No one, to my knowledge is calling for Ferguson's resignation – they'd be too scared – but there is still, it seems, a career on the line. Apparently, referee Wiley was so upset by Ferguson's comments that he considered quitting the game. There's been a controversial remark – someone has to lose their job. Oh, for goodness' sake. Mr Wiley should know it's impossible to referee a football match without upsetting someone. He should close his eyes, outstretch his arms, and let the abuse pour down on him like a warm shower.

With Cristiano Ronaldo gone, Sir Alex is merely re-establishing himself as the club's most dislikeable representative.

Surely it should be possible for someone in the public eye to say something silly – and I'm not talking about holocaust denial or similarly calculated unpleasantness – without everyone calling for their blood. This is why public figures have virtually stopped saying anything at all. They're all having media training that reduces language to a sort of cosy verbal muzak – a series of ultra-safe, slightly over-rehearsed clichés that could be replaced by a repeated blah-blah-blah with no real loss of meaning. This is the world that people like the FA, David Cameron and those online Dannii-bashers are building.

I'm not actually trying to defend Sir Alex, Dannii, or Alan Duncan for these specific controversial utterances. Ferguson undermines my sympathy for his fiery passion by combining it with an ultra-sensitive reaction to any criticism of him or his team; Dannii has chosen a job on *X Factor* where she regularly swings a critical axe – as ye judge so shall ye be judged; and Alan Duncan is a Conservative MP. My point is: people say stupid things and if you then gag them, or, worst of all, sack them, the loss is often ours. If you get rid of people who make mistakes, they never learn from those mistakes and we never benefit from them learning. I'm getting that last sentence put on a T-shirt in time for the General Election.

My 'critical loyalty' to the Roman Catholic Church

23 OCTOBER 2009

I really feel there is a God. I know atheism is extremely fashionable nowadays but I just can't kick this believing thing. I must say I have a lot of time for atheists. I respect anyone who gives this most momentous question a good deal of thought, whatever conclusion they finally arrive at. I'm less keen on the glut of bandwagon-atheists who've just unquestioningly joined in because they think the atheist label makes them sound clever and grown-up. It's bad enough that many believers never question their own convictions but at least their dumb acceptance comes with an element of 'safest option' insurance. I'd have thought, in the bandwagon-atheist's case, it's worth having a proper think – maybe even spending an hour on Wikipedia – before turning your back on what might just be a life illuminated by faith. It seems rash to screw-up eternity on the strength of something you read on the side of a bus.

I was baptised Roman Catholic but left the Old Church when I was 17 because I was an angry young man who couldn't accept doctrine like papal infallibility, praying to saints and the gaining of indulgences. I read every book I could find on Catholicism – most of them condemnatory – but, 11 years later, I returned to the church. It may have been, I admit, mere socialisation – some yearning for identity – or it may have been the instinctive recognition of a great truth but, either way, the urge got stronger and I gave in. I never had an epiphany – a single moment when I knew I must return – but I do remember identifying strongly with something I read by Hans Küng – a Swiss theologian rejected by the Vatican in 1979. He said the Roman Catholic Church was essentially on the road to truth but sometimes turned into cul-de-sacs – exactly what one might expect from a divine institution run by ordinary human beings. That was more or less the attitude I returned to the Church with – what Kung called a 'critical loyalty'. I've met many impressive, even saint-like Catholics who properly walk the walk; people whose faith has led them to a life spent helping others. When I see how the Church inspires such people it fills me with optimism for its future. I suppose it also allows me to put some of the more problematic aspects of Catholicism on my moral back burner.

Then, this week, I read about the Pope inviting Anglicans to rejoin the Mother Church. It felt, at headline-level, as if the still-weeping wounds of the Reformation might, at last, be healed by tolerance and love – our separated brethren returned. Then I read further. If the Anglicans seeking this shelter were doing so because of *their* instinctive recognition of a great truth, because some part of them yearned for the poetry of the Old Church rather than the prose of Anglicanism, because they had come to believe that the Pope was a direct, if some-times fractured, link with St Peter, or even just because they felt an unexpected surge of joy when Glasgow Rangers lost 4-1 at Ibrox on Tuesday night, I would rejoice at their return to the fold. The fatted calf would already be on the rotisserie. But the truth is not so uplifting. The Anglicans knocking at the door of the Vatican are doing so, it seems, because they don't have much respect for women or gay men. Two aspects of church teaching which I find extremely unnerving are the attractive lure that draws these new converts in. I say 'converts' but I worry that spiritual matters are not the main criterion here. I don't get a sense that these Anglicans are crossing the great divide because of their belief in transubstantiation. It feels more like they're seeing my Church as a safe haven for homophobes and misogynists. I, like many liberal Catholics, have been fighting an angst-ridden battle with that image of Catholicism for many years. I want people to be drawn to the Catholic Church because it travels the road to truth not because they want to hang out in its dingy cul-de-sacs. I was hoping the Church's antipathy to female and openly gay priests would, in time, weaken and dissolve. Now, instead, it seems, a whole lot of bigoted reinforcements are arriving to galvanise those more unpalatable aspects of Roman Catholic doctrine. Should I stay in a club that would welcome these people as members? It's as if *The Times* had suddenly headhunted Jan Moir. I've dreamed of a reunion of the Catholic and Anglican churches in the past but I always imagined it would be a marrying of the best of both, not a rallying of the worst. No doubt we'll hear one of the more high-profile converts airing their offensive views on a forthcoming edition of *Question Time*. Should I continue my policy of 'critical loyalty' or consider a counter-conversion to an Anglican Church presumably much-improved by this natural editing process? I suspect I'm on the long-term car park as far as Catholicism is concerned. I should welcome all converts and just hope the Church keeps at least one eye on that long road to truth. Maybe there'll soon be a more reassuring influx, when the bandwagon-atheist's deathbed-conversions start steadily rolling-in.

Don't shake hands with Jesus

30 OCTOBER 2009

The Health Protection Agency says footballers should avoid spitting during games because of the dangers of spreading swine flu. I always assumed that players actually *needed* to do all that spitting but the HPA would hardly counsel them against it if that was the case. I now wonder if spitting, for men, is, in fact, some instinctive display of fertility. I won't spell out the symbolism in a family newspaper but you hopefully get my drift. This would explain why professional footballers – those virile young stags of our modern culture – are near-perpetual fountains of sputum.

I'm guessing the HPA's concern is that one player spits on the pitch and then a second player, perhaps in the throes of a mock-injury multiple-roll, accidentally gathers up that spit and any harmful bacteria it may contain. I suppose it *could* happen but it sounds to me like another instance of that swine-flu hysteria which has made so many of our everyday activities suddenly feel like a game of Russian roulette. For example, I was recently leaving a public toilet at the same time as a friend. He stayed to wash his hands but I didn't bother. I would very much like to see the results of a survey on this but, speaking for myself, I never wash my hands if my toilet activities have only involved using the urinal. To do so seems, to me, rather grand. Later that evening, the same friend reprimanded me for my lack of hygiene and I explained my general policy. 'That might have been all right in the past,' he said, 'but with the swine flu pandemic you have to be much more careful.' The implication seemed to be that I ran a genuine risk of catching swine flu from my own genitals. How could this possibly happen? Am I to believe that my penis has been going out on its own and, furthermore, that during these excursions it has completely flouted the government guidelines? Forgive me as I move from the ridiculous to the sublime. When I take Holy Communion in church on Sunday mornings, it involves eating a thin disc of bread and then sipping from a chalice of wine. As a Roman Catholic, I believe that this bread and wine, through some supernatural process, has transubstantiated into the body and blood of Jesus Christ. Being a recovering alcoholic, some sceptical friends have accused me of using transubstantiation as a loophole. I can't blame them for this. I've had similar doubts about Catholics on a no-carbs diet. Either way, in recent weeks, my local church has withdrawn the wine element as a precaution against the spread of swine flu. Given that they too believe in transubstantiation, the inference is that I might catch it from Jesus. Surely that strain would at least be self-healing. I sometimes wonder if the precautions against this pandemic are more dangerous than the actual illness. The other day, I had to save my girlfriend from falling over as the bus we were on took a sharp corner. Had she been holding on to one of the many support-poles or handrails there would have been no problem but she refuses to touch any of these in case they're covered in swine flu.

Maybe these prophets of doom are right and I'm being complacent. Maybe the HPA is right and football really is a swine-flu minefield. Take the handshake, for example. Footballers customarily shake hands at the end of games. If the spit don't get you, the handshake will. To be fair, the football managers are doing their bit to lessen the risk by reducing the handshake to its absolute minimum requirement. When shaking an opposing manager's hand, at the end of a game, they seem to adopt a method not dissimilar to the five-second rule one applies when deciding whether or not to eat food that's fallen on the floor. In fact, these post-match handshakes are often less than a second in duration and are usually accompanied by what is perhaps another swine flu preventative measure – the complete turning away of the head. Meanwhile, the players cast caution to the wind by wilfully embracing each other after every goal. If this reckless habit continues, by the time we reach the World Cup there'll only be Emile Heskey left standing. I asked my doctor the best way to deal with swine flu. He said, 'Get it – hope you're not one of the tiny minority who don't survive it – then get over it'. This sounds much less hysterical than the HPA's scare-mongering.

Due to a temporary obsession with a film called *Ghost Dog: the Way of the Samurai*, I once spent a period of my life trying to live by the Samurai code. One thing it says there is that, in a heavy rainstorm, we should not scamper from eave to doorway, frantically seeking shelter. In doing this we'll still get wet but will add frustration and anxiety to the experience. Better to march boldly onward and accept the inevitable soaking with calm resignation. I suppose one could go further. I recall a journalist who said he always got sick when visiting India so, nowadays, as soon as he arrives, he seeks out the nearest puddle of stagnant water and drinks from it. He thinks it best to accelerate the process and get it over with. Maybe I should snog a handrail.

True love – a mathematical formula

6 NOVEMBER 2009

If your partner is a lot older or younger than you, be prepared for a barrage of hostility.

This week I've read newspaper stories concerning a 71-year-old man, married to a 25-year-old woman, who has just become Britain's oldest father of twins; a 112-year-old Somali man who is marrying a 17-year-old girl; and the artist Sam Taylor-Wood, 42, who just got engaged to her 19-year-old boyfriend.

I like to chew over news stories with friends but big age differences in relationships, as a conversation topic, rarely bring out the best in people. For example, the women over 30 I know – even the most laid-back or postmodern ones – tend to get disproportionally vicious when discussing a relationship between an older man and a younger woman.

I have first-hand experience of this. I was away filming in 1997 – I was 40 – and was sitting in a bar one evening with the production team, when I mentioned my then girlfriend. One of the two women on the team, both of whom were over 30, asked me what my girlfriend did for a living.

When I said 'She's a student,' dark clouds seemed to gather. 'What, so she went back into education, did she?' one of the women asked. I decided to head straight for the eye of the storm.

'She's 20,' I said. If I'd added 'and I occasionally punch her in the face,' I don't think it could have made the atmosphere much worse. It was an off-duty event and I wasn't expecting star treatment but the ensuing debate got really quite aggressive. 'What can you possibly find to talk to her about?' I was asked.

Although both these women were bright and interesting, my 20-year-old girlfriend was, in truth, brighter and more interesting but it seemed unwise to use this as a 'for instance'. Instead, I just said that I picked my partners on criteria other than age. 'Oh, I bet you do!' said one of the women. UP to that point, the three of us had got on famously but, post-revelation, I was clearly now in the same condemned cell as Woody Allen.

A few years later I was watching the nightclub owner Peter Stringfellow on a daytime TV show, talking about his teenage fiancée. He got asked the same 'What do you find to talk about?' question by an irate female member of the audience but he replied: 'Oh, well, you see, I'm lucky because I'm quite shallow.'

I looked hard for irony but found none. He went on to explain that he didn't require much from conversation, so rarely felt short-changed. The crowd was silenced.

The dismissal of all relationships with a considerable age difference as intrinsically dysfunctional is so common, so unquestioned, that any dissent smells suspiciously of hidden agenda. Maybe I should say that my relationship with the 20-year-old ended, as have my relationships with many women of varying ages, and that now, aged 52, I live with a 39-year-old woman who I'm crazy about. I know that's still a 13-year difference but no one seems to get angry about it. I'm told the accepted formula for a successful relationship is that the woman should be half the man's age plus seven years. My female friends definitely approve of the fact I'm not claiming my full allowance.

The Sam Taylor-Wood debate among my lady mates was much less predictable. Where I had expected 'Go, girl!' I got, 'Well, she'll probably have two or three years of fun before he clears off.'

Cougars – women who date much younger men – tend to get a patronising smile rather than the cold hostility reserved for men who date much younger women. Why do so many women get angry about the latter? I'm not talking gobby fishwife-types who rattle off anti-men clichés between each draw on their high-tar cigarettes. I'm talking caring, intelligent, successful women, often in happy relationships of their own. I don't believe it's as simple as fear of their own ageing, or some sort of inter-age-group rivalry – 'they come over here, stealing our men.'

I'm concentrating on female responses I had to this subject because they were so extreme. Male friends were either just dismissive or lapsed into laddishness. The worst reaction I ever had to my 20-year-old girlfriend was a male friend taking me to one side at a party and giving me an enthusiastic congratulatory handshake. The horror!

There are communication problems caused by the age-gap – when I dated a younger woman I tended not to discuss anything that happened before the *Teenage Mutant Ninja Turtles* – but every relationship involves unshared areas of the mind. There are, I'll admit, difficult moments. It was slightly wince making when I relaxed with a post-coital cigarette and she did revision. And it was awkward when her parents – I felt deliberately – encouraged me to share, in front of her, reminiscences about decimalisation. But all relationships are difficult and both partners being the same age is hardly a guarantee of success.

It worries me that anti-age-gap prejudice assumes youth and beauty to be intrinsically more valuable than experience and its hopefully resulting wisdom, and thus the younger partner is always somehow perceived as getting the spiky end of the pineapple. Is the physical – the obvious – always the greater prize? We've accrued enough common sense and compassion to accept interracial relationships and, more recently, civil partnerships; maybe it's time to broaden our minds a little farther and accept that love should always have our respect, even if we think its participants ill matched in years.

How the MPs' expenses scandal restored my faith in politics

13 NOVEMBER 2009

E ven the drunken youth who urinated on the war memorial and the couple who used their baby's buggy to steal Poppy Appeal tins haven't been able to prevent Gordon Brown from topping the Remembrance week villains' league table.

A misspelled name, a forgotten bow and being seen to preside ultimately over the Ministry of Defence bonus scheme has now left the Prime Minister maybe not an anti-Christ but certainly an anti-Dame Vera Lynn.

The MoD bonuses are surely the most difficult action to defend. At a time when our teenage gangs appear to be better armed and equipped than our soldiers, it really isn't good enough to be saying that bonuses and equipment money come from two different pots. As the latter pot seems far from overflowing, the correct action was, surely, to pour the former pot into it. The MoD should work like a football team: you only get your bonus after you've won.

Apart from the obvious pain and frustration these revelations have caused our soldiers' loved ones, I find this scandal particularly annoying because I fear that 'greedy' MoD civil servants might be used to provide a human shield for much, much greedier bankers. I can just hear those bankers saying: 'Get off our backs about bonuses now. If it's OK for the civil servants at the MoD . . .' Well it isn't OK. We're talking vastly different sums of money, and I don't see why the people who, indirectly or otherwise, brought about the credit crunch should be allowed to wriggle off the hook.

In last week's *Sunday Times*, the boss of Goldman Sachs, Lloyd Blankfein, said that his bank was doing 'God's work'. I'm sure this line was ironic but, coming from a fabulously highly paid banker amid the rubble of the credit crunch, it did feel like the rapist winking at his victim from the dock after his highly paid legal team has got him off scot free.

Bankers are back, as brazen and unapologetic as ever. They wedged a filing cabinet against the office door when the storm was raging. They leant back, feet on desk, and said, 'Don't panic. The public have got short memories. Show them the slightest hint of recovery and most of them will forget their moral indignation and we can start where we left off – making the biggest splashes we can and not worrying about the ripples.'

Now, as the green shoots glisten, it's cigars-in-the-wine-bar time again. It looks suspiciously like the bankers have got away with it and, without a hint of remorse or reformation, are happily returning to business as usual.

It's not like that in the House of Commons. Another of this year's great scandals, MPs' expenses, has had a very different outcome. Politicians, in the main, have simply admitted they did wrong and shown due contrition. The MPs have held up their hands, whereas the bankers have limited it to just one middle finger. Take Jacqui Smith – she apologised in the House and has admitted that she is 'disgraced', very different from Sir Fred Goodwin scampering off abroad with a gleeful 'too late, suckers' look over his shoulder.

Of course, it might be that the MPs aren't really any more repentant than the bankers but democracy – the fact that we can vote them in or out – does offer a helpful incentive to don the sackcloth and ashes. The MPs may even have somewhat over-ashed. It's possible that the Kelly report has gone too far and we'll look back on measures like the ban on employing family members as a case of throwing out the baby with Jacqui Smith's bathplug.

We're unlikely to look back on the post-credit crunch regulation of bankers as having been too severe because there hasn't been any. Well, not much. All the attempts at preventing a return to massive bonuses – three-year delays, payment in shares, transaction tax, G20 capping – have been ignored, savaged or watered down. Barclays, having announced a fat profit this week, said that it will take into account public concern about the size of bankers' bonuses. As a result of this sensitivity, their investment bankers look set to receive bonuses of only £200,000 this year. It's going to be a cold, hard winter.

Prince Andrew, speaking as the UK's special representative for trade and investment, said recently: 'I don't want to demonise the banking and financial sector.' Well, I do. If senior bankers were subjected to a public vote like MPs I suspect bonuses would be down considerably this year.

This is the problem with democracy. It's like *The X Factor*: one can give people the vote but true power will always remain with the unelected rich. I'm sick of hearing about the sanctity of the free market when all that freedom seems to ensure is that boom leads to big bonuses for the bankers and bust leads to big debts for the people.

Nevertheless, it may sound contrary but the MPs' expenses scandal has actually restored my faith in politics rather than destroyed it. When it came down to it, those at fault really were accountable to us. They bared their backs, took their public lashes and time will tell if they've been forgiven. The credit crunch has completely destroyed my faith in our financial institutions because it's shown them to be essentially a law unto themselves.

As for the MoD, which of these two routes will they take: 'we made a mistake' public penance or 'we earned it' insensitive indignation?

Life in Jedwardian England

20 NOVEMBER 2009

When I was a child we had a canary. My dad always told me that if it ever escaped into the garden, the other birds – the scruffy starlings and extremely commonplace sparrows – would tear it apart because they'd be so jealous of its specialness. I imagined our lovely, yellow canary naively believing an audience of garden birds was gathering to enjoy its beautiful singing. Then the horror would unfold. Specialness is hard to like. At first it's impressive, but pretty soon it reminds us that we ourselves are not brightly coloured or filled with beautiful music.

This may go some way to explaining the phenomenon that is *The X Factor*'s Jedward – John and Edward Grimes. They came in from the garden. They are two cheeky sparrows who somehow found themselves in an elaborately gilded cage. The garden birds, agog at the window, celebrate the duo's profound un-specialness, delight in their unmerited glory and revel in the displaced canaries' angry disbelief.

Some years ago a former BBC executive, in what I believe was supposed to be a pep talk, told me I had the great gift of apparent ordinariness. 'People don't want to admire,' he said. 'They want to identify with. They don't want to be thinking "I wish I could do that," they want to take comfort in the fact that they easily could.' His face said 'compliment' but I struggled to find it in his words. Freedom from sparrow-attack didn't seem much of a consolation.

When I read that Jedward were doing a Wham! song on tomorrow's

X Factor, it brought the phenomenon into sharper focus. Jedward are a sort of Wham! but one which comprises Andrew Ridgeley and Andrew Ridgeley (though they look like Beavis and Beavis). They are an anti-talent rallying point for everyone who's sick and tired of the gifted hogging the limelight.

We have not stopped admiring the talented but we have become more honest about our resentment towards them. When the former *X Factor* winner and very talented Leona Lewis got attacked at a book signing the other week, her assailant was dragged away shouting: 'I love you, Leona.' Had the security staff been a little slower he may have gone on to say: 'But I still want to punch you in the head.'

The X Factor is, as Sting said, 'televised karaoke' and karaoke is a democratising force in live entertainment. Completely untalented people can take the mike and provide great entertainment for the crowd. In fact, my least favourite part of any karaoke night is when somebody really good gets up, takes the singing very seriously and thus completely misses the point. I hate good singers at karaoke nights and I'm getting pretty bored with them on reality shows.

I really like Susan Boyle – also on tomorrow's *X Factor* – because she combines her talent with an unattractive exterior. She is a challenge in that respect. If you want her beauty you must pass through her ugliness – you must pick the gold coin from the urinal. Her appearance keeps her safe from the sparrows but her beautiful song still brightens the garden. To see her and Jedward together will be interesting because the twins represent the pop music trend that she bucks – they are pretty people who can't sing.

Their cuteness is a sugarcoating to the bitter pill that is their performance. They are part of a longstanding pop music tradition. You should take a look at Fabian, a pop heartthrob of the fifties, on YouTube.

Interestingly, *The X Factor* has, till Jedward's arrival, been largely a school of excellence. Before the safety-net backing tracks that have blanded-out much of this series, it presented competitors with a momentous challenge – singing live, week after week, on national television. We once asked pop-superstar Jennifer Lopez to sing live on my old chat show. If we'd asked her to levitate it could not have caused a more incredulous response. Whenever big stars like Whitney Houston or Shakira sing on *The X Factor* they rarely sound as good as the contestants.

Their obligatory standing ovation from the judges pays tribute to their fame rather than their performance. Judged by such criteria, Jedward should win the whole thing. There have always been pop stars who can sing, but it's a bit like being a strong swimmer on a pedalo – it might come in handy but it's no real advantage.

Jedward are interesting in other ways. They have helped to establish the convention of combining names to signify a couple, as in Brangelina. If only this had been the norm when Posh Spice started dating David Beckham – what could have been more perfect than Peckham? Jedward also seem to be a culmination of reality television's obsession with twins, from the Cheeky Girls, through *Big Brother*'s Samanda and on to Jedward. In such company the Cheekys now seem like a latter-day Lennon and McCartney.

The point is, the sparrows and starlings all have a vote and they can use it to empower one of their own. Democracy gives them the opportunity to champion the hopeless – thus Jedward, thus John Sergeant, thus Boris Johnson. We're not doing away with the talented but we need the occasional random talent-free representative to be our Everyman.

Big Brother embraced this fact. *The X Factor* is still struggling against it. Simon Cowell can't really be shocked that Jedward, though they show no signs of talent, have become household names. Surely that is a precedent that began with the judges.

The red carpet
to Hell

27 NOVEMBER 2009

I went to the Royal Film Premiere at the Odeon, Leicester Square on Tuesday night. It's the last film premiere I'll ever attend. If you've never been to one of these things you may imagine them to be extremely glamorous and exciting. In fact, for me, they are like navigating the first five circles of Dante's Hell. When I began to get, what I'm going to call for the purposes of this column, famous, I was particularly excited about being invited to film premieres – the red carpet, the ranks of photographers calling my name, the celebrity-encrusted after-show parties. It really felt like I'd arrived. I did everything I could do to get my picture in the paper. I'd strike a series of comical poses, wear eye-catching combos like a football shirt under a tuxedo, and drop as many hints as I could to whoever happened to be my female plus-one for the occasion that she had a specific mission to fulfil – flesh exposure equals press exposure. I was so excited to be at these events that I never stopped to wonder what it was doing to my soul. I never considered the dangers of the premiere-goer's dark decision-making processes. For example, how much time should one spend on off-carpet digressions into the watching crowd? The key is to sign enough autographs and pose for enough phone-camera snapshots to appear like a warm-hearted man-of-the-people but not enough to seem desperate. It's also important to take into account the growth or shrinkage of one's own celebrity. If you really want to know how famous you are at any given time, a film premiere is a savage indicator of the truth. When you're number one in the singles chart, the crowd want to embrace you like a returning loved one. In less triumphant times they opt for that nodding smile one might give a stranger in a lift. In fact, no matter how brightly my own particular star has shone, I've never had a conversation with a crowd-member at a premiere when they haven't been looking over my shoulder to guard against missing a more-prestigious attendee.

Having negotiated the crowd one must then take on the line of microphone-wielding interviewers that stand at the edge of the carpet. These almost always work for radio stations or Internet channels you've never heard of and are often still smarting from having just been snubbed by Denise van Outen. Every interview conducted carpet-side is marred by the same fundamental flaw. You're being asked your opinion on a film you haven't seen yet. As I knew nothing about Tuesday night's featured movie, *The Lovely Bones*, I told interviewers I was looking forward to a warm-hearted film for the festive season. I figured this was a safe bet because the Royals – in this case Prince Charles and the Duchess of Cornwall – always, when it comes to entertainment, opt for chirpy and unchallenging. In short, the paedophile serial-killer plotline was a surprise to me.

The next harrowing decision that must be made at a film premiere is how long to give the press-photographers. Posing for the paparazzi is like kissing – it's important to be the one who stops first. This may seem unnecessarily coy but anything more giving only serves to back up the paparazzi conviction that you'll wilt without the life-giving light of their flashbulbs. About four years ago, when entering a rather smart West End restaurant, I was charged by a group of paps who continued past me to take photographs of a woman who'd recently finished eighth on *Britain's Next Top Model*. To attend a film premiere is to actively seek out such humiliations. On one occasion, during some red carpet paparazzi posing, I noticed one photographer not joining in. He looked on, unmoved, as the others flashed. I winked at him and he smiled. We knew the truth. If you're not in the film, in the gossip columns, or in a slut-chic designer-dress, all those pictures just disappear into delete.

The actual movie is the easy bit. The probing light of the paparazzi is replaced by the sanctuary of the darkened room. However, at Tuesday's royal premiere, we had to wait a little longer for that comforting gloom because five uniformed trumpeters took the stage to play a fanfare for Charles and Camilla as they entered the auditorium. I wonder if the royal couple have a Keep Fanfares Live sticker on their car. The national anthem was then played on the Odeon's Wurlitzer organ but I seemed to be the only one singing, and got a few unimpressed stares for my troubles. I've never much cared for the instrumental version. For what it's worth, I thought the film was rather fine.

The after-show party was pretty much what every after-show party is. I stood swirling a sparkling Vimto around and around my glass while my girlfriend talked about how uncomfortable her shoes were. I made the occasional lunge for a cocktail sausage but at last we turned to leave, like two penitents who'd completed their ten Hail Marys, and stepped into the cold London night. We passed a group of half-a-dozen autograph hunters. 'Frank Skinner', one of them observed, in the same flat tone he would have said 'ten-to-eleven' if asked the time by another of the group. Their books remained closed, their pens un clicked. I shuddered. It may have been the cold.

Groundhog Day in Wootton Bassett

11 DECEMBER 2009

I was booked to be a guest on last night's *Question Time*, filmed in Wootton Bassett. It would have been my second appearance on the show and I was looking forward to it in an egotistical 'Look, everyone, I'm much cleverer than you'd expect' kind of way.

I was also intrigued at the prospect of seeing Wootton Bassett in a context other than mourning. I planned to have a wander around the town, have my photo taken with some giggly middle-aged ladies, get ribbed about my football team, that sort of thing. I wanted to see its people laughing and swearing and getting a parking ticket – just doing normal things that didn't involve stern faces and standing to attention. I wanted to see Wootton Bassett at ease.

It's so tempting to view the town as being trapped in a perpetual loop of Remembrance Sundays – a bit like that Bill Murray film, *Groundhog Day* where the residents' radio alarms wake them not with 'I Got You Babe' but with 'The Last Post'. One imagines the black armband on a coat hook by the door; the poppy sewn-on rather than pinned.

I hadn't heard of Wootton Bassett 12 months ago. I've come to see it as a town that exists only for that endless cortège that's made its main street a modern-day River Styx – a town that has sacrificed itself in order to represent us all at the funeral – a town of death.

I was keen to replace that mythological Wootton Bassett with one I'd seen for myself but I never got the chance. *Question Time* blew me out. It seems I was considered a bit too light-entertainment for a show set in Wootton Bassett. I wasn't serious enough. Years of public flippancy, lowbrow preoccupations and populist TV appearances had made me an inappropriate guest. I was replaced by Piers Morgan.

It was probably for the best. Having my own, real experience of Wootton Bassett might get in the way of the myth and I find I've come to rely on the myth. It suits me to see it as a place where there are no difficult grey areas in the minds of the townspeople. While the rest of us soul-search, argue and protest about Iraq and Afghanistan, Wootton Bassett stands in simple silence. This week the town's mayor said he was worried about the arrival of *Question Time* because debates about these wars should take place 'anywhere in the country except Wootton Bassett'. The mayor added, 'We have stayed out of all the politics.'

It's as if they've deliberately cleansed themselves of any difficult thoughts in order to fulfil their function as the nation's mourners. I suggested, in a column I wrote in mid-July, that the townsfolk of Wootton Bassett perhaps had to 'put their knowingness on hold' in order to mourn the dead soldiers in that uncomplicated way that dead soldiers were mourned in the past, before patriotism was replaced by cynicism, certainty by doubt. It seems this personal choice has since developed into official council policy.

It's as if the town has deliberately placed itself in the unquestioning past – in a time before anti-war riots and Iraq inquiries. Wootton Bassett seems, from afar at least, a glimpse of that Great Britain that makes a lot of people, including the BNP's Nick Griffin, go dewy-eyed with nostalgia. Maybe Nick Griffin is a bad example. Well, obviously Nick Griffin is a bad example but I mean a bad example in this particular context. One would guess there isn't often a tear in Nick Griffin's eye – unless, of course, the wind suddenly changes at a book burning – however, he does seem to get genuinely sentimental when he hankers for a lost Britain.

One often hears references to a sort of British golden age – a period of patriotism, hard work, community spirit and blissful naivety – not just from people with extreme right-wing views but from anyone who experiences a vague sense of things being not as good as they were.

This idea of our golden age seems to be based, in some strange way, on two or three minutes of black-and-white documentary film footage that shows simple working-class people laughing and smoking at a sunny Butlin's holiday camp in about 1955. Everyone's white, everyone's jolly. No one knows that tobacco gives you cancer or that the sun gives you a bit more cancer. We know, deep down, they weren't always jolly but some people's desperate need for the past to have been happier than the present has overridden the facts. England's golden age probably seems so perfect because we've never been there. Those who were there inevitably compare not so much then with now as youth with age.

Likewise, Wootton Bassett seems to me like a little outpost of that lost England because I've never been there and because a part of me needs it to remain just that. I imagine its tradesmen whistle and always keep a pencil behind the ear and I imagine its mourners remain oblivious to the rights and wrongs of these complicated wars and concentrate on the personal tragedy of each fallen soldier. But that's me looking at them from over here. There's probably as much doubt, anger and terrible not-knowing in Wootton Bassett as there is everywhere else in Britain.

Let's face it, there's probably more. We just need them to keep it to themselves. That's become their job.

Why I love Silvio Berlusconi

18 DECEMBER 2009

I can't guarantee it, but by the time you read this, Silvio Berlusconi's wife might have finally stopped laughing. As for myself, I was genuinely upset by that footage of the Italian Prime Minister getting his face smashed by a souvenir model of Milan's Gothic cathedral, thrown at him during an informal walkabout.

I know we're constantly being told that Berlusconi is morally and politically corrupt – he must react to our measly little MPs' expenses scandal like Amy Winehouse responds to picture of the Soap Awards after-show party – but seeing him bloodied and afraid, and trying so hard not to look afraid, swept away all the derision and dark rumours and caused me to respond to him as simply one human being to another. It reminded me of those heart-breaking shots of Norman Tebbit in his pyjamas. At times like that you realise your dislike of a public figure, perhaps your dislike of anyone, doesn't go quite as deep as you imagined.

Berlusconi might be a silly, egotistical old man who can't keep his trousers on, but he didn't deserve that. Some, in Italy, have suggested that he did. They point out that there was something particularly apt about this alleged adulterer being struck down by a model of God's house. By that logic, Tiger Woods should have been hit with the actual cathedral.

At least with Berlusconi there's an element of what you see is what you get. Anyone who's seen that YouTube clip which allegedly shows him simulating sex with an oblivious meter maid as she leans over a car will know that Silvio is a man who wears his penis on his sleeve. He's one of those old Italian geezers who was brought up on bottom-pinching and hasn't quite readjusted to a post-feminist world. If you wanted to assault him with something really apposite I guess you'd go for an action figure of the Giant of Cerne Abbas. With Tiger there were no hints of impropriety and then suddenly there were women all over the place. It was as if they all dropped out of that tree when he drove into it.

I feel a sort of guilty-pleasure affection for Berlusconi that I don't feel for Tiger. We're always more forgiving of folly if it isn't aligned with hypocrisy. That cheeky meter-maid mime and a whole string of borderline sexist and racist remarks suggest that naughty-uncle Berlusconi's real, admittedly sometimes unsavoury, self keeps spilling out of the politically correct, serious-statesman container that it's supposed to fit discreetly into. In short, he's the Italian answer to Prince Philip.

Despite the horrific footage, the fact that Berlusconi's assailant used a model of Milan's cathedral to attack the Prime Minister in Milan does have a local-reference neatness that seems to make the crime not quite so bad. It's a bit like being threatened by a man with a knife in Sheffield. I'd be afraid, but I'd respect the fact that he was at least supporting local industry. However, I hope the miniature local building weapon thing doesn't lead to copycat crimes. If Gordon Brown, out and about in London, was suddenly approached by someone carrying a nine-inch version of the Gherkin, you'd worry about the exact nature of the impending assault.

I occasionally use this column to suggest ways in which Mr Brown might yet win over the electorate at the eleventh hour. Well, I suspect an incident that reduced Mr Brown, like Mr Berlusconi, to an obvi-ously frightened, fragile human being, no longer hidden behind a blustering, rhetorical shell, could be a real vote-winner. Maybe an irate squaddie could hit him on the nose with a flintlock musket he'd recently been issued with. However, if Mr Brown's suddenly exposed human frailty is to be a vote winner, he mustn't leave it too late. When the *X Factor* finalist Olly Murs was shown last-minute 'we're so proud of you' messages from his family during Sunday's show, he sobbed and snivelled and said to host Dermot O'Leary: 'What are you doing to me?' What they were, in fact, doing to him was giving him one last chance to blub his way to victory.

Had his tears come earlier, it might well have worked because his rival, Joe McElderry, watched his own family messages with an 'I've told you never to call me at work' expression that must have sent a chill through a lot of his fans. Cheryl Cole cried, I cried, but Joe just stared. He did, as an afterthought, make as if to brush away a tear, but 20 million viewers gasped at the sound of dry finger against dry cheek.

Maybe my frantic downloading of Rage Against the Machine's 'Killing in the Name' will finally help melt his ice. And that triggers my final Christmas message of hope to Gordon Brown. Three or four weeks ago, an *X Factor* Christmas No. 1 was a bigger certainty than a Conservative victory in the next election, but if the people can somehow be mobilised, there's always hope. Some might say the downloaders' rage against the Simon Cowell machine disregards the personal feelings of a sweet 18-year-old lad from South Shields, but I think Joe would probably take defeat like Mr Spock taking a barbed comment from Dr McCoy.

I admit there might be a little but of spitefulness on my own part in all this but, like Mr Berlusconi, I'm only human. And let he who he is without sin cast the first cathedral.

The elasticated waist of self-loathing

1 JANUARY 2010

It's become clear that intruders have broken into my flat over the Christmas period and deftly taken in the waistband of every pair of trousers I own. As I tried them on this morning, each waist button seemed to gaze despairingly across the swollen expanse between it and its estranged buttonhole.

Though the world only recently celebrated the twentieth anniversary of the fall of the Berlin Wall, I have erected over the course of the Christmas season a new and even uglier barrier separating my waistband's east from its west. I find myself checking my diary, counting the days before I have an appointment where wearing tracksuit trousers would be unacceptable.

Poor old tracksuit trousers! When I was a kid they were the exclusive garb of sportsmen and -women. Now they're the cosy refuge of the slob. I have worn trackies for the whole of the yuletide season. They, with their non-condemnatory elastication, have been like a loyal and forgiving friend. They're all wrong for sportspeople. If I had a waist like Jessica Ennis I wouldn't hide it behind an elasticated waistband. I'd do my warm-ups in skin-tight jeans, wearing a tape measure as a belt, just to rub it in.

Some readers might find my weight-gain anxieties surprising because I seem to be essentially a thin man. This is true of every part of me except my stomach. Naked, I look like one of those pythons that have swallowed a goat.

Even before Christmas I'd taken to hoisting my belly upwards so it sat atop my waistband like Humpty Dumpty on his wall. This last week has seen Humpty fall but remain completely intact, nay, thrive and expand. It's the waistband that I couldn't put together again.

I feel moved to confess all this because I've just read that a breakfast cereal company has surveyed 2,200 women about their 'trophy jeans' – that pair of jeans that 35 per cent of women keep, although they no longer fit into them.

Don't come crying to me, I've got a wardrobe full. The survey says that women fantasise about, one day, getting back into their trophy jeans more than they fantasise about sex.

It's about time cereal companies, glossy magazines and everyone else came to terms with the fact that it isn't just women who fret about getting fat. Women talk about it – that's the difference. Men take on the nonchalant air of not caring, but they gaze down just as anxiously at the scales beneath their feet. I'd love to tell you my expanding gut doesn't fill me with self-loathing or that a tight, flat stomach wouldn't illuminate my life with joy, but I'd be lying. Even that fat, boozy bloke we all know, who seems to celebrate his giant paunch and all that it says about his carefree lifestyle, sometimes looks in the mirror and mournfully asks 'What have I become?'

In my defence, I must say that I've been seriously let down by the swine-flu pandemic. One of the few advantages of getting fatter is that every illness has a silver lining. As soon as those first signs of shivering and nausea come upon me, I'm thinking, with ever-increasing excitement 'Oh, this feels like a bad one. We could be talking half a stone – maybe ten pounds if I have a relapse.'

Again, I emphasise these are the thoughts of a 52-year-old man, not a 15-year-old girl. When you're bedridden with flu, friends will often visit and try to cheer you up. The best way to cheer me when I'm too ill to eat is to make up my sick bed in the bowl of some enormous weighing scales so that I might lie and watch the ounces slowly dropping off me.

I started my Christmas excesses in early December because I felt sure the swine flu would take me in its strong arms and pound and pummel me back into shape. This Christmas, as I grew upon my armchair like fungus on a tree trunk, watching 12 hours of telly a day and eating anything I could reach, I waited for those first shudders of illness to rescue me from myself. It was the Christmas gift that never came.

Don't imagine that I've let my brain get flabby along with the gut. I only watched rubbish television when the remote control couldn't be reached without standing. In the main, I sought educational programmes as an accompaniment to my lemon-flavoured Turkish Delight and cranberry-topped pork pie – both dubious contributors to my somewhat ailing five-a-day regime.

I watched three movies directed by Orson Welles and two documentaries about him. These provided intellectual stimulation and also slowly won me over to the idea that fat people can still be admirable. The truth is, every Christmas I notice that my temporary half-man, half-armchair lifestyle gets more difficult to give up. It used to be that, come 27 December, I was itching to get out and about, to start work, to eat salad. Now I find the joys of communing with soft upholstery while maintaining the calorific intake of a five-man Everest expedition drift on into the New Year.

As you read this today, of course, many of you, hangover permitting, will be beginning new and rigorous exercise regimes that will take you right up to the end of next week. My New Year's resolution is to learn to play chess. It won't do much for my stomach but I think Orson would have approved. This time next year I could be looking longingly at my trophy armchair.

Michael Parkinson in my toilet – the joy of daydreams

8 JANUARY 2010

As I walked along the Strand, yesterday, a passing stranger said to me, with grim sarcasm 'Aston Villa away? Thanks very much.' I instantly knew two things about him – he supported Brighton and Hove Albion and he'd watched me draw the Fourth Round of the FA Cup on TV last Sunday teatime. Doing the cup draw gives one a slightly unnerving sense of God-like control. Though the balls, nestling in a concealed plastic bowl beneath the table, were hidden from me, as I thrust my hand into their midst I felt the seductive thrill of power. Should I take that ball against my thumbnail, or the one my little finger now taps against, or have another swirl that moves both out of my reach? These tiny decisions had enormous consequences, like moving pieces in a game of cosmic chess. That ball at my thumbnail would temporarily transfer 8,000 people from Leeds to North London. The one at my little finger would ensure that football legend, Roy Keane, spends a Friday night in a Southampton hotel, staring at a ceiling that I've condemned him to stare at. This was the butterfly effect in action. If, in two weeks' time, a Brentford fan gets punched in the mouth on a Saturday afternoon in Millwall, is his blood on my hands? Someone picked the ball that gave Ronnie Radford the opportunity to score one of the greatest-ever FA Cup goals, for Hereford United in 1972, but someone also picked the ball that sent Liverpool to Hillsborough. Such were the thoughts that passed through my mind as I made my blind selections last Sunday. How does Tony Blair sleep – or any world leader who goes to war, cuts health spending, or makes some other similarly portentous decision?

For all that, the Fourth Round draw was an exciting and enjoyable experience. After my fellow cup-drawer, the former Chelsea star, Paul Elliott, and I had done flexing our God-like muscles, I got a text from my friend, Dan, asking me if what he'd heard was true – that some of the cup-draw balls are specially heated so you can feel which ones represent the big teams. Richard Dawkins has got a lot to answer for. I explained that all the balls were at an even room temperature and confirmed the purity of the whole cup draw process. I felt Dan's faith was restored.

Someone asked me 'Did you ever dream you'd be doing the FA Cup draw?' And I was able to honestly say that I hadn't. I'd dreamt about being a player and a manager. In fact, a lot of my daydreams have centred on football. There was a period of three or four years when, every time I sat on the toilet, I recommenced a long, imaginary interview with Michael Parkinson in which I discussed, in some detail, my illustrious playing career with Barcelona. I've also spent many hours dreaming I was not only manager of West Bromwich Albion but also a master hypnotist capable of turning the most uninspiring player into a world-beater. However, the FA Cup draw, formerly associated with portly FA officials in suits, soberly taking balls from a velvet bag, was never on my wish list. Becoming a fat, dull, yes-man seemed too big a price to pay. I did not foresee the draw's showbiz reinvention.

I enjoyed being able to say I'd never dreamed of doing the draw because it seemed somehow humble and self-effacing. I remember quite the reverse effect, on *A Question of Sport*, when Sue Barker asked me if, when I recorded the song 'Three Lions', I'd ever dreamed it would become an iconic football anthem. I said yes. It sounded arrogant but it was true. She could have asked me about almost any personal achievement and the answer would have been the same. That's the thing with daydreamers – it's generally a waste of time asking them questions that begin 'Did you ever dream . . .' because they invariably did. Just to even things up a bit, I also dreamed that the second series of my ITV sitcom, *Shane*, would win a clutch of awards and become a well-loved classic like *Steptoe and Son* or *Hancock*. As it was, ITV judged it to be so bad it was never even broadcast. I hadn't dreamed that. I was once invited to appear on a TV show in which childhood dreams could be fulfilled retrospectively. When I told them the child-hood dream I'd selected, they said snogging Honor Blackman 'wouldn't be visual enough'.

We should be more upfront about our daydreams. We hide them away, worried others will mock them. It's actually very liberating to share. Reality TV seems to be the only place where it's acceptable to speak openly on such matters. When, on *Celebrity Big Brother* the other night, the cross-dressing cage-fighter, Alex Reid, told actor Stephen Baldwin he spends hours dreaming of being a Hollywood star, I wasn't embarrassed or dismissive. I found his honesty exhilarating. I bet Gordon Brown spends time imagining himself giving his General Election-winning speech. I bet even Nick Clegg does. And their imag-ined applause probably isn't half as loud as the applause I receive during my Columnist-of-the-Year fantasy. Let's wear our daydreams on our sleeves. They don't need to lead anywhere. They have their own beauty. What kind of ice-heart doesn't have any? Speaking of ice, I'm now dreaming of that call from the Pools Panel.

The alluring charms of capital punishment

15 JANUARY 2010

They say you get more right-wing as you get older. I haven't noticed this general trend in myself, but I do occasionally like to holiday on the right-wing – to spend some time exploring right-wing thoughts – just for a change of scenery. My generally liberal ego takes a breather in the passenger seat and my right-wing id gets to take the wheel. It was in this mode that I found myself considering the report by the cross-party Justice Committee that says building expensive new prisons would be a 'costly mistake' and that we should, in fact, reduce current prison populations by a third.

It costs, on average, more than £40,000 a year to keep someone in a British prison. Why doesn't one of the main parties offer to reintroduce the death penalty as a cost-cutting measure? I think most of us, at our untutored core, feel the population of modern Britain could do with a bit of an edit. A priest told me he'd once seen a sign on a monastery door that read 'everyone who enters this place brings joy to its inhabitants, either by their presence, or by their departure'. That sign could be the key to a genuinely constructive death-penalty policy. Every citizen should have a duty to bring at least a sliver of joy to other inhabitants of the planet. If they're, instead, such a profoundly negative force they bring joy only by their absence, the solution is obvious. There's a theory that only about 3 per cent of people are truly bad and a similar amount truly good. The rest of us are followers, choosing the easiest course of action, dependent on prevailing social pressure. If I'm giving the Archbishop of Canterbury a lift home, I'll stop for that old lady at the zebra-crossing because I know the Archbishop will like me for it. If Charles Manson's my passenger, I'll blast my horn and give that old girl the V-sign because Charles will think it's hilarious. You might argue that Manson's evil influence is curtailed simply by his being locked away in prison but we can't afford such indulgences any more. Any political party who promised to chip away at that corruptive 3 per cent while saving all those £40,000 annual outlays would surely be on to a winner.

Let's consider the case of 16-year-old Jordan Horsley who poured bleach over a woman because she asked him to be quiet in the cinema. He was given a 12-month sentence. I'm not saying Horsley is truly bad. I choose him merely as a random criminal from this week's news. The 46-year-old woman, Annette Warden, though physically recovered is still too scared to leave home without her husband but, to most people, a death-sentence for Horsley would have seemed excessive. OK, let's dig a little deeper. The original falling-out took place during a screening of *Harry Potter and the Half-Blood Prince* – an unlikely movie to attract a gang of five rowdy, disrespectful youths, one of whom was Horsley. It makes me wonder if there wasn't at least one lovely lad amongst them – a secret Potter-fan, entranced by the glittering moral fable. But Horsley, six foot three with a beard, would clearly be a dominant force in the group. The reports say he purchased a bottle of Domestos from a nearby petrol station and 'demanded' to be driven to the restaurant where Mrs Warden and her family were eating. Could he be one of the bad 3 per cent? If Horsley was, by nature, a follower, surely the good-versus-evil yarn that is a Harry Potter film would have influenced him for the better that night, but no. Despite all the film's persuasions to the contrary, he chose the way of Voldemort. Instead of a life-enhancing road-to-Damascus experience, he took the road to Domestos. Horsley had been previously convicted for hitting someone with half a brick. Let's imagine he'd been identified as one of the 3 per cent back then and thus edited out of that night at the cinema. The four lads would have watched the movie, perhaps somehow absorbing its uplifting moral lessons, and Mrs Warden would have had one of those simple but beautiful nights that epitomise the joys of family life – a good film followed by the chance to discuss it over a restaurant meal with her husband and two sons. And the taxpayer would have saved £40,000 and countless other expenditure. This is not to mention how many otherwise ruined nights would have been rescued.

Many liberals will be horrified by my id's nasty thought-processes but consider the good this policy would do our prison population, forced to endure overcrowding and the presence of intimidating bullies who create a context where any urge to go straight – which would, in the long run, save the nation even more money – is a betrayal of the gangster code. The bad 3 per cent, whoever they really are, bring joy only by their departure. Let's hurry that along. Of course, the problem with the death penalty, we're always told, is that some are wrongly convicted. I could be hanged for a crime I didn't commit. Yes, but I'm much more likely to die at the hands of someone who wouldn't have been around if we had the death-penalty policy I'm suggesting. That's enough now. I worry if I sojourn too long on the seductive right-wing, I might not be able to get back again.

Inspirational British politicians – why they don't exist

22 JANUARY 2010

Wednesday was the first anniversary of Barack Obama's inauguration but there's still a detainment camp in Guantanamo Bay, fighting in Afghanistan and polar bears teetering on ever-diminishing icebergs, like a bad-taste publicity-stunt for Fox's Glacier Mints. Did we all get a bit overexcited? Maybe, but let's celebrate the fact that we still have the capacity for such excitement. We're always being told that people have become disillusioned with politics but it seems what they've actually become disillusioned with is politicians. The euphoric popular response to Obama showed that people are still aching for an inspirational politician to relight their fire. A Special One in British politics could soon get the disillusioned masses back into the polling booths. We all remember those incredible scenes in Berlin last July when Obama, a foreign politician not even, at that stage, the head of his country, drew a large, euphoric crowd to hear him speak. On the night of his election, I went to a venue in Central London to see Enter Shikari, an unnervingly cool band whose audience seemed to be almost exclusively teenagers. The drummer wore an Obama T-shirt and proudly drew attention to it at the end of the gig, evoking massive cheers from the crowd. What British politician could provoke such responses? They are an inspiration-free zone.

Take oratory, for example. I can think of only two speeches by recent British politicians that have genuinely moved me – Neil Kinnock on how he was the first in his family to go to university and Robin Cook denouncing the decision to invade Iraq. Everything else is like the

CEO's speech at a double-glazing company's annual do. And I know because I've listened to several of the latter whilst waiting to go on as the evening's comedy turn. Suffice to say, as the CEO makes his way back to his seat, I've always found the opening line 'Follow that!' is guaranteed to get a collective guffaw. I've met a lot of politicians and they, with the odd exception, are sadly disappointing. This may be down to my own perhaps unreasonable expectations. I yearn for the people running the country to be noticeably brighter than the rest of us. In truth, they're pretty much exactly like the people I chat to at the double-glazing gigs. MPs are pleasant enough but not the obvious heirs of Cicero. They're essentially office workers, just like the ones you hear on their mobiles on the train, telling some colleague they'll speak to Dave Willets in sales about the Bellfield contract, and then making a derogatory remark about Manchester United. I want politicians to be sharp, highly articulate characters, charismatic, dazzling me with their knowledge and individuality. I imagine Winston Churchill was like that. Perhaps that's why he's still so present in the public imagination. Stuff like 'Never in the field of human conflict was so much owed by so many to so few' is in a different league from 'the lady's not for turning', 'education, education, education', and 'we will never return to the old boom and bust'. Gordon Brown clearly has a taste for the inspirational, as he recently revealed when admitting he sought solace in the W.E. Henley poem, 'Invictus', so why is there so little evidence of the inspirational or poetic in his public speaking?

I suspect the kind of oratory that makes the hairs stand-up on the back of your neck is viewed with suspicion by the modern British politician. They regard it as old-fashioned and overblown. They want something they'd be happy to write on a flip chart, something corporate, uncomplicated by metaphor or allusion. They've replaced the stentorian with the statistical. The overuse of statistics – often downright misleading rather than coldly factual – has virtually killed political eloquence in this country. And, what's more, how are we to know whether the numbers are true? The producers of the televised pre-election debate should take note of test cricket's new referral system. If one of the party leaders quotes a statistic, one of the other leaders should be able to give a sign calling for clarification – I'd suggest a large 'C' formed with the arms, as used when singing the Village People's 'YMCA' – at which point we cut to independent scrutinisers, like the dictionary lady on *Countdown*, who question and clarify the statistics used.

Of course, we don't need a Parliament crammed with grand orators. Every hive needs its worker bees. The corporate politicians are perfectly fine in those roles. It's the House's upper-echelon that I fret about. Where is our Obama? I doubt that person is currently in politics. The bottom-rung of British politics – the method of entry – is unlikely to attract sharp-thinking, charismatic people. For example, I watched the novelist, Will Self, on *Question Time* a couple of months ago. He was challenging, clearly intelligent, a fabulous dark presence among the shiny corporate politicos. He would, I suspect, have made a great minister – a sort of brooding but brilliant undertaker figure in the House. However, he doesn't seem the type of man who'd be keen to spend his time knocking on strangers' doors, wearing a rosette. The worker bees are fine with that sort of stuff. There needs to be a fast-track facility for the Special Ones, something that accelerates them into the top jobs. Our Obama is out there somewhere. And, if he achieved nothing else, at least he could get the T-shirt industry back on its feet.

The Spanish Inquisition could save the planet

29 JANUARY 2010

I laughed out loud when I watched the Defence Secretary, Bob Ainsworth apparently give away the date of this year's General Election on Sky News. Blabbermouth Bob, looking and sounding, as always, like a 1960s school caretaker, said people would be sorry if they woke up with a Conservative government 'after the sixth of May'. It was right up there with 'Don't tell him, Pike.' A much less comical gaffe came from China's chief climate change negotiator, Xie Zhenhua, when he said at a conference in Delhi this week: 'There are disputes in the scientific community. There's an alternative view that climate change is caused by cyclical trends in nature itself.' Of course, maybe this wasn't a gaffe. Maybe it was an unashamed explanation of why China's climate change negotiations seem to lack conviction. At that same conference, the Indian environment minister said, 'We still need more science to understand whether global warming is causing the glacial melt or whether it is the natural cycles.' My unquestioning acceptance of the whole man-made global warming phenomenon was beginning to wobble.

Then yesterday I discovered that the massively influential researchers at the University of East Anglia want us, it seems, to simply take their word on climate change and have consequently adopted a mind-your-own-business approach to any requests for evidence. Now I've had enough of this. There's definitely global warming. Is it destroying the planet? Is it caused by carbon emissions? What's the truth? You never get universal agreement on anything but when the scientists seem to be hiding something and the climate change negotiators are suddenly sounding unconvinced, we've got a problem. All this has combined to give me a loophole. I'm not going to scamper around the house turning off lights if it's all down to 'natural cycles'. I suspect governments are starting to think along similar lines. If we need 'more science' to clear up these potentially lethal doubts, where is it? There's a conference of scientists, in London this week, discussing extra-terrestrials. Have they got their priorities right? Scientists confidently tell us there's no God – a view which, even they'd admit, cannot be proven – but they can't voice a similarly unified opinion on climate change. This is somewhat more than an interesting intellectual debate. If I believe I descend from Adam and Eve, chimpanzees, or was brought by the stork, it probably doesn't threaten the lives of millions of people. If the man-made global-warming doubters are mistaken but influential, we're all going to fry. Science needs to get its house in order before it's swept away by a post-glacial tidal wave.

The trouble with the whole climate change thing is that it doesn't feel like proper grown-up news any more. It's gone a bit *Newsround*. It's the sort of thing schoolkids do projects about. As I write, there'll be a hundred classroom walls covered in paintings of rainforests, polar bears, and smoking factory chimneys, with neat, marker-pen signs saying stuff like 'What is global warming?' and 'What can we do?' And meanwhile, just outside the classroom, I see Bob Ainsworth, wearing a brown overall with pens in the pocket, climbing a stepladder, to fit energy-saving light bulbs.

Climate change has become the refuge of the used-to-be-important – like Al Gore and John Gummer – a political hinterland for people who are looking for something to do – something that makes them sound as if they're still important, maybe more important than ever. If carbon emissions really are causing global warming it's crucial the topic is not allowed to become passé. I honestly thought, when I first heard about the climate change threat, that it would be like when those alien ships hovered over the planet in the *Independence Day* movie. I thought the common enemy – the universal danger – would unite us. I honestly believed we'd put aside our differences and fight, shoulder-to-shoulder, to save the planet for future generations. I can be such a prat sometimes. When I watched the hard-nosed politicians in Copenhagen, having to be cajoled and persuaded to save mankind from extinction, I saw the grim truth of it.

I've no doubt the media gives credence to alternative views, merely because of their novelty value, but it's the scientific community who need to put us straight on all this. I'm sure Richard Dawkins would cite the Spanish Inquisition as a classic example of religious evil but the Inquisition's motivation was that heretical views might lead people astray and ultimately to Hellfire. Science can learn from that. Holocaust denial is seen as a crime but is it ultimately as dangerous as man-made global-warming denial? We need to know if the dissenters are wrong or right and if they're wrong they need to be shut up. I'm not suggesting we burn them at the stake – I'd worry about the carbon. I just want to see their claims, if false, finally refuted by the scientific community in some form of official unified statement, clearing up any grey areas. If that's going to require 'more science' bloody well get on with it and leave the extra-terrestrial musings to nutters on the Internet. Alternatively, if the whole carbon-emissions thing has been sexed-up and is no more a threat than Saddam's WMDs, tell us the truth and let's burn some fuel. Maybe one of the UEA scientists could have a confidential chat with Bob Ainsworth. I'm watching Sky News with anticipation.

An affair of the hearth

5 FEBRUARY 2010

John Terry shouldn't feel too downhearted. George Best was football's crown prince of sexual infidelity but he ended up getting an airport named after him. Football fans will excuse almost any behaviour as long as a player delivers on the pitch. If Wayne Rooney shot and killed six people in a kebab shop this coming weekend, I would still sign a petition demanding he be allowed to play for England in this summer's World Cup. If I had to choose between Team Terry and Team Bridge I'm afraid my decision would be totally based on current form. Terry seems to have made football his main priority too. His decision to miss Chelsea's Fifth Round FA Cup tie against Cardiff City so he can spend Valentine's weekend with his wife, Toni, in Dubai, sounds lovely till you consider she's already out there – 'a lonely figure in paradise' an 'onlooker' told a tabloid reporter. Big JT could have raced out to be with her immediately but there's the small matter of a game against Premier League rivals Arsenal this Sunday. Cardiff in the Cup or a high-profile Premiership six-pointer against the Gunners? It'll do her good to have some time on her own.

Incidentally, I've been very disappointed by what the tabloids' various unnamed 'onlookers', 'friends' and 'sources' have had to say about this whole affair. Surely, the whole point of quoting an anonymous person is that you use them as a vehicle for outrageous lies. I want stuff like 'A source close to the French lingerie model said, when she met Terry, she forced his hand down into her undergarments and said "Have you ever felt one of these before?" Terry replied, "Not since I missed that penalty in the Champions League Final."' Instead the sources just say everyday stuff like, 'John realises what he's done and is very upset.' Thus, an opportunity to make outrageous and unsubstantiated remarks is completely wasted. And all the time, Max Clifford circles overhead, waiting for the carcasses to ripen. Terry has, we're told, brought in a media man who specialises in 'crisis and reputation management'. His other clients include Sir Fred Goodwin. Nothing to worry about there, then. It reminds me of an interview I read with a woman who proudly told how she'd been Michael Jackson's personal make-up artist for 30 years. There are some things best left off the CV.

One might expect public sympathy to be with Terry's wife, but it seems to be mainly with Wayne Bridge, Terry's England teammate and father of the French lingerie model's child. In fact, when someone said to me they felt sorry for Toni Terry, I thought JT had done the dirty on some Italian footballer as well. All four characters in this tale of lust and betrayal knew each other. As the *Sun* says, 'They were even seen enjoying a family day out at Chessington World of Adventure.' The problem is that British footballers are so parochial. They generally, like Terry, marry their childhood sweetheart so we shouldn't be surprised that, when they wander, it's not very far. Terry didn't even venture out of the back four. Having an affair with a teammate's girlfriend was a bit like side-footing a ten-foot pass – easy and unadventurous.

Apparently, the most-ticked box on British computer dating sites is 'must live within five miles of my home' so it's not just footballers who like to keep it local. We all seek love and passion but we don't want to have to catch two buses. When JT got the urge, he didn't even get to Burger King. It had to be someone whose number was already in his phone.

The whole England captaincy thing is a red herring. Who believes that football captains make any difference nowadays? Do you really think Terry or David Beckham or Alan Shearer, ever gathered the England players in a circle, pre-game, and spoke to them of St Crispin's day? Any player who can enunciate either the word 'heads' or the word 'tails' can be captain of England. They don't even have the challenging task of exchanging pennants any more. Having said that, if they asked me to pick the England captain, I'd go Wayne Rooney every time. When the team march out of the tunnel, he's the player I want to see first, mainly because I want to make absolutely sure he's playing. When I see those three lions, his is the chest I'm most happy to see them on. A 'source' said 'Wayne would love to be England captain now. He was far too busy last year, what with the Darwin Bi-Centenary and everything. He took part in two major exhibitions and was subjected to several very exacting scientific tests.' I know he's had his own sexual scandals in the past but the fact they involved older and, not wishing to be unkind, slightly unattractive women, only serves to make him even more of a down-to-earth working-class hero. Besides, that was all part of his wild youth and, in the end, true love prevailed. A 'friend' explained 'Colleen and Wayne are very happy now, though she was livid at the time. Once, she followed one of the women for nearly three miles to find out where she lived.' I don't know what's happened to the world – the WAG's tailing the dog. Anyway, must go now. I'm getting the midday flight from Sven-Göran Eriksson International.

Why we love to see celebrities suffer

12 FEBRUARY 2010

Brad Pitt and Angelina Jolie are reputedly suing the *News of the World* for saying their relationship is crumbling. It seems the famous couple don't fully understand their role in society. Celebrity is a modern-day pillory. You have to endure a certain amount of rotten vegetables. A few years back, I was one of several British comedians taking part in a penalty shoot-out at Villa Park. A generous sponsor had agreed to give a thousand pounds to Comic Relief for every goal scored. As the jeering and catcalls rained down upon us, one well-known comic said to me 'You know, when celebrities did something like this 25 years ago, they got cheers and affectionate applause.' He was right, of course, but people nowadays have a more complicated relationship with fame. Celebrities get good money, the best tables in restaurants and more sex than they intrinsically merit so it seems right there should be some payback. Though I myself have some experience of celebrity, I still participate in that collective resentment towards the well-known. I don't want to read about them winning gongs and playing happy families. I want to read about trouble in paradise. Brangelina need to accept that their massive wealth, fame, talent and physical beauty place them completely beyond the pale. These attributes are each a sufficient reason for loathing. To combine all four is bordering on the deliberately provocative. If Brangelina had jogged out at Villa Park they may well have been lynched. The sad thing is that, as the waiting noose dangled from the crossbar, they wouldn't have understood why. Sir Elton John once told me he was treated with enormous respect and admiration in

America, to the point where he was sometimes made to feel almost Godlike. Then, when he returned to Britain, he would pick up a red-top newspaper and see himself described as 'a ridiculous old poof'. To his credit, he admitted that, once the initial anger had passed, he was able to see this as a healthy antidote to the star-worshipping he encountered stateside.

Celebrity is completely wasted on people like Brad and Angelina. Beautiful people can never fully appreciate fame. When I first became well known, it was like my popularity light had been switched on. Suddenly, after years of being unnoticed, especially by women, all my fruit machines started paying out at once. This attention wouldn't have been anywhere near as enjoyable were it not for the fact I'd spent the previous 30 years being ignored or downright rejected. At last, the sun had risen on a glorious morning. That transformation just wouldn't have been the same for Brad or Angelina. Beautiful people are always the centre of attention. They don't need celebrity's seal of approval. Beauty is a form of fame. Non-famous beautiful people get as arrogant and self-centred as some celebrities because they receive similarly special treatment.

Also, I don't approve of celebrities pairing up. It seems very selfish. Fame is still a relatively rare commodity. I feel there's a certain obligation to spread it around a little. I certainly did my bit. Celebrity is a novelty item, a conversation piece. All the friends and relatives come round for a gawp, have their photos taken, leave with an anecdote or two. Having two spotlights on the same household is just pointless. You've got to have light and shade. I feel the same about beautiful people. They should have the decency to breed with ugly people so the offspring have got at least a 50–50 chance of having nice personalities. Brad and Angelina have famously adopted some kids, from Africa and South-East Asia, to mix-up with their biological ones. I wasn't sure about the adopting-from-the-Third-World thing at first. I feared they might be setting-up a sweatshop. Now, I think it's sweet. I imagine the Brangelina household is like a lovely, big Benetton advert, though, obviously, with a certain tension in the air during the World Cup qualifying rounds. But, as I say, we don't want Brangelina to be happy. They've had too much good fortune already. In the old days, if we'd wanted to spoil a happy home headed by a beautiful woman with an international troop of kids, we'd have just sent in Woody Allen. I don't see Brad as that kind of dad grenade. Besides, we don't want to wait that long. We want a split-up-story now. If there's no drug or drink problems, no career dips, we're at least entitled to that old fallback – 'unlucky in love'.

Ironically, our own Katie Price was in *Hello!* magazine this week, saying she'd manufactured last year's split with Alex Reid to get more publicity for her reality TV show. I loved the warped echoes of Brangelina. DC Comics, the home of Superman, sometimes features a parallel world, a cube-shaped planet where everything is a crappier version of its Earthly counterpart. It's called Bizarro World. There is even a Bizarro Superman – chalk-faced, dishevelled and incompetent. He stands in stark contrast to Earth's great superhero, and is all the more lovable for it. Katie and Alex are the Bizarro Brangelina. They're proper British celebrities – quite rich, attractive-ish, and not too heavy on talent. Thus, whilst booing and jeering them, we're also able to love them. We don't want a perfect couple. We need Vernon Kay's sex-texts and Victoria Beckham's bunion. Brangelina have to take the rough with the smooth. And develop a taste for overripe turnip.

The anecdote minefield

19 FEBRUARY 2010

I write this sitting in a large country house, somewhere in the East Midlands, without access to phone, Internet, radio or television. I've been deliberately separated from all news by the producers of a new panel show, called *The Bubble*, which airs tonight on BBC Two. Regular readers – there may be a handful – will recall I experienced similar estrangement from the outside world when I did the pilot show for this same series last year. I'm guessing the show's title comes from that boy-in-the-bubble phenomenon one heard about during the eighties and nineties, when some people had so many allergies brought on by modern living they had to be separated from the world and put in a large, protective bubble. These unfortunate souls were always described as being 'allergic to the twentieth century'. One never hears of them now. I wonder if, ten years ago, as the strains of 'Auld Lang Syne' permeated their plastic globes, heralding a new millennium, they suddenly started feeling a whole lot better. The idea behind the BBC's *Bubble* is that my fellow inmates and I are shown a series of authentic-looking news items by the host, David Mitchell, and we have to guess which of these reported events really happened this week.

Although we seem to be surrounded by endless green fields, we're not allowed to wander away from the house in case we hear a news bulletin from a passing car radio, or find a discarded newspaper in a hedge. In other words, I've had five days of enforced staying in. There was a time when such confinement would have horrified me. For much of my adult life I hated staying in because I was scared of missing out on exciting happenings in the outside world. I always imagined that, on my deathbed, I would look back and bitterly regret those wasted nights. A surprising amount of my behaviour, over the years, has been governed by thoughts I might possibly have on my deathbed. I applied this test to much of my decision-making with varying results. I got off my backside and became a comedian because I was terrified at the prospect of looking back, never knowing whether I could have made it or not. But, then again, that fear of being tortured by any missed opportunity was also a one-way ticket to chlamydia. Nowadays, I love staying in. Those friends who call to beg my pardon because they must, at the eleventh hour, pull out of a scheduled get-together, seem relieved and grateful that my response is so forgiving. They don't realise that I'm experiencing the warm joy of cancellation. I don't have to put on sturdy shoes, or park my car, or wait 15 minutes for a restaurant bill. I can lie on my sofa, eat out of a saucepan and wear clothes that have neither zips nor buttons – cosy, cuddly, baggy-waggy clothes. Severe weather, minor illness, a slight sense of foreboding – any excuse to stay in and become the fleecy, floppy man is gratefully accepted.

However, staying in at the Bubble house is a somewhat different experience. I share the place with my two fellow panellists and two members of the production team. Inevitably, we've become embroiled in an unofficial anecdote contest. The swapping of anecdotes in any group can be a hair-raising roller coaster through delight and despondency. Every anecdote is recorded on a never-acknowledged league table that's burned into the heart of each competitor. We all know which story got the biggest laugh, which one trailed off into silence, and every slight gradation in between. Don't get me wrong. I love to hear a funny anecdote but not quite as much as I love to hear a duff one – the palpable disappointment of the listeners, the teller's desperate attempts to add extraneous details that might constitute some sort of rescuing coda. One knows a long round of anecdotes will almost always produce at least one flop per contestant. For a professional comedian, it's only slightly less terrifying than Russian roulette. An old friend of mine told me he once switched on Radio Four and caught the last seconds of a random programme. He never found out what it was about but its closing phrase had a massive effect on him. It was a woman's voice saying 'and that man was Robert Dougall'. My friend saw this reference to a much-loved presenter of the time as some sort of gift from God. From that point on, whenever he found himself amidst the ruins of a failed anecdote, he would tag on 'and that man was Robert Dougall' by way of a final flourish. He swore it never failed him but, as it was his gift from God rather than mine, I can't imagine using it myself unless I was getting particularly desperate.

Despite my lust for glory, I'd never derail another's yarn. I see an anecdote as a sacred thing. It will always culminate in pleasure of some kind. It's long been my contention that restaurant tables should each have an anecdote light that one switches on at the beginning of a tale, and off again at the end. I've come close to striking that idiot waiter who asks if everything is OK with the meal, just as I head into an anecdote's home straight. I'm an attentive listener to other's tales, mainly because I'm seeking the hook that will enable me to recall an anecdote on the same theme that is, well, better. But who knows where the loaded chamber will stop? Perhaps only one person – and that man was Robert Dougall.

My bully beef
26 FEBRUARY 2010

So Gordon Brown has gone from Joseph Stalin to Mr Bean and now to Gripper Stebson. Andrew Rawnsley's flinch-and-tell revelations have been a great source of fun this week. I particularly enjoyed the intervention of the National Bullying Helpline. I find it hard to respect this organisation, largely because no one who works there has realised that they desperately need an 'anti' or a 'prevention' somewhere in the title. One wonders how many misled bullied have called them up asking for tips on demanding dinner money with menaces, or requesting a factsheet on the Chinese burn.

I'm sure the organisation's founder, Christine Pratt, who is large, ginger, wears glasses and is called Pratt, knows a fair bit about being bullied, but she didn't help anyone this week. When she seemingly grassed up the civil servants who'd asked her organisation for assistance, she couldn't even get the facts straight.

Consequently, poor Ms Pratt became a figure of fun. Phil Woolas, the Immigration Minister, led the assault by calling her 'this prat of a woman'. Yes, he cleverly spotted that her surname could be used as a term of abuse. Amazingly, Pratt had no quick-fire comeback for this. It surely can't be the first time she's faced that particular line of attack. I really wish she'd given a gutsy example to the bullied of this nation by putting the opportunistic Woolas in his place. Maybe she could have fought fire with fire and pointed out that 'Phil Woolas' is what you do when sodomising a sheep. Instead, she let the bully go unchallenged.

As for the charges against Mr Brown, they don't seem to indicate bullying at all. Every bully has a target, someone they've identified as weak and vulnerable. Mr Brown had no target. The only consistent victim of his rage seems to have been a car passenger seat.

Mr Brown railed against the universe. In the Rawnsley extracts, the Prime Minister comes across like a Shakespearean tragic hero. At one point, after he discovers the police are to investigate potentially unlawful party donations, Mr Brown says: 'For this to happen to me, it eats my soul.' That's fantastic. It's like King Lear in the storm. I wanted Peter Mandelson to appear at his side, call him Nuncle and lead him to shelter.

And what about those poor aides and civil servants who, Rawnsley says, fell victim to the PM's rage? When Bob Shrum was discovered to have recycled bits from the speeches of Al Gore and Bill Clinton to use in Mr Brown's speeches, was the PM not entitled to go properly ballistic? I used writers on the latter series of the TV chat show I used to do. If one of them had recycled a joke and sold it to me as an original, they've have been out on their ear. Mr Brown also went crazy when told that a civil servant had mislaid two computer disks containing the personal and banking details of 20 million people. Quite right too. Was he supposed to just tut and say, 'Never mind'?

When I was doing that chat show I got a reputation for being difficult to work with. I introduced a ritual whereby people who'd messed up, including myself, had to raise their hand and say: 'I'm sorry, I made a mistake.' Then everyone would applaud. I think some people saw this as a humiliation. I never shouted or threw things but I did use withering sarcasm as a weapon. I'm not proud of that, but trying to make a funny TV show, week after week, can be a high-pressure activity.

My moods weren't really about anger; they were about fear – fear of failure and the resulting ridicule. I've always said that when I get to the pearly gates, I hope St Peter will offer a special dispensation for show days. Well, if I got stroppy because someone didn't get the right video clip to enhance my Westlife interview, how mad is Gordon Brown entitled to get when someone's cock-up makes it even harder for him to run the country?

It seems to me he's a rough-hewn, passionate Scotsman who really cares about the job. People respect Sir Alex Ferguson and Gordon Ramsay for that, so why not the PM? Personally, I've been more impressed by these tales of the volcanic Brown than I was by his teeth-and-tears performance on the Piers Morgan show. I prefer him as the god of thunder.

I did a bit of bullying at school. I wasn't big enough for the physical stuff. Instead, I provided a sort of mocking Greek chorus for the bullies as they fell upon their prey. I wasn't quite part of the bully gang – more an artist-in-residence. Now I realise that my verbal attacks were at least as bad as the physical bullying. Derisive words can really rip the self-respect and confidence out of someone.

So any journalists, politicians or, indeed, comedians who condemn Mr Brown for his supposed bullying should consider how they've verbally bullied him. Has he not, despite his undeniable work ethic, been the butt of every joke? Has he not provided the weak and vulnerable target that every bully needs? Shouting, throwing newspapers and punching passenger seats is small fry compared with mounting a relentlessly scornful character assassination. Surely the latter constitutes bullying. If only there was some sort of helpline for Mr Brown to call.

The warm glow of persecution

5 MARCH 2010

I'm a Roman Catholic and I go to church every Sunday. Towards the end of Mass, there's a thing called the Sign of Peace. We all shake hands with everyone in shaking-distance and say 'peace be with you'. Last Sunday, the priest told us to drop the hand-shaking element to show our solidarity with Wayne Bridge, who'd refused to shake hands with the adulterous John Terry just 24 hours earlier. That's one of the things I love about being Catholic. You can tell the highly suspicious non-Catholics – their imaginations fired by talk of kissed statues and venerated fibulas – about almost any odd behaviour in a Roman Catholic church and they'll believe you.

To many British people, Christianity seems like a weird but unexciting theme park. Personally, I like our ever-dwindling status. I even like our ever-dwindling numbers. There was a time when social pressure made people go to church. If anything the reverse is now true. Most adults you see in church nowadays are there because they want to be there. That's not decline, it's progress. The wheat has been separated from the chaff. We get quality, not quantity, in the churches and the chaff can enjoy a nice lie-in. That's just as well because there'll be little opportunity for slumber when they've got a demon's pitchfork up their arse. Christians have always worked best as an unpopular minority. We were surely at our most dynamic when we knelt, eyes to Heaven, hands clasped in prayer, with a Colosseum lion bounding towards us.

That's why I think Lord Carey, the former Archbishop of Canterbury, is wrong to get his cassock in a twist about changing attitudes to

Christianity in this country. He speaks of a 'strident and bullying campaign' to marginalise Christianity. But that's great news. 'Blessed are ye when men shall revile you, and persecute you, and shall say all manner of evil against you falsely, for my sake.' We're going to have Brownie points coming out of our ears. The evidence of such bullying, many Christians would argue, was evident in two recent incidents when a teacher was sacked and a nurse suspended – both because they offered to pray for sick people. I agree that those punishments seem wrong-headed but both women will receive huge blessings for enduring such injustice. Surely their mistake was up-fronting their intentions. I've prayed for loads of friends, most of them atheists. I tend not to tell them. If I do tell them I fear my motivation for doing so is largely ego-based. I'm just trying to show how nice and caring I am. It's much healthier to do it on the sly. 'When thou prayest, enter into thy closet, and when thou hast shut thy door, pray to thy Father which is in secret, and thy Father which seeth in secret shall reward thee openly.'

Lord Carey feels Christians have been too soft. He said if you behave like a doormat, you get treated like one. I'm a little wary of muscular Christianity. It's been used to justify everything from the crusades to the shooting of abortion doctors. It seems to be in direct contradiction to 'Resist not evil, but whosoever shall smite thee on they right cheek, turn to him the other also'. This is the doormat as positive role model – a doormat who's more concerned about the 'Welcome' than the muddy feet. Surely the central image of Christianity is someone who can shoot fireballs out of his fingertips allowing himself to be nailed to a wooden cross – submission as the ultimate show of strength – love as impenetrable armour. Most British Christians are badly dressed, unattractive people. We're not pushy and aggressive members of society. We're a bit like Goths – no one can remember us ever being fashionable and we talk about death a lot. I love the glorious un-coolness of that.

The oppression of Christians in some other countries is completely unacceptable. I obviously wouldn't want to see such genuine persecution of Christians in the UK, though that blessing for the reviled and that championing of the turned cheek would, strictly speaking, still apply. As Lord Carey admits, here it's more about a local council not wanting to call Christmas 'Christmas' in case it offends someone. I'm hoping that, with the rise of secularisation, Christians will be able to claim Christmas as exclusively their own again. I'm sure the New Atheists, many of whom point out that Christianity cynically appropriated pagan festivals, would not want to be guilty of similar hypocrisy. Don't come begging for church weddings or christenings either. Maybe a bit of strictly observed us-and-them will lead to a new Christian unity.

I went to a public debate this week. The motion was 'England should be a Catholic country again'. I ended up voting against. The marriage of church, any church, and state seems alien to the teachings of Christ. Power corrupts and British Christians should be happy to continue relinquishing it. The Catholic Church lost more than it gained when it got into bed with the Emperor Constantine. Christians tend to save their best work for the 'voice in the wilderness' genre. We are most impressive when operating as a secret sect, kneeling in small, candle-lit rooms and scrawling fishes on walls. I'm enjoying this current dose of persecution. It's definitely good for the soul.

How to kill a dog with your bare hands, and other childhood memories

12 MARCH 2010

I was driving through West London, this week, when I saw a young man walking a Rottweiler. I'd read several articles about new measures to control dangerous dogs that day, so I watched the pair carefully as I sat at traffic lights. One shouldn't, I know, judge a book by its cover but if I'd been driving around the streets desperately searching for someone to partner me on *Who Wants to be a Millionaire*, and this man and his dog were all I could find, I don't think it would have much mattered which end of the lead I'd chosen from. I don't like to dismiss someone as an idiot without good evidence but, as there were quite a few unused holes on the adjustable band of his baseball cap, it seemed clear that this was a man whose brain didn't require much storage space. I'd seen this type out with big dogs before. The scary dog is the modern-day equivalent of the codpiece. The owner is endeavouring to tell the world how strong and virile he is. 'I'm an idiot', however, tends to be the banner headline. The man was eating sweets. I couldn't help thinking that if they were aniseed balls, the problem might soon solve itself.

Pedantic dog-lovers will point out that the Rottweiler is not actually classed as a dangerous dog. However, these same people will tell you their dog understands every word they say, so their opinion is obviously null and void. I'd say every dog is potentially dangerous. I used to have a cute little mongrel who bit me about 25 times. Admittedly these incidents were largely the result of me wrestling with him, tapping him on the nose or refusing to hand over his ball but then surely one of the joys of dog-ownership is aggravating your pet to the point of snarling retaliation and then drawing back before it tears you to pieces. Nevertheless, any animal with teeth and claws is capable of doing completely unprovoked damage. Even on satellite TV's *The Dog Whisperer* – a show about a world famous dog-training expert – blood is sometimes drawn. To single out certain breeds seems like a form of dog racism. However, I think these current proposals – to microchip every dog and to make third party insurance compulsory for every dog-owner – aren't quite right. When I was a kid, everyone had to buy a licence for their dog. It was seven-shillings-and-sixpence and, no, it wasn't cheaper if the dog was black-and-white. Maybe dog licences should be reintroduced and the government could come up with a method for not issuing them to idiots. I think one can generally tell just by looking. Isn't that the rule-of-thumb they use when issuing firearms licences? What's the difference? It's all about not trusting idiots to handle dangerous things.

People had very different attitudes to dogs when I was a kid in the Black Country and I think we could learn from them. Everyone I knew had a dog but nobody I knew bought dog food or even owned a lead. The dogs lived on scraps and were let out on their own to roam the streets. They were free-range and probably happier for it. The local dogs became communal property that we all felt some investment in. One didn't just look out for one's own dog but kept an authoritative eye on the behaviour of all of them. There were certain set procedures. If there were dogs fighting in the street, someone would always get a broom to separate them. If dogs were having sex in a public area, someone would dash off for a bucket of cold water to throw over them. I fear one might get sued for taking such action now. Of course, some of the dogs did bite people but it was a rare occurrence. I don't recall any of the tragedies one reads about nowadays. My dad once had an argument with a neighbour whose dog was barking and snarling at him. My dad said if the dog got any nearer, he'd 'pull apart its front legs till its heart burst'. I don't know if that's anatomically possible but the incident shows, admittedly rather graphically, how dogs were disciplined by whoever was nearest rather than by the individual owner. Thus, the idiotic owner's influence was diluted by the responsible attitudes of a sort of dog-owners' cooperative. One could even see it as an *Animal Farm*-type fable, showing how private ownership leads to corruption but communism makes us free.

I remember stories of Teddy Boys throwing cats at people's faces, in the hope they'd instinctively cling on, and when football hooligans carefully folded newspapers to form a rock-hard 'Millwall brick' which could then be used as an offensive weapon. Almost anything's dangerous in the hands of the truly unpleasant. How dangerous are dogs per se? About a hundred British people a week need hospital treatment for dog attacks. Idiot-control would reduce that but, even as it stands, it seems a small price to pay for the sheer joy of, say, watching a still-circling dog, with its tail in its mouth, look up at you with that gloriously confused facial expression that says 'what do I do now?'

Why I won't share a plane with anyone more famous than me

19 MARCH 2010

William Shakespeare is about to get another play published and Michael Jackson has a new 10-album deal with Sony. It really has been an excellent week for dead people. Meanwhile, Sony dropped the *X Factor* whipping boys, Jedward, after only one single. Now I'm not suggesting that Jedward were dropped because they're still alive but it was definitely a contributory factor. How galling it must have been for the Irish twins – let's call it Donegalling – to be leaving the Sony building, still dusting the boot-prints from the seats of their trousers, only to have to suddenly step aside so that Michael Jackson's casket could enter through the same door. I know everyone said Jedward were a passing fad but when a dead person is judged to have more long-term potential than you it must hurt. Luckily, the twins are imbeciles. One imagines that, minutes after receiving the bad news, they were in a park somewhere, shrieking with delight over a game of leapfrog. It genuinely pleases me that Universal has agreed to give these grinning fools another shot at stardom.

Reading the new Shakespeare play, *The Double Falsehood*, is, I must admit, an exciting prospect. Of course, it isn't quite a Shakespeare play. Firstly, it was co-written with John Fletcher and, secondly, what's actually being published is an eighteenth-century adaptation by a scholar called Lewis Theobald. He was convinced that the manuscript he worked from was partly written by Shakespeare but everyone else at the time thought it was a forgery. Now, it seems, he's been vindicated. Maybe it's time to revisit some other supposed forgeries like the Hitler Diaries, the gun-toting Sarah Palin in her stars-and-stripes bikini or that competition to find a name for the Blue Peter cat. Imagine discovering in 300 years' time that David Cameron was completely genuine after all.

This new Shakespeare play suddenly coming to light has made me wonder if I could get my money back on that Complete Works of Shakespeare I bought in good faith. Also, I must say, I feel a bit sorry for John Fletcher. He was a big-name dramatist in his day but he is to this modern publication what Midge Ure was to Live 8. Us egotistical entertainment folk like to come before the 'and' rather than after it. I was once on an aeroplane when there was a loud crack and we dropped about 20 feet in the air. The playwright, Tom Stoppard, was sitting a couple of rows in front of me. Just before I began praying for my eternal soul I took time out to consider my billing. If the plane was going to hit the ocean, leaving no survivors, would the headline be something like 'Tom Stoppard dies in plane crash' and then a subtitle 'Comedian also perishes' or would poor Tom end up as the afterthought. This was the late nineties, I was doing three TV series a year, so I was pretty confident I could edge Tom into silver-medal-position. I remember thinking, as panic ensued all around me, that, in a game of Celebrity Top Trumps, the sketch with me dancing in my pants to the Venga Boys would probably beat his *Rosencrantz and Guildenstern Are Dead* and, furthermore, my 'Three Lions' would trounce his *The Real Inspector Hound*. But, with my PR machine completely undermined by the short notice, nothing could be guaranteed. As it was, the plane recovered and any indignity was avoided.

Of course, now this play is attributed to Shakespeare, we'll all suddenly realise how brilliant it is. If there are any unarguably crap sections we'll just attribute them to Fletcher. The play ends with the heroine marrying her rapist. What was that idiot Fletcher thinking about, the misogynistic git? I bet Shakespeare was tearing his hair out. Presumably he calmed down before he reached the side bits. I've always been fascinated by the whole process of joint-authorship. W.H. Auden said that writing with someone else is like riding a tandem – you're utterly convinced that you're doing all the hard work while your partner is just freewheeling. Of course, we'll never know for sure who wrote what in this work. We only know two things for certain about Shakespeare. Firstly, his head was shaped like a light bulb and, secondly, no one ever told him that.

I find previously unreleased works were often unreleased for a very good reason. Anyone who's ever seen the video, *The Unseen Frank Skinner Show*, will know exactly what I mean. What we're essentially getting here is a Shakespeare outtake. We shouldn't expect too much, nor impose too much upon it. There's a lot to be said for authorial anonymity when it comes to judging works of art. I make a special point of not reading those highly informative labels next to paintings and sculptures in art galleries. If I see a famous name – a Picasso or a Rodin – I'll then find greatness in that work, even if it's awful. Consequently, despite all my efforts, I'll probably be so star-struck when I finally read this play that I'll love it, no matter what. Sony knows a lot of people feel like that about Michael Jackson's work too. I hope Universal don't discover exactly the opposite about Jedward.

For Adolfs Only

26 MARCH 2010

I stayed in on my own the other night. I put on some slightly ripe lounging clothes, got my feet on the coffee table and began tantalisingly running my index finger up and down the television remote control. Many British middle-aged men reading this will think they know what's coming next. A night in with complete control of the remote? They'd do what lots of other British middle-aged men would do. They'd scour the satellite television channels for Adolf Hitler documentaries. This is a bit like looking for hay in a haystack. It's often possible to plan the whole evening around the Führer. I had a quick look at the listings. There was a documentary about his final days, another about his attitude to the Channel Isles, another about the Night of the Long Knives, and so it went on. I'm amazed that someone hasn't polarised this phenomenon and come up with The Hitler Channel. Then they'd no longer have to water down the content by including programmes about Elizabeth I or the invention of the hovercraft. It would be Adolf all the way. For some reason, it seems British men of a certain age can't get enough of him. He's their Lady Gaga. One can imagine them laughing scornfully at their teenage kids and pointing out that Gaga's not the first celebrity to wear crazy outfits and suffer undermining speculation about testicles.

I used to occasionally make reference, during my stand-up comedy act, to old-age pensioners constantly wittering on about World War II. I eventually came to realise that, though this was true during my childhood, it's no longer the case. Nowadays, pensioners witter on about the Beatles. However, the glut of Hitler docs is slowly reversing this trend and tomorrow's pensioners will be wittering on about World War II again. Well, Hitler, mainly. The press have the Hitler-bug too. In this last week, I've seen stories about Hitler's attitude to cricket, about his student drawings, and about a letter from him to a British journalist, which sold for £8,000. The readers' comments on the online version of the latter article all talked about what a fantastic bargain it was. It's Hitlermania, for goodness' sake.

So, what's going on? There's a general fascination with bad guys. Just take a look at the amount of True Crime books there are in the average bookshop. A bad man is like a bad relationship – intrinsically more interesting than a good one. It's why we look for the warts on our heroes – anything to convince us that good doesn't have to completely equate with dull. It's why the malevolent Richard III gets a whole play to himself but the squeaky-clean Henry VII has to settle for a bit part. But why don't other iconic bad men get the coverage Hitler does? I did read, this week, that the Moscow authorities are thinking of putting up Joseph Stalin posters as part of their Victory Day celebrations, but this seemed to be regarded as a minor piece of news compared to the revelation that Hitler thought cricket pads were unnecessary. Way to go, Joe. Osama bin Laden had a period of being a by-word for evil but when did you last see an article about him in the paper? He's not even suitable for a 'where are they now?' One can almost imagine bin Laden cropping up on the next series of *Dancing on Ice*. I reckon Jason Gardiner would still get the most boos. Bin Laden was a flash in the pan. Hitler's been around longer than Cliff Richard. He's the Peter Pan of evil.

Is it the whole Nazi-chic thing that draws people in? I remember when lounge-singer Bryan Ferry got into trouble for saying that the Nazis really knew how to 'present themselves'. People still go for that shaved-head/black-leather-boots/long-coat look. It's a grim irony for the Germans that the darkest days of their history just happened to coincide with the only time they've ever been regarded as well dressed. It may seem horrible to think people could overlook the horrors of Nazism for the sake of what they perceive to be a cool look but I'd rather they were drawn-in by the style than the ideology – better the fashion than the fascism. However, I like to believe that the fascination with Hitler comes generally from a better place than all that. The difference between him and Stalin or bin Laden is that Hitler was properly defeated. He's a one-man morality play. He was evil in what seems to be a clear-cut and uncomplicated way and he also got a proper comeuppance, dead on a concrete floor, in the arms of an Alsatian. Well, I suppose, technically, in the legs of an Alsatian. Perhaps the knowledge that he ultimately failed and was beaten in a war that seems, at this distance, more obviously justifiable than most recent wars makes him a reassuring example of what happens to bad men in the end, or what we wish happened to them. There's a lot of True Crime stuff on satellite too. Inevitably, it also tends to be about bad men who got caught and punished. I think people – admittedly, maybe subconsciously – are tuning in for reassurance, not macabre titillation.

Gut-reaction, nostalgia and sheer chance – the science of political allegiance. Part 1

9 APRIL 2010

I remember watching a news item about an American politician on the campaign trail. There was footage of him standing on a small stage, holding aloft the hand of a slightly confused-looking party colleague. Rather than risk the uncertain colleague messing-up the whole photo opportunity, the politician leaned forward to whisper some clarifying private words. 'It's the symbolism we're after,' he said. Unfortunately for him, he said it a bit too close to the microphone and the secret strategy was revealed. It was an embarrassing moment for the politician, it was commented on by the media, but the campaign continued – no resignations or even apologies were required. We know, don't we? We completely accept that election campaigns are about sleight-of-hand and sly persuasion. Senior politicians talk openly about having an 'election strategy' and we don't seem to mind that the strategy's aimed at us. If we're to be cajoled and persuaded to vote for someone couldn't they at least have the decency to be more covert about it? The media know all the tricks of the trade and we're made fully aware of the tactics being used to win our vote. 'Let's keep calling ourselves the party of change and then Labour will look old-fashioned and tired' or 'If we go on about David Cameron being posh we can cash-in on the majority's antipathy towards the privileged classes.' The current round of political billboard posters may all have different slogans but the rationale is always the same. People aren't bright or interested enough to genuinely weigh-up the difference in party policies so we'll give them their information in a form that's decidedly idiot-friendly. There are detailed manifestos out there somewhere – I'm not sure where – but these posters are more like children's books – big pictures and not too many words. It's a worry that, despite their simplicity, the posters are often badly misjudged. Equating David Cameron with much-loved television icon DCI Gene Hunt was obviously unwise and saying he'd take us back to the eighties just made me think 'Hooray! I can start drinking again.' The Tories' efforts haven't been much better. Their Gordon Brown poster that says 'I increased the gap between rich and poor' could cause many dyed-in-the-wool Conservatives to start seeing Mr Brown as their kind of guy. It's also a worry that the party leaders feature so heavily on the other side's posters. Even advertisers who sell apparently less important products like crisps or perfume tend to concentrate on how good their product is rather than slagging off their rivals. The latter approach would suggest a struggle to find good things to say about their own product – worth remembering as we watch the election campaign unfold.

A row about National Insurance wasn't the most exciting way to get the Election ball rolling. The subject was so dull and complicated the media had to concentrate on the fact that Mr Brown dared to suggest that successful businessmen are capable of being 'deceived'. An economics dullard like me can't help thinking that if these businessmen are so sharp, perceptive and clever why is it generally accepted that British business is on its knees? But there's the problem. I don't like being patronised by silly posters but nor do I want to do a three-year degree in, say, Business Studies in order to develop a more informed opinion. Besides, the credit crunch showed us how much financial experts really know. The issues relevant to running a country are extremely complex and that bloke in the pub who you're impressed by because he 'knows about politics' still only knows a minuscule fraction of the whole story.

I went to a talk about the Spanish Civil War. The speaker knew so much about the subject that he was unable to answer any questions on it. I know that sounds contradictory but what happened was that someone would ask a question and the speaker couldn't bring himself to give a simplistic, graspable answer. He knew how complicated the truth was and he was determined to try and cover the various nuances and contradictions involved. Thus his responses were ultimately unsatisfactory. We wanted a nugget of simplified truth we could take away and bring out whenever the subject cropped-up. Then we'd be that bloke in the pub who knows about the Spanish Civil War. But the speaker refused to lie to us. Our politicians are much more amenable. All we want are a few simple sound bites we can hang our fragile opinions on – just enough to give us a sense of joining-in. Those party slogans that we're seeing everywhere now are like chat-up lines. We know they're probably not sincere but we still like to hear them. Choosing a government is as random as choosing a girlfriend or boyfriend. Some small, probably irrelevant or misunderstood thing can draw you in or drive you away. They put on their best front and hide all their bad stuff until they've won you over and you stay with them until the opportunity for change comes along. Then you have to decide between the lure of fresh meat or the cosy, warts-and-all security of the familiar. Just accept that your final choice will be based on not much more than gut reaction, nostalgia and sheer chance.

The FA Cup Final – the science of political allegiance. Part 2

16 APRIL 2010

The televised Leaders' Debates are an interesting sideshow but I'm not sure they'll rinse away the bitter taste that informs this General Election. We're told that most people are voting for 'the lesser of two evils' and that the main thrust of the electorate's decision-making is against rather than for. Theorists suggest this is because of the general cynicism brought on by the expenses scandal, or a general distrust of both main-party leaders, or the inability of the Liberal Democrats, or any other party, to offer a viable alternative. I watched the launch of the UKIP manifesto on TV this week. Their 31 per cent flat tax rate caused me to look up from my muesli but, after the outrages of MPs' expenses, could anyone really vote for a party whose symbol is a pound sign? The 2010 General Election is a study in despair – a drama with no heroes. The main protagonists are either despised, distrusted or dismissed, and often all three. I remember flitting around the country in a helicopter as part of the BBC's 1997 Election coverage. As we flew back down to London, the darkness lifting and our beautiful island waking beneath us, I turned to the pilot and said 'The dawn breaks on Blair's Britain.' I was not being ironic. We had spent the night, in between assignments, listening, on the helicopter radio, to the Tory government crumbling – Michael Portillo gone, Malcolm Rifkind gone – a glorious landslide of optimism washing away the old guard like the Red Sea closing on the Egyptian army. Now that thrilling night was being followed by a new morning. Never, for me, had politics seemed so dynamic, so exhilarating. How I'd love to feel that way again.

Still, I'm all for making the best of a bad job. I like the Beckettian bleakness of this year's election. Never has that X on the ballot paper seemed more apt – a negative symbol for a negative vote. If only the polling booths could be wired-up so that each X was accompanied by that squelching sound-effect they have on *Family Fortunes* when a guess turns out to be not on the list. I like the fact that the Conservative Party is looking to win on the 'we can't be any worse' ticket while Gordon Brown is banking on a 'better the devil you know' appeal.

I find myself really taking against every politician I see on TV or hear on the radio, regardless of what party they represent, or whether I agree with what they're saying. I am so convinced that their motivations are all about power and personal glory, rather than public service, that I find myself screaming at the telly like I only used to do when Cristiano Ronaldo was playing for Manchester United. And it doesn't take much to get me going. I watched David Cameron – I chose him at random rather than for any political reasons – in an 'intimate profile piece' on TV earlier in the week. He said 'our aim is to make Britain the most family-friendly country in Europe.' Family-friendly? Doesn't that suggest a lowbrow, brightly coloured plastic wonderland of unchallenging, unquestioning blandness – a CBeebies Britain so relentlessly cuddly that the poor, the angry and all the other socially ugly phenomena will have to be shovelled up and carted away in case they obscure the synthetic scenery? That was the question I bellowed at my four walls. I don't want to be that kind of voter, all angry and disillusioned. I don't want to vote Labour just because I'd get such a kick from seeing David Cameron beaten and washed up, the sheen scuffed, the bubble burst. I hate myself for savouring that thought. It's not too hard to conjure up the image because Gordon Brown looked that way for most of 2009. All I have to do is a bit of mental photoshopping.

So what's the answer? It seems that to come up with a more positive motive for voting we need to distance ourselves from the election. We need to replace it with something we are not so embittered and disillusioned by: an analogy for the election that we can consider objectively, learn from, and then use to inform our vote on 6 May. Let's try the FA Cup Final. This year's game features Chelsea, the billionaire-owned representatives of one of the most affluent areas in Great Britain. They have filthy rich players with a distinct air of decadence about them. They are the elite. Then we have Portsmouth FC, from a strong working-class town traditionally associated with people of all races and backgrounds. The club has massive debts and has just been relegated from the top flight. Their manager is dishevelled and eccentric-looking but somehow admirable. It's pretty obvious that, for the purposes of our analogy, Chelsea are the Conservative Party and Portsmouth are Labour. Now all we have to do is search our hearts and discover which one of these teams we'd instinctively like to see win the FA Cup. Then we apply what we've learned to the General Election and all the clouds will suddenly clear and we'll know not only who to vote for but also that our motives are honest and heartfelt. I can almost hear that helicopter.

Why the Elephant Man wouldn't win *Britain's Got Talent*

22 APRIL 2010

Samuel Johnson famously said that to hear a woman preach is like seeing a dog walk on its hind legs 'it is not done well but one is surprised to see it done at all.' When I watched Chandi, the performing dog, on *Britain's Got Talent* last weekend, I noted that this simile is not reversible. Watching Chandi walk unaided on its hind legs was nothing like hearing a woman preach. On the contrary, the border collie's erratic prancing had an air of pagan lasciviousness about it. It was like watching some lewd she-wolf from a disturbing fairy tale. It seemed intelligent but in a sly, manipulative way. Was it controlled by its trainer, Tina, or she by it? On *Britain's Got Talent*, all things are possible. The show's producers are not afraid to dip the ladle deep into the dark soup of British society in order to bring forth such wondrous oddities. Jeremy Kyle picks and prods at the jagged edges of broken Britain but he seems to find only sadness. *Britain's Got Talent* celebrates the misfits and outsiders. Showbiz is a beautiful city that shines so bright it dazzles, but on the outskirts of town lie the homes of the strange. *BGT* reaches out and beckons them forth into the light.

Some think this cruel. They imagine that those insulted by Simon Cowell and his fellow judges are forever pointed at in the street and scornfully reminded that they got humiliated on *BGT*. I doubt this is the case. Too many are abused – too many buzzers pressed – for any one victim to stay in the mind. It would be like remembering an individual blade of grass. Besides, on this show, the losers are at least as important as the winners. Britain has got talent but it also has self-delusion, blind-hope and strangeness. All these are integral ingredients of the dark soup *BGT* serves up. The show is like a census of alternative Britain – a Domesday Book of weird people. Those old talent shows like *Opportunity Knocks* and *New Faces* were afraid to dip too deep. They felt the need to exclude, to edit, to spare us any uneasiness. *BGT* is what those shows would have looked like if they'd been directed by John Waters. The odder contestants are somehow heroic. They seem to offer themselves up as colour, as texture, as the part of the fabulous journey between one genuine talent and the next. Even if their performance is woefully misjudged it's right and good that they're part of this national event. They have stepped into the light. *BGT* is beyond a television programme. It's a happening. It's no place for those who worship the great god Normal. Indeed, on *BGT* golden ability, as Susan Boyle showed, can be at one with strangeness. That strangeness is the show's house-style. We miss it when it's absent. Tina and Chandi were high on talent but also the stuff of nightmares. The ten-year-old girl from Wolverhampton who sang Vera Lynn's 'White Cliffs of Dover' had her own take on that house style. The Black Country accent she exhibited in her preamble soon disappeared to be replaced by the clipped and proper tones of the 1940s BBC. Her singing voice seemed to come from another place, like she was the mouthpiece for a lost soul, called-up at a séance in some grim living room, attended by lonely and bereaved old women. I loved it. I should like to see an entire World War II dramatisation featuring such children. The little brother and sister from BBC One's *Outnumbered* could be enlisted. He'd make a marvellous Winston Churchill and she a convincing Unity Mitford. It would be a sort of Doodlebugsy Malone.

BGT never seems completely of the modern world. The winner gets to perform at the Royal Variety Performance. The three judges still seem to see this as an amazing honour, even though the RVP lost its magic about 20 years ago. The judges employ the anticipated gaze of the Royals as a moral rule-of-thumb with which to measure the acceptability of each act. One contestant this week was a theatrical burper. He began with two enormous burps and was immediately buzzed into silence. 'Do you really think the Royal Family would want to watch that?' he was asked, as if Queen Victoria and Prince Albert were to attend rather than the oft-pilloried, scandal-ravaged walking-wounded that constitute today's Royals. Is belch-based entertainment anywhere near as disturbing as the conspiracy theories that surround the death of our Queen of Hearts?

Of course, an appearance at the Royal Variety Performance is exactly the right kind of surreal star-prize for *BGT*. If money or some sort of professional contract was involved, the normal world would begin to seep into the show like water entering a sinking ship. It's not a freak show. The Elephant Man could succeed on *BGT* but he'd need a gimmick. Otherwise he might get lost in the crowd. *BGT* dabbles with freak show-ness, the way an experimental musician dabbles with discord, but it always regains harmony before any damage is done. Ant and Dec may laugh at the acts, but always with joy rather than scorn. I already ache for tomorrow night's extravaganza.

Science is cool.
In fact, it's so cool
it's downright cold

29 APRIL 2010

Clearly, Professor Stephen Hawking is a heroic figure – a man who's so damned clever even extreme physical disability couldn't prevent his ascent to intellectual star-status. But, this week, he's pushing product. He's taken time-off from top-drawer thinking to plug his new TV show. There are certain tried-and-trusted approaches to this kind of thing. For example, the popular actress Denise Welch was plugging her auto-biography this week. She took a well-trodden path to column-inches. She revealed a few painful and humiliating personal scandals – such as the fact she snorted cocaine between takes whilst filming *Coronation Street* – which will now be written about extensively in articles that include the phrase 'in her new book'. Professor Hawking chose an even darker method for gaining publicity – scaremongering. The professor warned that we shouldn't try to contact aliens because they may not necessarily be friendly and inter-galactic conflict could ensue. He explained 'I imagine they might exist in massive ships, having used up all the resources from their own planet.' I have to say, this is a bit route-one as far as alien-based speculation goes. I'm surprised he didn't go on to suggest that these ships might possibly be saucer-shaped. I suppose some TV-type said to him 'Let's not mention the blackboards crammed with calculations at this stage. We'll lure them in with science fiction and homeless extra-terrestrials.'

I hate it when scientists try to be all populist and accessible. It's like politicians talking about football – it just doesn't ring true. Science isn't fun. It's just maths in fancy dress. Most bookshops have a Popular

Science section but these books are only 'popular' because impressionable people, having noticed that science, due to some unfathomable mix-up, has become quite trendy, now want to clamber onto the bandwagon. These books are, in truth, very complicated, deathly boring and not really for laymen. Twenty years ago they would have, quite rightly, only been bought by people with bad skin and dickey-bows. Now cute girls with purple hair and boys in skinny jeans are joining the club. Needless to say, they'll soon become disheartened and few or none of them will ever reach page 50. Indeed, the pages of Professor Hawking's own blockbuster, *A Brief History of Time*, are completely blank from page 55 onwards. I only discovered this, accidentally, when wind disturbed the pages of my own copy, shortly after I placed it in a skip. All Popular Science books have a warm, even human, opening chapter that fills one with excitement and enthusiasm for the subject. The next chapter begins to flesh out some of these ideas. The third chapter is maths. A Popular Science book, or, indeed, TV programme, is a bit like science itself – it starts with an exhilarating sense of discovery but soon becomes unbearable. 'Hurrah! Man can fly! Now we can drop atom bombs on Japan.'

The whole Popular Science charade can be blamed on one photograph – Albert Einstein sticking his tongue out. This image caused gullible but essentially well-meaning people to completely ignore what they learned at school – that science is most definitely not popular – and start thinking that a science book could be like a night at the circus. It can't. It can, at best, only ever be a maths book with a ramp. I imagine that Einstein was sticking his tongue out at all the ordinary people who enjoy stuff like dancing, cupcakes and cartoons – y'know, genuinely popular things. He wasn't being light-hearted, he was being contemptuous. Why pretend that scientists are fun when they're clearly, by definition, detached, dispassionate killjoys. The difference between your average person and a scientist is that we love to read about the warm and loveable Ratty, in Kenneth Grahame's *Wind in the Willows*, whereas they like to see a real rat, pinned to a board. Of course, we need science – it gives us good things like headache cures and glow sticks – but let's not pretend it's warm-hearted. There's a reason that scientists in comic books and B-movies usually get the prefix, 'evil'. That's the wisdom of the people.

I wonder if Professor Hawking is against us communicating with aliens because such contact could prove embarrassing for the scientific community. Though scientists miss out on fun stuff like ghost stories and pulling wishbones, their great consolation is that they know more than anyone else about science. What if a bunch of aliens turn up and know a whole lot more? What if some dude with antennae and sucker-feet takes one look at the Large Hadron Collider and says 'Aren't you going to take the lens-cap off?' We're in awe of our boffin-types but we take what they tell us on trust because no non-scientist can break through the boredom-barrier and check-up on the facts themselves. Any contact with sucker-foot could blow the whole scam. Whatever reasons Professor Hawking has for warning us against alien intruders, the effects could be widespread. Many, like Hawking, will be scared at the thought of strange outsiders arriving here in bizarre costumes, spreading disruptive, unearthly ideas. Hence the press response to the forthcoming papal visit. I imagine the Foreign Office representative who got caught sending a satirical memo about the Pope is already preparing a similar memo about the space invaders – with jokes about aliens attending the opening of an abduction clinic, Martians launching their own branded chocolate bar and endless references to Uranus.

Beauty and the ceased

7 MAY 2010

I saw a picture of national-treasure-in-waiting, Cheryl Cole, in the papers this week, looking very attractive and rather saucily attired. There's nothing unusual about that, of course, but I did also notice that a particular phrase has begun to appear alongside pictures of Mrs Cole, just lately, especially if she's in glamorous mode. I always keep an eye out for newspaper leitmotifs but this one has crept up on me. It has slight variations but the general gist goes something like 'here's Cheryl Cole, showing Ashley what he's missing'. I've also seen it attached to recent alluring pictures of Kate Winslet and Jennifer Aniston, with 'Ashley' of course, replaced by the names of their respective exes. I know one shouldn't take showbiz reporting too seriously but there's a lot of pernicious and reductive assumptions attached to this 'what he's missing' theme so it's worth a bit of close analysis. The most obvious assumption is, I suppose, that what one misses about an ex-partner is their flat stomach or long legs. This is almost never true. The three relationships mentioned above were surely well into the stage where the what-once-seemed fathomless depths of physical attraction had been plumbed, charted and no longer concealed any exciting mysteries. The narcotic-like draw of raw physical attraction can hold together the flimsiest of partnerships but only for about 12 months or so. By that time you've tried all the sweets in the sweetshop and it's time to get your confectionery elsewhere. Unless, of course, you realise you've come to enjoy the sweetshop for itself – the worn oak counter, the dusty but hypnotic chandelier, the quirky clientele. You're not quite sure what it is, but you just don't want to go anywhere else. This feels like home – familiar, safe even, but also profound and inexpressible. This is what you miss if you miss anything about an ex-partner. Any longing for previous physical delights tends to be more about a fear of the new, or the amount of often fruitless effort it takes to acquire the new – a running away from rather than to. Of course, the whole 'what he's missing' trope assumes that the former partner misses anything at all. He may be looking at those photos with a sense of blessed release. I say 'he' because I have yet to come across an example of a male celebrity who's said to be showing his ex 'what she's missing'. This omission suggests, of course, that the concept is partly based on the tired old theory that men are chiefly concerned with the physical element of relationships. Those who adhere to this view would say the very fact that Ashley and Cheryl are no longer together is their Exhibit A. He wanted more sweets than she had in stock. But Ashley can get sweets all over the place. For him, it's a buyer's market. There can be new, untried sweets every night. One can never conclusively see into the mind of one's fellow man but I'd wager, based on my own experience, that if Ashley misses anything about Cheryl, it won't be sweets. It will be the way she wrinkled her nose when she got cross, the distinctive rhythm of her breathing as it lulled him back to sleep, and that time she cried at *Shrek* and tried to pretend it was hay fever – the hard-to-explain knot-in-the-stomach memories that transcend the sexual and stubbornly cling to your consciousness, partly because you can't really explain them to anyone else. People understand flat stomachs and long legs but this lingering, heart-wrenching stuff is in a foreign language and the only other native speaker isn't around any more. When a once-solid relationship ends it takes a long time to shut down all those parts that were 'we' rather than 'I'. They linger. 'It's a beautiful day. We could go . . .' and then you remember we can't go anywhere because there is no 'we' any more. That's what you miss. But it's hard to put that in a photograph.

This 'what he's missing' thing is supposed to make wronged and abandoned women seem strong and independent. It's a more sanitised version of a drunken girl, with mascara on her cheeks, screaming Gloria Gaynor's 'I Will Survive' at a late-night karaoke. In fact, it makes women seem superficial, manipulative and backward-looking. It suggests their self-worth is somehow defined by what their ex-partner thinks. It reinterprets post-split weight-loss so it's not a sign of grief but rather a sort of spiteful rebirth – a revenge-driven process that punishes the rejecter by taunting him with now-forbidden fruit. It suggests that if anyone misses anything about this woman it could only be her flat stomach and long legs. Of course, it's reassuring to reduce Kate Winslet, Jennifer Aniston and Cheryl Cole to their physical attributes. We like to think that people who look that good couldn't have much going on inside. Such abundance would be unfair. Thus the 'what he's missing' angle keeps them in their place and tells us that, yes, they're beautiful but even their wondrous beauty was not enough. 'He' had that beauty but he walked away. And if he misses anything it could only be that beauty because what else could there possibly be to miss?

Happiness is a menu-torch

21 MAY 2010

There's a scene in the film *Lost in Translation* when crusty old Bill Murray lies on a hotel bed with the beautiful young Scarlett Johansson and she asks him if things get easier as you get older. He hesitates and then grudgingly admits that one does begin to feel a little more relaxed with oneself. It's a small admission but a significant one. To my great surprise, though I'm clearly closer to the grave than the cradle, I've become, in recent years, what I'd dare to describe as happier – a feeling all the more solid for its unspectacularness. Indeed, no longer craving the spectacular is part of this subtle evolution. Caring just a little less about what you look like, how you're supposed to behave, whether you're cool, is the compensatory gift that makes getting older much more pleasurable than I ever dared hope. A few weeks ago, I watched a guy, probably about 60, struggling to read a menu in a moodily lit restaurant. He calmly reached into the inside pocket of his jacket and took out a Maglite torch, switching it on and twirling it into position with a deft one-handed movement. He'd done this before. The now-distressed young waitress attending his table looked around the restaurant to see who else had noticed – like he'd made her his unwilling accomplice in a wantonly embarrassing act. She seemed to represent youth, self-conscious and uncomfortable. He was simply doing what was practical, a calm decision uncluttered by considerations of what others might think. He made his suggestions, clicked-off the torch and, this time, placed it, glass-down, on the table. They say you have truly found freedom when you can dance as if there's no one watching. This was his dance. I was almost disappointed when he used the torch to check the food on its arrival. I was dreaming he might produce a pair of clip-on cutlery headlights – one for the knife, another for the fork – twin-beams exploring the gravy. Headlights he'd politely dip if someone came to sit at an adjacent table. The glory of all this was that the torch was no grand gesture, no self-styled colourful affectation. It was just that the man's behaviour had sort of levelled-out. The way he behaved when alone and the way he behaved when in public had not perhaps fully merged but they were now much closer, I'm sure, than they were in his youth.

This vague sense of becoming at ease with oneself got some academic back up, this week, from an American university research project. 340,000 men and women between 18 and 85 were interviewed and the researchers concluded that 50 is the age when people finally begin to have fun. Well, 'fun' was the word the newspapers used, mainly, I suspect, because it offered some alliteration with '50'. The joy of the menu Maglite – the joy of finally growing into oneself – seems to me to be far removed from my definition of 'fun'. I find that fun and the pursuit of fun, often has a desperation about it. It's the very opposite of the joyous ease I'm talking about. I think children can have unself-conscious fun, splashing about in paddling pools, eating lollies or trying to kick a pigeon but once you get beyond about ten years old, it's less about having fun and more about needing to be seen as someone who *has* fun. The heroine of Stella Gibbons' *Cold Comfort Farm* tells of a Greek vase, ringed with bacchanalian revellers, twisted and contorted in a frenzied dance. Their thrusting limbs, almost dislocated by trying too hard, suggest the dancers are desperate to convince the observer that they're having fun. How many groups of loud and demonstrative teenagers have you seen in the street, going to similarly extreme lengths to prove that same thing to the world and, indeed, to each other?

According to the American researchers, 50 is the magic number. That's when one's white-knuckle grip on life starts to ease-off a little. I had a slight crisis at 50 – a fleeting sense of being a rejected outsider in a desolate universe – but this was soon supplanted by a longing for boiled sweets. My closest thing to a mid-life crisis came when I was 30. A whole bunch of us got to be 30 at the same time and it was suddenly like being in the company of madmen. Everyone was buying pixie boots and doing press-ups. Our youth was disappearing and we were too far from 50 to see getting older as anything other than horrifying. But, hey, that was mid-life. Nowadays, two-thirds of the way through, I seem to care more about stuff that matters and less about stuff that doesn't. Mind you, I am as yet still only half-emerged from the pupal cocoon. I still have twitching remnants of my insecure youth but happily they are slowly falling from me. I sometimes notice them gone. For example, it's become apparent of late that my back aches if I lift heavy objects. Imagining such an example of diminishing strength, even four or five years ago, would have terrified me. As it is, I've just stopped lifting heavy objects. I'm already over it.

The terrors of
the L-word

28 MAY 2010

The great American stand-up comedian, Lenny Bruce, did a routine during which he'd ask how many people from ethnic minorities were present in that night's audience. Each question would begin 'How many . . .' and then he'd use the most abusive, racist term he could think of for each minority group. He'd end by explaining that if we take these words and keep saying them until they lose their scary magic powers, no little kid would come home from school in tears because somebody called him one of these names. As Lenny knew only too well, the demonising of any word only makes it more powerful.

So, today, I'd like to talk about the L-word. 'Lonely' has a scary, magic power. Who admits to being lonely? It's one of the great social taboos and seems utterly unaffected by progress in other areas. It's now OK to be gay, depressed, deaf or dyslexic but lonely is still a social disgrace. Fear of loneliness governs so many of our actions. We use deodorant, dress like our peers, keep abreast of the latest water-cooler topics, and try to hide our alienating idiosyncrasies because we're afraid that, otherwise, people might reject us and we'll be lonely. A report by the Mental Health Foundation published this week said that one-in-ten British adults regularly experience loneliness. When you read that it's tempting to think 'Well, I see the occasional inhabitant of Lonely Street, walking their odd walks, with their broken spectacles and their mysterious shopping bags, but I never thought they were 10 per cent of the population.' Those people, it's true, often constitute the loneliness front-line. They start odd. Other people avoid their oddness;

the resulting loneliness makes them odder and on it goes. But we know, because we've heard it said, by the founders of dating agencies and frustrated therapists, that loneliness is a very broad church. It can strike cute red-headed women, or extremely witty male physics teachers – just about anyone. We've heard this but we don't quite believe it. There might be an isolated case when a well-dressed professional is at a loose end for 48 hours but true loneliness is surely the spiritual home of the strange. Well, I have known loneliness. It has stayed just long enough to frighten me – just a week or two, here or there, when every day feels like toothache. During such times, I've gone on my own to the theatre and been one of the handful of people who stay seated during the interval, reading a dull souvenir programme from cover to cover while the sounds of chat and laughter drift in from the adjacent bar. I could have stood and addressed those scattered souls who sat around me, suggested that we, the lonely, should head to the bar together, take it in turn to share our views of the show so far, and maybe even form a regular theatre club, attending performances as a group and always hanging back a little, at the interval, to recruit new members and open a few more closed hearts. But I didn't rally my fellow lonelys for two reasons. Firstly, I didn't want to own up to being lonely and, secondly, I didn't want to talk to other lonely people because they're all weirdos and I'd never be able to shake them off. This is the great dilemma of the lonely person. They know that *they* don't have severed heads in the fridge and an inclination to cause awful public scenes by screaming and getting undressed but they assume every other lonely person probably does. What can be done? In this country, loneliness has largely been a product of climate. I've been to villages in rural Africa and the Middle East where people only enter their homes to sleep. Life is al fresco and therefore almost inevitably communal. Here we have to lock ourselves away in insulated boxes or freeze to death.

This new government must be desperate for a defining policy that isn't about making the innocent masses pay for the excesses of the guilty few – something noble to be remembered for. An anti-loneliness campaign could be it. It amazes me that government after government have allowed this social disease to remain untreated. There must be a lot of lonely people sitting at home who'd much rather be out spending money and therefore helping the economy. There needs to be a network of regular events specifically designed to do what I hadn't the courage to do during that theatre interval. The lonely could be seeded so, for example, the stranger ones could be brought together, to swap shopping bag revelations and mend each other's spectacles, while the theatregoers would assemble elsewhere. I'm not talking about singles' nights here. The only widespread attempts to cure loneliness have been based on dating and motivated by financial gain. This new movement should be about finding friends. That should not be seen as less important than finding a spouse. The important thing is that all these events be under the umbrella term The Anti-Loneliness Club. Let's liberate the word and we'll liberate the victims. Any government that demystified and then, to some degree, eradicated loneliness could rightly call itself a positive force for change.

Why double-acts hate each other

4 JUNE 2010

Eddie Large, formerly of the comedy double-act, Little and Large, revealed, in an interview with *TV Times* this week, that he and his former partner, Syd Little, never speak to each other. This shocked me for two reasons. Firstly, as a sometime member of a comedy double-act myself, I hate the idea that comradeship forged in the white heat of the comedy crucible could ever be put asunder and, secondly, I thought *TV Times* closed down about 25 years ago. I guess Eddie and *TV Times* had their golden years at about the same time so there's a certain neatness in their current juxtaposition. Mind you, by that logic, I should do an interview with Eddy Shah's *Today*. The story of Little and Large's estrangement is not just sad, it's weird. Mr Large explained to the *TV Times* that 'he lives up near Blackpool and I live near Bristol, so I haven't spoken to him for a long time'. I understand that these last years have been lean times for Eddie but have bookings dried up to such an extent that he's actually forgotten what a telephone is? How primitive is Eddie's current communication-system-of-choice that it cannot cope with the distance between Bristol and Blackpool? It has to be either that thing that kids used to do with two tin cans and a length of fishing twine or, alternatively, it's just shouting.

Syd and Eddie's professional partnership lasted nearly 40 years and included a BBC One Saturday night show that ran for 13 series. You'd think such a long period of intense shared experience would have formed a unique and unbreakable connection between them. For Eddie and indeed for Syd, there's only one other person on the planet who understands what it was like being Little and Large. Their estrangement makes me feel sad. Hearing that Little and Large aren't speaking is like hearing that John McCarthy, Brian Keenan and Terry Waite don't exchange Christmas cards. I fell into a similarly melancholy mood when Chas and Dave split up. I experienced a sort of cockney knees-down.

Of course, I'm fully aware that double-act feuds are a showbiz tradition. Abbott and Costello didn't speak for two years, during which time Bud Abbott threatened, in print, to give Lou Costello a public thrashing. The massively popular Dean Martin and Jerry Lewis came to hate each other, the former telling the latter 'you're nothing to me but a f****** dollar sign' and things got so bad between Mike and Bernie Winters that Bernie replaced his brother with a St Bernard dog. I think it must be something to do with sharing the limelight. Some members of double-acts resent their dependency on the other half. When they dreamt of the gold medal they never imagined it would be for the three-legged race. I read a review of *Unplanned*, a completely impromptu show I did with my double-act partner, David Baddiel. The reviewer liked the moments of uncertainty, the pauses where we looked to each other for support, as they put it 'the moments between the trapezes'. And it is like a trapeze act. You launch-off into your swoops and twirls hoping the other half is there to catch you. Sometimes one member will feel that they're the one who provides all the magic. The truth is a double-act is a single creature with two heads. David and I had a rule that when we worked on scripted stuff we never said, no matter who asked, who wrote what joke. Our stubborn reply was always '*we* wrote it'. I regard the double-act part of my career as a bit of a treat – like being accompanied by a close friend on a walk you'd normally do on your own. Of course, I'm a part-time double-act member. Maybe, if I was full-time, I'd be fantasising about how it would be to draw my hands away at the last moment and watch the empty trapeze just swinging there as the shrieks and sobs rise-up from the crowd below.

We're told Little and Large came into being when Syd, doing his solo act at a small club, got severely heckled by a fat bloke with curly hair. Suddenly, the heckler got onstage and started doing a Cliff Richard impression that wowed the crowd. He continued to heckle the sad-faced, bespectacled Syd, now from close-range, and this whole comedy *coup d'état* went so well they decided to remain a twosome. It's every heckler's secret dream come true and it makes Syd Little seem not so much a straight man as a hostage. Maybe Eddie has finally set him free. Nonetheless, we love double-acts and we, in turn, need them to love each other. I wish Syd and Eddie would make contact before it's too late. I remember Brian Clough's desperate grief when Peter Taylor died in the midst of their estrangement. Abbott and Costello, Lewis and Martin, Mike and Bernie, they all made friends again in the end. There must be something that still connects Syd and Eddie, if it's only Stockholm Syndrome. Where's the conciliation service, ACAS, when you need it?

This could be the last thing I ever write

11 JUNE 2010

Mark Twain once said there'd been a lot of terrible things in his life but most of them didn't happen. Thus lives the worrier. I'm about to fly out to the World Cup in South Africa and I'm a bit frightened. Believe me, I'm not the only one. I went to sign an updated version of my will on Wednesday. I was loath to admit to anyone, even myself, that my impending trip was the reason. It turned out there was no need to be coy. The lady who overlooked the process told me there'd been 'quite a rush on' over the last few weeks, with people openly citing their World Cup jaunts as their motive for putting everything in order. I suppose this is both a twisted testimony to the reckless enthusiasm of football fans and, conversely, a grim insight into what supporting England does to your general pessimism levels. I did a gig with Keane on Monday night and, at one point, their singer, Tom, suggested to the crowd that England would lose on penalties in the quarter-finals. An indignant woman, wearing an England shirt, corrected him by shouting 'semi-finals'. I'm actually quite optimistic about the football but the trip fills me with a sense of impending doom. One friend did reassure me I wouldn't be sliced-up by machete-wielding bandits but he based this on the fact that, before that could happen, I'd almost certainly be blown to pieces by al-Qaeda at the England–USA game. Should I survive that, three days later I'm going to see the mighty Brazil play North Korea. The resulting almost-certain humiliation of a country with rogue nuclear capabilities should really up the potential for disaster. At this rate, I'll be lucky to get past the group-stages.

I sound like I'm making light of this but gallows humour seems the only option when you're off to spend five weeks in a country that has a higher murder rate than *Kill Bill*. Still, one beneficial side-effect has been a reordering of all my usual pre-World Cup anxieties. I used to worry about us being involved in a penalty shoot-out but, if given the option this tournament, I'd happily make that my shoot-out of choice. Spalding Gray, in the excellent film *Swimming to Cambodia*, tells of a time when he agreed to swim across a particularly dangerous stretch of water. In order to distract himself during this ordeal, Gray left his sneakers on the beach with a large wad of cash and his gold Rolex watch inside them. He called this 'displacement of anxiety'. He was so fretful about his unattended cash and wristwatch he hardly noticed the hazardous swim he was undertaking. I seem to be experiencing a less-satisfactory version of this. I'm often nervous before an 11-hour flight but an 11-hour flight to Johannesburg is different. Usually, I'm worried about what's going to happen to me if the plane crashes. This time I'm worried about what's going to happen to me if it doesn't. Johannesburg, I've read, is a city where people get murdered for their mobile phones. God knows what will happen when they see my iPad. The bandits will have to go one better than murder to ensure my punishment is apposite.

The thing is, I really don't want to feel like this. Not only is it spoiling what ought to be a joyous anticipation – going to the World Cup is something I should be giving thanks for – but also it feels really unfair to South Africa. It only seems like yesterday it was morally reprehensible to eat their fruit and now they're hosting the biggest football tournament on the planet. I should be celebrating their moral makeover. I've been trying to conjure-up Rainbow Nation images of dancing locals welcoming visitors with a warm grin but they always culminate in me getting my throat slit. I hate myself for this. I firmly believe that life is a series of choices between two basic mindsets. If ever I'm flapping about any decision, I ask myself whether my overriding motivation is love or fear. If it's the latter, the decision is usually a bad one. Similarly, I want to find the love in this trip and beat the fear into a pulp. My choice of metaphor suggests this is still work-in-progress. I love football and I love the whole Long Walk to Freedom dream of the new South Africa. I felt very moved when I first saw that statue of Nelson Mandela in Parliament Square, even though the pose suggests a man who's just washed his hands and is now desperately seeking something to dry them on. From convict to international hero – the closest we've ever got is Jeffrey Archer. How must Mandela feel about the World Cup being there? I dare say the old South Africa was safer for visitors but if someone offered me five weeks of retro-apartheid would I say yes to save my skin or no and risk the terrors of transition? I need to have a real good look at myself in the mirror while I'm answering that question. That should eradicate any unsavoury faltering. I'm sure the next 30-odd days are going to be amazing. Pray for me.

Why gay men have more fun

16 JULY 2010

I've decided to offer my thoughts on the homosexual friend-finding iPhone application known as Grindr. This is partly because I enjoy any opportunity to enrage the inflexible authoritarian spellcheck on my computer and partly because I'm intrigued by plans to introduce a heterosexual version of this service – that's Grindr, not spellcheck.

The latter, in conjunction with its grammar-police cronies, couldn't get much more masculine – that is, uptight and unimaginative – than it is already. Our language is in chains and we simply bow in obedience.

Anyway, Grindr is a devilishly simple idea. You announce your location and you're shown photos of all the Grindr-participating men who are, as it were, in spitting distance. The fact that everyone involved subscribes to Grindr suggests a freewheeling openness to new, perhaps extremely short-term, friendships. In other words, the main purpose of Grindr is to get sweet, uncomplicated sex as soon as possible.

I spent much of my adult life on that same quest and I often felt envious of my counterparts in the gay community, with their apparently cavalier attitude to physical encounters. In every sexual situation I'd experienced, or heard about from my friends, the male was the accelerator and the female the brake. I figured that if you took the female out of the equation you could really burn some fuel. There is, after all, no chance of unwanted pregnancy – no new life curtailed or made miserable by a few minutes of abandoned thrusting. As long as you observe the obvious health precautions, what's not to like?

This may sound an out-dated, even bigoted view in the age of the civil partnership but I don't really understand how gays could think, 'What can we plunder from the heterosexual world that will bring us happiness – something that's an unqualified success and continues to go from strength to strength? I know – marriage!'

My first-ever gay friend told me he'd been on holiday to a gay hotel that adjoined a small wood where men would roam looking for action. He said, partly owing to language differences, a nod and a smile would often suffice, and they would then head to the nearest arbour – apologising if it was already being utilised – and share a special moment. He assured me that he had sometimes not yet finished his post-coital cigarette before another opportunity presented itself.

However, the place was not completely idyllic. There was another wood, separated from the first by a railway line and, over the years, a few distracted men had been hit by trains while crossing from one love glade to the other. My friend assured me that this, however, would be 'a lovely way to go' – burning bright in the fervour of pursuit. I remember telling him then that if someone could find a way of establishing a heterosexual version of that magic forest, they would become very rich indeed. It may be that the people behind Grindr had a similar thought. I doubt heterosexual men would even require a photo.

Some may find such baseness unpalatable. There was a period in my life when I indulged in one-night stands. I admit it eventually left me feeling empty and inhuman, but that took about 12 years. By that time I'd crossed a lot of railway tracks and the fervour of pursuit had been reduced to smouldering embers. When I was still young and lascivious, a heterosexual version of Grindr is something I would have happily swapped perhaps not my soul but certainly my self-respect for.

If I was unattached now, I think I'd want to know what the single women in the vicinity were thinking rather than looking like. I'd sacrifice a bit of sex appeal for a conversation about Walter Sickert. I'm not sure if that's maturity or elitism. Having said that, if there were two bright women nearby, the photos could make for a handy tiebreaker. The truth is I'm not sure females would be that interested in Grindr.

Perhaps I should say, at this point, that the heterosexual version will not be called Grindr because homosexuals now feel that's very much their word. Let's hope the owners go for something whimsical like Strangers-in-the-night and avoid the obvious Slut-search. I just don't think girls will sign up. It may be that lesbians use the current application but, if they do, I suspect the friend finding is considerably less bish bash bosh than the male version. A not-at-all-narrow-minded female friend once said to me that, with a one-night stand, the man gains something and the woman loses something.

A heterosexual Grindr would have to deal with the fact that women, not always but often, want a bit more. I should probably acknowledge, at this point, that there are, of course, saucy bluestockings who have occasional casual sex like they have an occasional menthol cigarette: because they damn well feel like it. Or perhaps I should reference those pictures one sees of drunken girls lying on the Saturday night pavements of Britain, subconsciously stating that they are as reckless and irresponsible as any fella.

But I still think that while an all-male Grindr is probably like a fabulous dessert trolley, a heterosexual one will essentially be an agitated man staring at a blank screen.

The Girl Guides and their search for cellulite

6 AUGUST 2010

Girlguiding UK said, this week, that airbrushed photos of models and celebrities should have 'compulsory labelling' telling us that the subject's appearance has been digitally enhanced. I had no idea that the Girl Guides issued such socio-political statements. I look forward to hearing the Brownies' views on human trafficking. Anyway, in the light of this, I've decided to write this week's column about knots. No, in truth, I'm a great admirer of the Guides, and the Scouting movement in general. Who wouldn't be impressed by each Guide's promise to 'respect all living things and take care of the world around her'? The Scouting movement instils a sense of duty, a love of adventure and outdoor pursuits, and encourages group bonding through the medium of inspirational community singing. It's essentially *National Service: The Musical*. One wonders if there's a badge for peeling potatoes. When I was a youth, I often heard reactionary old men viciously criticising young people and saying 'bring back National Service.' Worryingly, I'm starting to have similar thoughts as I get older but, by channelling these thoughts into a championing of the Scout movement, I feel slightly less fascistic than those old curmudgeons. I like the idea of uniformed youth gathered around a bonfire but I'd rather they weren't tossing books into it. I would urge any child to join an appropriate branch of the Scouts or Guides because I think it will probably make them better people. Having said all that, I think Girlguiding UK are wrong about airbrushing.

Head Guide Liz Burnley's argument is that young girls see digitally enhanced babes in magazines and then develop eating disorders and other body issues as they attempt to emulate the unreal. I'm afraid Ms Burnley won't get her Original Thinking badge. This theory has been bandied about a lot but is it really valid? I know some celebrities and models are cited as 'thin-spirations' on those scary 'pro-ana' websites but they are invariably celebrities and models with genuine eating disorders. No one needed to airbrush Mary-Kate Olsen. Besides, airbrushing is such a commonplace topic nowadays can teenage girls really be unaware of it? Don't they do any post-production on their happy-slapping videos? If we accept that most girls know about airbrushing then Ms Burnley is in danger of depriving them of a very useful get-out clause. At the moment, if a susceptible young girl is confronted by a picture of a female who seems to be much prettier, slimmer and generally more unblemished than she is, she can console herself with the thought that 'she doesn't really look like that. It's all airbrushing and photoshop'. However, some women really are pretty, slim and unblemished. If you introduce the labelling system, there's no escape. That girl with no label really does look like that. You're stuck with it.

Is airbrushing any different from make-up? Both are in the same pretend-to-be-more-beautiful-than-you-are Venn diagram. It's quite possible that I could see a picture of Boy George, in full slap and a stylish Philip Treacy hat, and think to myself 'What's wrong with me? He's only four years younger than I am but he looks amazing. I need to have plastic surgery' not realising that underneath it all he looks like Uncle Fester from the Addams Family. No one who wears make-up has the right to condemn airbrushing. Maybe the latter was more sinister when the process was still something of a trade secret but not now.

I'd say the current showbiz press do everything in their power to expose the smoke-and-mirrors pretence of celebrity beauty. All those paparazzi shots with magnified details of cellulite, veins and pustules surely make the readers feel much better about themselves. However, when the trashy magazines expose and emphasise these defects they're charged with cruelty. Do we want the truth or not? I'd say the flattering portrayal of public figures is fading fast. We used to be fed more or less what their publicists wanted. Now the golden wall has come down and we see much more of the unedited mess. We not only know Britney has bad skin but also what her genitals look like.

Imagine if Girlguiding UK start a trend and all the pretences get thrown out with the airbrushing bathwater. TV comedy shows would no longer be edited. The rubbishy, unfunny bits would remain. Does a comedy show that's recorded for two hours and then cut down into a half-hour of the best bits make insecure young viewers feel pressured to regularly reel-off funny remarks with no dead-ends or terrible silences? Would you have me write this column in one breathless stream-of-consciousness, uncorrected, with no rethinks, Googling or verification of facts? If I see something in a newspaper or magazine or on TV, I like to know it's had a bit of a polish – a crafting of some kind. Otherwise I might as well just look out the window or at the *Big Brother* live feed. Anyway, to my Girl Guide readers: if you keep your solemn promise and respect all living things and take care of the world around you, you'll be beautiful on the inside, and that type of beauty lasts much longer. And as for your physical appearance, just dyb, dyb, dyb.

My difficult relationship with the speed-limit

13 AUGUST 2010

The government has said it will cut £38 million from this year's UK road safety budget. I fully expect, the next time I pass a patch of waste ground, to see a dirty and bedraggled Green Cross Man sharing a can of Special Brew with Tufty. Doesn't a person feel a bit wary when, in a meeting about potential areas for cuts, they put up their hand and say 'What about road safety?' Aren't they afraid of being condemned by a head-shaking silence? Or has a sort of Bond villain how-evil-can-we-be bravado developed amongst the cuts coordinators? Were the cheers and applause that followed the road safety moment taken to another level by the wild-eyed Michael Gove as he suddenly bellowed, with arms raised in devilish exhilaration, 'Let's cut play-grounds.' And, meanwhile, in the corner of the meeting room, a silent plasma screen flashed up the return to profit of another high street bank. Either way, the first victim of the road safety cuts is unlikely to be rescued by a wave of public sympathy. The government has said that, for the foreseeable future, it won't fund any new speed cameras.

Research published this week suggests that 28,000 accidents have been actually caused by speed cameras since they were introduced in 2001. It says cameras make drivers look at their speedometer instead of the road and also encourage sudden braking. It's interesting they blame the inanimate object rather than the motorist. Many drivers screech forth, cutting people up and overtaking on the inside, until they reach a camera. Then, having glided serenely past – maybe pausing to sniff at a roadside hanging-basket or wave to a passing pensioner

– they immediately start driving horribly again. It's the sort of on-camera off-camera discrepancy you only normally find in show business. I suppose the researchers could also argue that speed-cameras make these motorists drive even faster because they're desperate to claw back those few seconds stolen from them by the enforced slow-down.

It's very hard to know how to make people drive safely. A friend of mine was involved in some research into this subject. He told me an expert had said to him that the great problem with modern drivers, in a world of seat-belts, cages and air-bags, is that they feel safe enough to drive dangerously. The best thing for road safety, the expert said, would be an eight-inch metal spike sticking out of the middle of the steering wheel. This Bond-villain thing seems to be contagious. The truth is we're encouraged to drive fast by that nudge-nudge wink-wink attitude to the speed limit that everyone, including the police, seems to share. Take, for example, when there's a police car on the motorway. It cruises, at exactly 70 mph, along the inside-lane, forcing the surrounding motorists to enter a world of make-believe. The police, of course, know that no one drives at 70 when they aren't around but that doesn't matter. It's just a game. The accepted etiquette is to join the procession for a mile or two, then, ever so gently, so as not to appear disrespectful, gradually overtake. When you feel you're obscured by other cars, you can speed off, procession time served, and liberate yourself from the whole charade. The police know exactly what's going on. They're playing the observing-the-speed-limit game and we have to make a show of joining in. That's all they ask. I've been told that the true motorway speed limit is 85 and one is unlikely to get nicked for doing less than that. I've no idea if that's true but it feels about right.

The Chief Constable of Gwent police said this week that road casualties have been halved in the eight years the county has had speed-cameras. In Oxfordshire, where they've gone a step further than the government and switched off all 72 of their fixed cameras, it's claimed that speeding has now increased by 88 per cent. All this may be true but, under the current system, speed bumps would do the same job the cameras do at a fraction of the price. I think speed cameras should be retained but they should be as well hidden as possible. There'd be none of that between-camera recklessness if no one knew where between-camera was. You could be caught anywhere at any time. The cameras could be moved or extra ones could be added and it would all be funded by the torrent of fines that would initially come flooding in. I've heard it said that the cameras are made obvious because they're supposed to operate as a warning. Put simply, the cameras tell us when we can get away with driving above the speed limit and when we can't. It's like putting 'occupants out' signs on houses, to assist burglars. The best thing to make people drive responsibly is fear of reprisal. I've been a much better driver since I've had six points on my licence. Another three and I'll be driving so carefully I might as well have the spike fitted. If the cameras were hidden, any speeding would be a risk. The motoring lobby would be angry but one always assumes that the motoring lobby are complete prats so that doesn't matter. We drivers need saving from ourselves.

How the police save my life – about once a fortnight

20 AUGUST 2010

In Altrincham, Greater Manchester, this week, thieves broke into a motorcycle showroom and stole three bikes. The police watched them roar off into the night but didn't give chase because they felt it would be unsafe to do so. You see, the thieves weren't wearing helmets or protective clothing. This story is tailor-made for those people who think political correctness has ruined this country. It involves not only an instance of criminals being treated with kindly concern but also an apparently ludicrous application of Health and Safety regulations. It's an irate middle-Englander's dream-ticket. The police, it seems, don't care if the country's going to Hell in a handcart as long as no one goes to Hell on a Honda Fireblade – not on their watch. It certainly wasn't cowardice that prevented these police officers from pursuing the motor-cycle thieves. It's national police policy to only chase motorcyclists if they're wearing the right safety gear. I wonder if the criminal fraternity were aware of this policy before now. I can imagine some convicted motorbike thief, in his horrid prison-cell, reading about the Altrincham case and making the same Homer Simpson doh! sound that the recently disgraced Peter Crouch made when he read Monday's story about an unnamed Premiership footballer taking out a super-injunction to keep the lid on his dirty doings. If it had been commonly known that the police never chase motorcyclists who aren't wearing protective gear, a bareheaded Raoul Moat would still be doing provocative wheelies up and down Rothbury High Street.

What else should we know about the police Health and Safety-based criminal-pursuit policies? If you deliberately don't put on seat-belts when you get into your getaway car, are you free to gently drive away, with the clearly frustrated, fist-shaking police officers growing ever-smaller in your rear-view mirror? Should an officer not release a snarling police dog if the scampering burglar doesn't have the regulation forearm-padding they always wear in those training videos? It's such a waste of the officers' specialist skills. I saw a police motorcycle display team at a summer fete in Smethwick in 1971, and they were genuinely impressive. I'd like to have seen the faces of those motorbike thieves when they realised they were in the shadow of an ever-nearing nine-man human pyramid, supported across three bikes. Barring low bridges, immediate surrender would have been the only option.

All these things went through my mind when I first read the motor-bike heist story but then I asked myself whether the police really should have chased those vulnerable motorcyclists. Stealing a motorbike is a bad thing but do we honestly want to see someone – even a thief – forced to drive at high-speeds in a chase situation and perhaps die in the process? The trouble is the police are, if you'll forgive me, piggy-in-the-middle between the hanging's-too-good-for-them lobby and civil rights proponents who expect officers to make an omelette without breaking any eggs. The police dash breathlessly between the two, trying to please, trying to do the right thing, but the ball keeps passing over their heads, to and fro, from one side to the other. They were too reckless with Charles de Menezes, too reticent with Derrick Bird, too hard with the G20 rioters, too soft with those three men on bikes. Some want to see them terrorising criminals, like DCI Gene Hunt, while others want to see them awkwardly joining-in with a communal knees-up at the Notting Hill Carnival.

I always assume that people who say they don't like the police never went to an away game in the 1980s. I can think of three separate occasions, following West Bromwich Albion, when I honestly thought I was going to end up in hospital. Supporting a football team, in those days, could be a dangerous business. Only the police stopped it from being a regular bloodbath at some grounds. I remember being cornered in a side-road at Derby County, with no escape route. It didn't feel all cutting-edge and cool, like in that Danny Dyer film. It was squalid and frightening. One of their fans was staring right at me. I was pale and scrawny. He was bigger, with bad skin. He'd probably marked me down as an easy trophy – his own little episode in the drunken post-match telling of the tale. But then, I heard shouting and the clatter of hooves and the mounted police came around the corner to rescue us. It really was like the cavalry arriving in a cowboy film. I was scared and then I wasn't scared. The finer political points of policing tend to fall away when you've experienced that. One comes to see the role of the police in a stark and simplified form – protection by courageous intervention. I feel I saw the uncluttered truth of it that day. Nothing I've seen since, on the streets, on television or in the newspapers, has substantially changed my mind. I don't mean that the police are beyond criticism, or reform, but I do think that every citizen, every politician, every newspaper, needs to decide whether they're essentially for the police or against them – relieved when the cavalry comes or angrily disappointed – because the default niggling criticism is making a hard job even harder.

Why I hate local libraries

27 AUGUST 2010

In the context of the great spending-cuts balloon debate – in which the government has to decide which lump of public service goes over the side next – news that the number of adult visitors to local libraries in England has fallen over the last five years does not bode well for the libraries' survival hopes. Seventy-five per cent of children from five to fifteen attended libraries last year but, even then, the fact that those ages correspond so closely to school-age makes me wonder how much of that attendance was voluntary. One expert says between 600 and 1,000 local libraries could close in the next 12 months. I'm always keen to defend the bookish community but my initial gut-reaction, save-our-libraries response was, on closer introspection, more about nostalgia than first-hand knowledge. It was like my dismay upon hearing that Woolworth's was to close down or that *Last of the Summer Wine* was to disappear. I bemoaned the culling of these two institutions but I'd had no personal experience of either for about 25 years. I didn't really like them, I just liked the fact that they existed. The same is true of local libraries. An image, probably in black-and-white, of aspiring working-class folk, soaking-up knowledge from borrowed books they couldn't afford to buy, makes me Dewey-eyed but I was an aspiring working-class person myself and I've probably been to my local library about ten times in my entire life. In my limited experience, local libraries contain a lot of battered, not-very-recently published books, most of them are in large print, and a fair proportion almost certainly carry the diseases of their previous borrowers. Yet, despite all that, I can't think of any phrase that more accurately expresses the image of myself I'd like to convey to the world than 'I'm just off to return my library books.' Unfortunately, it would be a lie. I like the idea of local libraries more than I like them. What I really like are books and the kind of people who like books and, even then, it's a certain kind of book. The only local library I got vaguely familiar with had a Mills and Boon section, which was easily the largest and most popular in the building. I'm not marching to save that. It's a sad fact that, in most sentences, the word 'local' can be replaced by the word 'rubbish' with no significant loss of meaning. Let me offer an example. 'I went to a local art gallery and read, in a local newspaper, an article about a local poet.' I wonder if 'local libraries' could be another example?

And yet, I am a library fan. I always make a point of visiting libraries whenever I'm abroad. Three years ago I saw a life-changing exhibition about the writer Jack Kerouac at New York Public Library. The picture I took of the exhibition poster, hanging over the main library entrance, is still my iPhone screensaver. Also, I spent about three hours alone in the Vienna public library during the last European football championships, just enjoying the scenery – the towering walls of books, and studious readers hunched over fat, impressive volumes. But defending local libraries on the basis of such experience is like defending *Loose Women* by saying you like *Newsnight*.

There's no suggestion, just yet, that local libraries will disappear altogether but the compromise solutions I've heard so far all seem unsatisfactory. The Big Society option seems to be replacing the qualified librarians with local volunteers. We used to call that scabbing. Then there's the idea of housing the facility elsewhere. There's already a library in a pub, and even one in a phone box, but both of these seem to just reinforce the idea that local libraries are quaint examples of British eccentricity – like big moustaches and real ale – rather than temples dedicated to the life-changing power of books. The most popular option seems to be housing the libraries in supermarkets. Customers, we're told, will borrow a book as they do their weekly shop. Well, I've written a couple of books and the publishers were particularly obsessed with getting them on to supermarket shelves. At book events, the buyers from supermarkets were the most important guests. It was big business and I can't see publishers, or the super-markets themselves, being very happy about a local library sprouting up behind the canned vegetables. Of course, bookshops employ people too. If public outrage led to a boost in the libraries' popularity, they might do to the bookshops what file sharing did to the music business. Would that be a good thing in the current climate? The truth is the rise in ebooks – paid for or pirated – will probably put an end to both. Still, I must say the government timed the publishing of the libraries report perfectly. Who's going to fret about a little thing like the local libraries system being dismantled when they've got cat-in-a-bin-gate to worry about?

I once found a book on a train. A sticker inside said please read this book and then leave it somewhere or pass it on to someone else. Maybe that kind of people's library is the way forward. OK you can still catch dysentery but at least you don't get shushed.

Hey, Fatso! I worship at the altar of your excesses

3 SEPTEMBER 2010

I saw those pictures from the 2011 Cliff Richard calendar, with Cliff bare-chested on a beach and looking amazing. He's 70 next month. He's had a 30-inch waist for the last 30 years. 'How does he do it?' the newspapers asked. It turns out he's spent most of his life eating only one meal a day. Meanwhile, in what feels like a different universe from Cliff, the American fried-food innovator, Mark Zable has, after years of trying, finally perfected deep-fried beer – little fat-sodden dough-envelopes full of Guinness. It seems to me, as society gradually splits into two camps – the eat-for-health people and the eat-for-pleasure people – we must all decide whether our hearts lie essentially with the self-deniers or the self-indulgers, the prigs or the pigs; are we with Cliff or Zable?

I first met Cliff about 20 years ago. I watched him sing his Christmas single for that year, in a dress rehearsal, and then went over to say hello. 'That sounded like another number one,' was my friendly opener. Cliff immediately rattled off his December chart positions over the previous few years, complete with rationalisations and helpful footnotes. It was a blizzard of statistics. He wasn't being defensive or putting me right – he was friendly and polite – but I'd never heard anyone speak about music like that before. I'd assumed it was all about emotion, about love. This sounded like a parent describing his children purely by listing their exam results. Looking back now, it seems to fit with 50 years of dieting. It's about exchanging joy for numbers. Anyway, Cliff's a well-known celibate so love handles would be wasted on him.

Mark Zable is a regular entrant in the Texas State Fair Fried Food Competition. Last year's winning entry was deep-fried butter. This year's contest includes fried salad. This is a world of excess but also of swashbuckling fun. It seems to me that the people who still eat this kind of stuff, despite the endless magazine articles, the 'are you over-weight?' questionnaires, and the cold promise of early death, are strangely heroic figures. They hear the slogan 'a moment on the lips, a lifetime on the hips' and they choose to celebrate the moment. Isn't that *carpe diem* mindset one we normally associate with a vivacious free spirit? We read about people who are seen as rebels, people who live their lives unrestrained by convention – maybe Amy Winehouse or Pete Docherty. But they choose lifestyles that sidestep the ultimate excess. They may party hard and get wasted but what they don't do is get fat. Pale, gaunt, emaciated – these are all profoundly cool attributes. Such rebels may seem to be dicing with death but, when it comes to it, they stop at the same safety-barrier as Cliff. That's the place where they at last say no. The excess of obesity is too scary, too ugly and too socially unacceptable. Cliff used to be known as the English Elvis about the same time as Vimto was known as the English Coca-Cola. Cliff made some fabulous records in the fifties and sixties but he always seemed manageable. Elvis was raw, dirty and extreme. He dripped rock 'n' roll. He got fat and died young. If Elvis was alive today, he'd be eating deep-fried beer off the buttocks of a naked cheer-leader. He sacrificed even his much-celebrated beauty to be utterly free – to consume everything and anything. He went where Cliff, Pete and Amy are too scared to go. Elvis wasn't like the fat people we see on *The Jeremy Kyle Show*. He could afford the finest, healthiest food on the market. Instead, he just ate what he really liked. He would not be contained.

I was at a Harry Potter film premiere, sitting next to a small child. I watched with fascination as he ate a Crunchie. He completely removed the wrapper, put one end of the Crunchie in his mouth, placed the palm of his hand on the other end, and pushed. It was like watching a particularly ferocious pencil-sharpener. I don't remember the last time I saw an adult eat a chocolate bar with such carefree abandon. When, risking a fingertip, he completed the process, he didn't say 'Oh, I shouldn't have eaten that' or 'the diet starts tomorrow.' He just ate another one.

I know that unrestrained eating is dangerous but I also suspect that being careful about what I eat and drink has brought about a certain meanness of spirit in me. I've ended up with Team Cliff but I envy the fearlessness of the wilfully obese – those who know better but don't care. I envy their De Sade-like defiance of social norms. Theirs is a sub-culture that gives a chubby finger to mortality. I run regularly, avoid caffeine and refuse desserts, scratching around to try and feel a bit better or live a bit longer. I was just up in Edinburgh where I ate haggis pakora and Irn-Bru Turkish Delight, but I undermined such pleasures by accompanying them with a guilty whimpering. Maybe obesity-related illness and death is no worse than a life of no-I-mustn'ts. Maybe it's time fat people were once again given the default adjective 'jolly'. The rest of us, it seems, have forgotten how it feels.

Wayne Rooney and Samuel Beckett – a further betrayal

9 SEPTEMBER 2010

I was, as they say in the football world, 'very disappointed' to read that Wayne Rooney has allegedly been having regular sex with a 21-year-old prostitute called Jennifer Thompson. Rooney was famously involved in a prostitution scandal a few years back when he was a teenage starlet at Everton.

However, on that occasion the woman who ended up in the papers was a 48-year-old grandmother from Diva's massage parlour in Liverpool known as Auld Slapper. I found the Diva's story strangely admirable. It made me think that Rooney was a young man unimpressed by the hordes of Pamela Anderson clones who shimmy their way through a world of pubs and nightclubs, desperately seeking a footballer – any footballer – who'll buy them drinks and listen to their worthless meanderings.

Rooney, I thought, prefers a salt-of-the-earth, warts-and-all kind of woman whose post-coital ritual involves smoking an unfiltered cigarette and reminiscing about the Toxteth riots. I liked the fact that he'd slipped past the superficial glamour girls, like he slips past desperate defenders, and opted instead for a sex life that had the air of a Samuel Beckett play. Now, I feel let down. Jennifer Thompson is just like all the other footballers' sneaky-sex choices. Rooney has gone route one.

Incidentally, Auld Slapper has never admitted to having sex with Rooney, but whichever of the old girls he frequented at Diva's, they only charged him £45 a time whereas Ms Thompson allegedly charged him £1,200. No wonder our elderly are freezing to death in their homes.

Ms Thompson's pricing structure was unorthodox to say the least. Her friend told the *Daily Star*: 'Jeni only charged the ugly ones.' Rooney was lucky to avoid bankruptcy. And it wasn't just Ms Thompson who was expensive. Rooney gave a hotel worker £200 to get him a packet of cigarettes. I wonder if Rooney's scally mates, who get his fags for him so he's not caught by a tabloid snapper, have told him that's how much they cost.

There are many odd facts around the story. Ms Thompson said that, on one occasion, when Rooney approached her in a hotel, Michael Owen looked at him with disgust. Apparently this caused Owen to pull a muscle in his face and he was out of action for six weeks. There are also claims that Ms Thompson has slept with 13 professional footballers – four strikers, three midfielders and six defenders. It makes a nice change from Fabio Capello's rigid 4-4-2 approach, though, in the light of recent England performances, he'd probably sympathise with her decision not to bother with a goalkeeper.

Rooney has supposedly told his friends he won't take any s*** from his wife or her family and that if she wants out he won't fight for the marriage. It seems brutal but it makes a change from the often insincere sackcloth-and-ashes stuff one normally hears from male celebrities who've been caught with their trousers down. You know, the 'I've been stupid', 'I don't deserve her' stuff that's supposed to give his partner a way of taking him back while retaining some dignity. Maybe Rooney, having noticed how badly that approach went for Tiger Woods, decided he might as well go down, all guns blazing.

Rooney's not a man who takes criticism with a bowed head. I remember how he reacted to the team being booed after the awful World Cup game against Algeria. He found the nearest TV camera and had a go at the England fans – a tactic almost unheard of among footballers.

Players usually stop short of criticising the fans, probably because they don't want to be pelted with coins, punched-out in a nightclub or woken up to find their Ferrari upside-down and on fire. I doubt Rooney is troubled by such considerations. He is a wild-eyed Irish Rover type who won't be tethered or tamed. Of course, looking back now, it does seem slightly ironic that he was reprimanding the fans for their lack of loyalty.

So what about the heart he's broken? Should he be forgiven? Should he be taken back, especially after such lack of remorse?

Well, at first I thought no, why should I? He was just awful in the World Cup, as were the rest of the England team. I went out to South Africa with six various England shirts and I deliberately left them all in my Johannesburg hotel room when I came home. They were chucked in a corner with my England scarf coiled on top. I felt betrayed. I resolved never to watch England again. But my anger is subsiding. I've watched the recent games on telly and I've found myself slowly remembering why I loved them. It hasn't been easy. I still have flashes of resentment – still call out 'why' – but it's better than it was. As for trust, well, it could be years before that comes back – maybe it never will – but you have to work at these things.

Rooney broke my heart but, deep down, I suppose I still love him. Well, I do today. I hope Coleen can rediscover that same feeling. After the Diva's massage parlour revelations, Coleen's response was truly magnificent – according to the *Sun*, she threw her engagement ring into a squirrel sanctuary. No one could top that, but I hope she finds something to make her feel better and eventually to heal the wounds.

Here comes
the Pope
17 SEPTEMBER 2010

The Pope's UK visit is costing somewhere between 12 and 20 million pounds, depending on how anti-Catholic you are. If you believe the media, the visit is more a rallying point for the haters than a source of spiritual renewal for the believers. Every secularist with a public voice is queuing up to rain on our parade. And it's not just the secularists. The Reverend Ian Paisley, recently transformed into a peace-process hero, decided to take one last walk down sectarian memory lane and join the protest too. It was a very different mood in my local Catholic church last Sunday. The priest gave details of how those travelling up to Birmingham to see the Pope on Sunday should pick up their 'pilgrim passes' and be on the coach by 2 a.m. He promised that, despite the hour, he would be there to wave them off. There is something beautiful about that. Those pilgrims, gliding through the dark night of drunken London, will be exhilarated at the prospect of seeing not Joseph Ratzinger, the man, but rather the representative of an office that has always epitomised Catholicism. That's why I got the tingles when I watched him getting off the plane, on TV yesterday. Like many Catholics, I grew up with a Pope's picture on the wall, at home and at school. The man in white reminded us of our difference. We were a mysterious club that no one else understood, and our leader had a hotline to Heaven. We were taught that Jesus gave the keys of the kingdom to St Peter and they were passed on, from Pope to Pope, ever since. Mind you, considering the history of the Papacy, one wonders how long it was before Jesus started to think about changing the locks.

I took part in a debate on Tuesday night, with a roomful of passionate but troubled Catholics. The subject was priestly celibacy but soon the other in-house worries came pouring out – chiefly paedophilia, misogyny and homophobia. I've been at many events where questions from the audience are requested and, in most cases, the response is disappointing. On Tuesday, the crowd was fighting to be heard. Dozens of hands shot up at every pause. These were people who really cared about what was happening to their Church. I don't know much about paedophilia – it's not a word I want to type into Google Search – but I do know that it's found in the family, in social services, in the education system, institutions that most of us admire. The Catholic Church's shame isn't that it was infected by a widespread social evil but rather that it conspired to suppress the fact. That seemed to poison every stream of discussion on Tuesday night. Those physically abused children were, of course, the real victims but every remaining Catholic is a kind of victim too. We were betrayed. The Church forbids women priests. If only it had forbidden male ones instead. As for homophobia, the Dalai Lama is big on that too but he, unlike Pope Benedict, seems to remain a universally respected figure. I guess the secret is to deliver your gay bashing with an otherworldly smile.

I'm sure lots of Catholics ask themselves, as I do, how many rules and attitudes one can disagree with before one no longer qualifies for membership. I've always been of that school of thought that says the people are the Church. Those frustrated, angry believers at the debate are out there in the secular world, every day, representing and defending Catholicism. Where should they find shelter? Liberal Catholics seem to have the worst of both worlds. We're blasted by the secularists for supporting the Church and dismissed by the Catholic traditionalists for not supporting it. Cannons to the left of them, canons to the right of them. Is it possible to be a Catholic who regularly disobeys the Pope? If it isn't, I'd say there are probably about 2,000 lay Catholics in the UK. St Paul said 'the letter killeth but the spirit giveth life' but what's a religion without rules? John Henry Newman, who's being beatified by the Pope on Sunday, said 'religion as mere sentiment is to me a dream and a mockery' but then he also said that if he had to propose a toast, he'd drink 'to conscience first and to the Pope afterwards'. I think many modern British Catholics are joining him in that toast.

Newman, of course, is on his way to becoming a saint. John Paul II created more saints during his reign than the preceding 17 Popes all put together. I greatly admire Newman but I fear this modern saint-fest is designed to whip-up local enthusiasm in places where religious fervour needs a boost. It's like the plate-spinner, tweaking a wobbling plate to get it really whizzing again. England is well overdue for a tweak.

Former Catholic nun, Karen Armstrong, in her excellent book on the Bible, tells a story of a rabbi who's challenged to stand on one leg and repeat everything in the Jewish scriptures. He raises his leg and says 'Love God and love one another.' He then lowers his leg and explains 'everything else is commentary.' If only Benedict would say that this weekend.

How an eighteenth-century lexicographer changed my life

24 SEPTEMBER 2010

Cleanliness is next to Godliness, but only in a very substandard dictionary. That's the sort of light-hearted lexicon-based remark I had up my sleeve when I was inaugurated as President of the Samuel Johnson Society, in Lichfield, last Saturday night. Happily, it was still up my sleeve when I left town on Sunday lunchtime. Johnson, of course, was an eighteenth-century lexicographer, writer, and scholar, born in Lichfield, who still retains literary-legend status, mainly because of a book written about him rather than by him – James Boswell's *Life of Johnson*. I read the Penguin abridged version of the *Life* in 1979 when I was studying English at Birmingham Polytechnic. It was a truly joyous experience. I loaned it to my course-mate and good friend, Ralph the Ripper (don't ask) and we spent much of the next few years quoting Johnson at every opportunity, to the point where it became almost involuntary. On one occasion, a clearly distressed fellow student told us his girlfriend was away camping with a group of people that included her ex-boyfriend. He completely trusted her, he explained unconvincingly, but the idea of her hanging out with her ex still caused him great distress. Ralph the Ripper's eyes lit up. I feared I knew what was coming next. 'Sir,' he said to our troubled friend 'never accustom your mind to mingle virtue and vice. The woman's a whore and there's an end on't.' An argument ensued. I recall the chap holding Ralph by the lapels and calling him a 'little scumbag'. I stepped in sure that, if I didn't, Ralph would almost certainly come back with what I knew to be his favourite Johnson riposte 'Sir, your mother, under the pretext of keeping a bawdy house, is a receiver of stolen goods.' That, I felt, wouldn't help.

Those student days were an incredible time for me. I'd previously been expelled from school, worked in factories and generally wasted my time but suddenly I was learning all this stuff. It was like someone had opened the door to my brain and finally let the light in. I knew that polytechnics were generally scoffed at but I was on a good course with a lot of really passionate lecturers. Johnson seemed to sum-up, for me, the idea of learning as something fiery and life changing. Lichfield is only about 20 miles from Birmingham – Johnson would sometimes walk the return-journey to help clear his melancholic moods – so I'd often go there to visit the house where Johnson was born and grew-up. When I moved to London in the early nineties I headed to Johnson's house in Gough Square, near Fleet Street. I remember standing alone for ages in the garret. This was the room where Johnson created his dictionary, sitting at trestle tables with his six amanuenses, composing definitions and selecting illustrative quotations. I stood there ruminating on the sheer effort of it all. It was exhilarating.

Anyway, I was, I'll admit, a little edgy about my inauguration. There was to be a grand dinner at Lichfield Guildhall, with speeches, toasts and plenty of protocol and the truth is I'm not very clubbable – incidentally, a word coined by Johnson. I feared a world of boorish, middle-aged men, stinking of cigar smoke, with red-wine remnants on their lips, making loud right-wing remarks and asking me if I'd had sex with Jordan or why I'm not a Freemason. It would be like a *Top Gear* after-show party. In fact, it was nothing like that. The society members were gentle and urbane and it was a treat to be able to discuss Johnson without the need for footnotes. Lichfield is a town where tradition walks hand-in-hand with modernity. The town sheriff was quick to tell me that the ermine on his gown was actually fake fur. After I'd received my heavy, silver president's medal, worn on a ribbon around my neck, I joined some Society members outside the Guildhall to smoke our churchwardens – white clay pipes with a small bowl and a stem about a foot long. I've always liked the idea of me as a pipe-smoker – mainly because someone once told me that stabbing one's pipe-stem in the general direction of an opponent was a great aid to emphasising a point in a heated conversation – but I've rarely smoked one without vomiting. I wasn't actually sick from Saturday's pipe but by the seventeenth time it went out I was glad it had done so. Back inside I delivered my half-hour Presidential Address on Johnson's Rambler essays, shook a lot of hands, and headed for my B&B.

On Sunday morning, in the beautiful, triple-spired Lichfield Cathedral, I, in the company of my fellow Society members, placed a laurel wreath on the church's Johnson memorial and gave thanks for the great man's life. Later, as I drove back to London along the M1, I hit a massive, virtually unmoving traffic jam. After I'd sat there frustrated for about 40 minutes, I had an idea. I took my president's medal out of its case and put it around my neck. Suddenly, my spirits were lifted. After about ten minutes, I took it off and put it away again, its work done. It was a very unusual weekend.

Why I love local libraries

1 OCTOBER 2010

I probably shouldn't admit this but I never look at the readers' comments that appear beneath my columns on *The Times* website. I'm not avoiding the paywall, I'm avoiding the pain. The online column is the modern-day version of the pillory. The author's locked firmly in place while the rotten vegetables splatter all around. I prefer, having released my words into the world, to imagine them covered only in golden praise. Then I received Don's letter. In a recent column, I discussed the threat to close hundreds of local libraries. I admitted that, in my experience, local libraries are musty, uninspiring places – dispensing Mills and Boon rather than Pound and Eliot – and not the temples of learning I romantically want them to be. In his letter, Don described my piece as a 'misinformed tirade' and held up his local library as an important 'communal asset' that was 'airy and light' and a 'centre of knowledge and information' used by people of all ages. As a Resident Representative, he invited me to go along and see for myself. The letter made me uneasy. I hadn't been in a local library for quite a while so maybe my opinion was indeed out of date. Consequently, I got on the tube last Tuesday and went off to meet Don for my guided tour, hoping I wouldn't be set-about with a Catherine Cookson omnibus the second I stepped through the door.

Don, a smartly dressed senior citizen, led me into what he described as 'a truly modern library'. My first impression was that there weren't anywhere near as many books as I expected. There were audiobooks – quite a lot of them – but, for some reason, they never seem quite so worthy of respect. There was also an extensive DVD selection, mainly popular movies. I became anxious. I realised I'd gone there eager to be proved wrong. I'd criticised local libraries because my personal experience of them hadn't been good and I always feel an obligation to be totally honest in these columns. However, I felt uneasy about somehow finding myself on the wrong side in the library-cuts debate, shoulder-to-shoulder with those who see books only as something to give ambience to a cosy pub – like a horse-brass or a Toby jug. Now I was worried that my out-of-date complaints about libraries had been replaced by a new horror – the books weren't musty, they were missing. I was told, by a senior library person, that, in the old days, they kept books for years, even if no one ever borrowed them. It was decided that these unpopular books would be sold off or given to charity shops. Now the aim was to only stock books that lots of people wanted to read. Books still mattered but times had changed and services like free computer access had become more and more important. I said, with a slightly desperate plea for reassurance in my tone, that perhaps some people came in for the library's regular Saturday knitting class and thought 'While I'm here I'll grab a book'. Heads nodded.

As Don promised, the library was airy and light. There was a separate children's floor that was colourful and welcoming, and also a teenage floor where, again, there were not as many books as I'd hoped. However, what books there were, I was told, were selected by the teenagers themselves. I was pleased to spot Plato's *Symposium* on the shelf. There were also dozens of Manga comics. It reminded me that I didn't read what you'd call a proper book till I was 21. Before that it was just comics. My passion for language, reading and, indeed, art, came from them. My book-based snobbery came later, although, if pressed, I'd probably still choose *Swamp Thing* over *Symposium*. I felt a little easier about the lack of books.

The library had loads of computers. The general feel of the place was a cross between a clean, efficient secondary school and a cyber café. No one was whispering. With the staff's encouragement, I actually joined the library, and proceeded to choose a book. I wanted Tony Blair's memoirs but that had already been stolen so I opted to reread *1984*. At last, the TV series decommissioned, George Orwell fans can reclaim the Big Brother franchise. The smiling lady on the front desk pointed towards a machine on the wall. I put my newly issued card in a slot, scanned the book, and got a slip showing the return date, which doubled as a perfect bookmark. I'm already seeing that date as a target. I work better with a deadline. Incidentally, I can return the book to any library in the borough and, you guessed it, renew it online.

There are many classes and events at the library. It really seems to be, as Don said, a communal asset. When I criticised local libraries I didn't know exactly what I was attacking. At the same time, Angry of Hampstead, when he's outraged at the idea of library closures, probably doesn't know exactly what he's defending. This was just one library but I think it's indicative of how libraries are evolving. I'm going to have to ditch my literary elitism and just enjoy the book swiping. And I'm not talking about Blair's memoirs.

The shelf-life
of comedy

8 OCTOBER 2010

I was sad to hear that Norman Wisdom had died. I know it's officially Sir Norman but all that title proves is that the Queen doesn't understand comedy. Audiences laughed at Norman because he was the little man, the loser. 'Sir' spoils the joke. Tony Benn understood. He knew he'd never be able to carry off that left-wing voice-in-the-wilderness thing if he became Viscount Stansgate. He wouldn't even risk Anthony. I wonder if Norman's working-class hero status in Albania was damaged by that Sir. Anyway, I met Norman a couple of times. The first time, he shook my hand so enthusiastically it developed into a hug. In fact, not so much a hug as a lean – I became aware that he was laying his whole weight on me. Those around all laughed at my plight. If I stepped back he'd fall at my feet, if I stepped forward it could lead to dancing. When you meet some comics they give you a signature or a photo. With Norman, you got a short but memorable spell as his straight man – or indeed woman. The next time I met him he did the same thing to my girlfriend. Obviously, two brief meetings don't constitute knowing someone. I'm not trying to get on the tribute bandwagon. I'm just celebrating the fact that Norman was one of those comics who was never off. Some comedians put on their funniness like a coat. It's essentially stage wear. I'd say, in Norman's case, it was more like a vital organ. Before comedy was my job, I used to be a desperate character when it came to making friends laugh. I didn't really have conversations. It was just routines and responses. I would use props, impressions – anything to get laughs. When I got a professional outlet for all that showing-off I was finally able to relax a little in social situations. I didn't need to get a laugh with every line. I would occasionally allow the bow tie to cease revolving. I'm not sure Norman ever reached that stage. I admired his relentless pursuit of the next laugh, onstage or off.

Perhaps the saddest thing about the death of a great old comedian is that the modern audience can never really appreciate how funny they were. Doing comedy is like sculpting in ice. It isn't meant to last for ever. A lot of people will have seen a clip from one of Norman's films this week and wondered what all the fuss was about. Comedy from the past can seem like an alien world. You might laugh at the odd gag – something that has, by chance, survived the journey – but often we find ourselves just staring at it, as the American comedian Bill Hicks said, like a dog watching a card-trick. I'm not talking about an artist's declining creativity here. That phenomenon rarely colours our judgement of his golden age. You might think Paul McCartney hasn't written a good song for years but you still enjoy his golden age songs. The same is true with the works of novelists, painters, and so on but with comedy the golden age itself tarnishes. And it tarnishes quickly. I found, during a recent viewing, that even *Fawlty Towers* is starting to slip away from me. I got the warm glow one sometimes gets from watching old comedy but that warm glow replaces laughter the way cosy friendship replaces passionate sexual desire. I don't laugh at *Dad's Army* any more. I don't even smile. I just glow. Norman Wisdom's comedy was essentially gurning and tumbles. Physical comedy seems to have an even shorter shelf-life than verbal comedy. I loved the Marx Brothers when I was a kid but Harpo is now just glow. Groucho, however, got funnier as I got older.

Look at Shakespeare. His serious stuff seems just as relevant as it ever was. He's commonly seen as superior to any modern writer in that area. His comedy, however, has rusted to dust. You could flick through the satellite channels on any given night and find dozens of shows that are funnier than Shakespeare. The drunken gatekeeper, the sardonic gravedigger – not a real laugh in sight. When we consider the complexities of his serious work, we imagine the audiences, back then, were much more sophisticated. When we hear his jokes, we imagine they were much more stupid. I'm not saying Shakespeare wasn't funny. I'm saying he isn't funny any more. His serious drama seems timeless; his comedy has perished. They contrast now like brown, rotted roses on a beautifully crafted and highly durable trellis.

The reasons for all this, like so many things in comedy, are mysterious. I think it's something to do with comedy's dependence on immediate audience response – laughter or silence, a tick or a cross. If the crowd don't like a joke, it has to go. In the end, the audience writes the comedian's act, or at least edits it. Consequently each generation gets its own bespoke comedy and when the next generation tries it on, it never fits quite as well. Let's just accept that Norman Wisdom fitted his generation perfectly. You don't get to be as big a comedy star as he was unless you're something special.

Why a little bit of cruelty does you good

14 OCTOBER 2010

The BBC announced, this week, a ban on 'humiliating, intrusive, aggressive or derogatory remarks for the purposes of entertainment'. This seems, on the surface, to be a compassionate anti-cruelty clause to protect nice, healthy, respectable people like swimmer Rebecca Adlington from nasty, cynical, embittered people like comedian Frankie Boyle. In practice, it could mean the time-honoured art of ridiculing public figures will be pruned to its spindly stem by nervous script-editors and producers desperate to avoid a reprimanding email from a superior. I know the BBC Trust say they've canvassed licence-fee payers on this topic before issuing the new guidelines but what about the studio audiences who are, one might say, canvassed at every recording? If Frankie Boyle's jokes about Ms Adlington hadn't got big laughs, they wouldn't have been broadcast. Isn't this a valid test of their offensiveness? Don't imagine studio audiences are sycophantic minions, all-accepting when it comes to matters of taste. Once, on *Have I Got News For You*, I said John Sergeant looked like a Churchill the dog candle that had been alight for several hours. The audience laughed. The joke stayed in. I also said that if fame turned Susan Boyle's head it would be an improvement. The audience tutted. The joke got cut. That seems, to me, like a healthy system. I like jokes that just about get under the wire. When that's what you're aiming for it's inevitable that a certain amount won't make it. However, I'm guessing the new guidelines would have removed both the Boyle and the Sergeant joke – the bathwater only slightly preceding the baby.

It's the comedian's job to make omelettes and accept some attendant breakages. Critics claim and enthusiastically exercise similar licence. Would you have wanted guidelines to have prevented Dorothy Parker from saying Katharine Hepburn 'runs the gamut of emotions from A to B'? Where would Prime Minister's Questions be without humiliating, intrusive, aggressive or derogatory remarks? They're part of public life.

I had a long debate with the Commissioning Editor of my recent BBC Two series, because I said, on one show, I regretted not having had nude photographs of myself taken when I was a young man. 'It would be nice to have proof that my genitals didn't always look like Michael Parkinson.' The CE said this line was personally abusive towards Michael Parkinson. I felt the impact was deflected by the fact that Parky was a mere simile on the way to a joke at my expense. We argued around the gag but, eventually, I won him over. This is how taste matters should be decided – by reasoned discussion and mutual respect. I didn't win every time but the decisions made were based on our experience and judgement. Next series there'll be a new sword-of-Damocles-like set of guidelines hanging over our heads as we debate – if, indeed, there's anything left to debate.

I'm happy to be a target for my own gags and this seems to somehow defuse the targeting of others. If I admit my head is shaped like a light bulb – 'it looks like my neck has suddenly had a great idea' – it then seems almost democratic to show an unflattering photograph of eight-times-married Elizabeth Taylor and say 'That's what happens to the human face if you keep throwing rice at it.' We have less sympathy with Clare Balding's complaint that A.A. Gill described her cycling show as 'a dyke on a bike' when we remember her pressuring jockey Liam Treadwell to smile for the camera so everyone could see how terrible his teeth were. The BBC Trust says it's important, if jokes about public figures are made, that 'comments and tone are proportionate to their target'. However, this area gets greyer every day. When *The Times* published derogatory cartoons about Disraeli, they could argue that the power and influence of the target justified the vigour of the attack. But all sorts of people are becoming household names now. Is Susan Boyle a legitimate target because she entered a TV talent contest?

Is Rebecca Adlington a legitimate target because she's done sexy photo-shoots for Speedo?

I interviewed Matthew Kelly just after he was cleared of sexually abusing teenage boys. He referred to a joke I'd done about him at the time of his arrest. We debated the issue. I asked Matthew if he'd ever told any jokes based on Michael Jackson's sex abuse allegations. He admitted he had, but never in public. That was, for me, the crux. Matthew was, as the host of several primetime shows, at the very heart of mainstream entertainment. It's a world where the edgy gags are saved for the green room. Onstage, it's all sweetness and smiles. The comedy revolution of the last 20 years has challenged that duality. The modern comic presents more of his real self to the audience – unfiltered opinions and all. They talk about celebrities like people talk about them at home, in front of their tellies. And audiences – large audiences – like it that way. New guidelines can't reverse that hunger for honesty. A lot of modern comedy fans like their pineapple with the spiky end still attached. The people who prefer those sweet, syrupy, more-manageable chunks need to live and let live.

Personal hygiene – a confession

22 OCTOBER 2010

I'm someone who's always about to begin a regime of self-improvement. This pursuit of a better me usually involves a declaration to take on some new daily activity. Regular contenders include Bible reading, meditation and hula hooping – a light-and-shade formula for happiness comprising both spiritual enlightenment and snaky hips. Of course, anyone who's ever made a New Year's resolution is painfully aware of the failure-rate of such enterprises. On New Year's Eve, I resolved I'd learn to play chess in 2010. Let's just say I'm anticipating a lot of last-minute cramming over the Christmas holidays. I like the idea of attaching a new beginning to a significant date but 1 January seems to have become more hindrance than help. Seeing all my friends' resolutions crumbling gives me licence to renege on my own. We celebrate each other's failure, toast our human weakness and feel reassured that, as we let ourselves down, we bring solace to, and avoid resentment from, those who are dear to us. I decided I needed my own private resolution-date so I could pursue my goal alone, without the safety net of quitter-based camaraderie. I opted for 21 October because I wanted a date I could associate with human endeavour and, according to the nearly dependable Wikipedia, that was the day Thomas Edison first switched on a light bulb – the great, glowing symbol of a bright new idea. So, I had a date but I hadn't yet settled on a resolution. Then, while idly scanning other events that took place on 21 October, I noticed it was the day, in 1973, when John Paul Getty III's kidnappers cut off his ear, and posted it to his billionaire father. I took this to be a sign. I had my resolution. On 21 October 2010, for the first time in a long time, I washed my ears.

That isn't a joke – some made-up nonsense to make me sound colourful and eccentric. I would, in all seriousness, say I've washed my ears about ten times in the last 40-odd years. My attitude to them has always been like Quentin Crisp's attitude to housework. He maintained that if one never cleans a room, it reaches a point, after about four years, where it never gets any dirtier. It is, he said, just a matter of keeping one's nerve. As far as my ears are concerned, I've kept my nerve incredibly well. In all other aspects of personal hygiene I'm absolutely meticulous. My girlfriend often remarks on my systematic showering technique. Everything, except my ears, receives a complete going over. I suppose I've always assumed they get a sort of secondary rinse when I wash my hair. My ears don't have many opportunities for accidental cleaning. I can't swim, rarely eat watermelon and don't own an overaffectionate puppy. I've seen cotton-buds in nice hotels but I'm not totally sure how to use them. I imagine they're designed to navigate that mysterious, mazy whorl of the ear that has, until now, remained a foreign land to me. As a child, my ears were cleaned by my sister, Nora. She had long, pointed fingernails. She'd put a thin face-flannel over her index-finger then poke and probe until my ears were red and glowing and I had tears in my eyes. When she got married and left home I, unsurprisingly, felt no urge to take on the torturer's task myself. I wonder now, how many people, down the years, have noticed my dirty ears. Is it something friends talk about behind my back? Is it a recurring theme when make-up ladies swap waspish celebrity anecdotes? Do I fall victim to humiliating remarks the second I close the barbershop door behind me? If my ears are burning it's a worry because there's probably enough wax in there to sustain an eternal flame. Expect to see me carried through the streets by various public figures during the lead-up to London 2012.

I've never spoken publicly – or, come to think of it, privately – about this before, probably because I wanted to leave open the possibility that not cleaning one's ears is completely normal. I've considered discussing it in the context of observational stand-up comedy but I never knew whether it would get that glorious laughter of recognition or just an uneasy silence. You may be reading this thinking, 'What's he talking about? No one actually cleans their ears – well, not in a thorough, exhaustive way. Ears just basically clean themselves.' But then again, you may not. Still, having already acted on the new resolution I'm now able to discuss the subject as a past misdemeanour, like Keith Richards talking about his heroin addiction. I won't bore you with the details but I did the deed in the shower yesterday and, though it added about seven minutes to my usual ablution-time, I saw clear evidence that the 'ears clean themselves' theory is utterly bogus. I was strangely moved by the thought that some of that wax may have been there since the late sixties – a bit like finding an old newspaper lining an antique chest-of-drawers. I looked at myself in the mirror, post-shower, and I did look different. With the bathroom light behind me, my ears looked almost translucent. Thomas Edison not only inspired the resolution, he illuminated the results.

My least favourite night of the year

29 OCTOBER 2010

I felt very nostalgic as I drove past my local fire station last Saturday morning. There's something so seventies about a picket line. Still, at least I didn't need to worry about what would happen if the brazier got out of control. It took me back, though. My brother, Keith, was a shop steward at Longbridge in the seventies. He appeared on local and sometimes even national news, warming his hands and talking about exploitation of the workers. Whatever the rights or wrongs of each dispute, I loved the fact that an ordinary working-class chap like our Keith could, with the support of his workmates, occasionally shove an oily stick into the machinery of commerce and cause the whole thing to crunch to a silent halt. The resulting stasis served to remind everyone that people like Keith had a say, that when the wheels turned it was because the workers agreed they should turn – a reasoned consent rather than a subservient acceptance. Still, as I say, it all seems a bit seventies now. Even that word 'workers' sounds strangely out of date.

The press has spent all week changing the firefighters' profile from heroes to villains – and it's working. I did a bit of impromptu canvassing on the topic and there's a definite tendency for people to talk about night-shift naps and paid meal-breaks rather than how it must feel to search a smoke-filled house or find a blackened corpse glued to the floor by its own body-fats. The firefighters' biggest sin, apparently, is the plan to strike on 5 November. The London Fire Brigade gets 250 call-outs on an average day. Last Bonfire Night they got 680. To my mind, that isn't a reason to not strike on 5 November, it's a reason to not have Bonfire Night. I don't see how anyone can justify an organised event that causes a 180 per cent increase in Fire Brigade call-outs. With the Blitz, we had no choice, but this is self-inflicted. Nevertheless, nothing is allowed to quench the Fawkesian flames. Boris Johnson said Londoners should celebrate Bonfire Night, regardless of the strike, but added they should be especially sure to follow the Fireworks Code. Can this thing get any more seventies? At a time when we read so much about the heavy-handed application of Health and Safety regulations, it seems incredible that Bonfire Night roars on. I know kids like a bit of sparkle and bang but surely there's a fireworks app they'd enjoy just as much – and without the danger of being permanently disfigured. A nation that goes berserk when a woman puts a cat in a bin turns a blind eye – and there'll be more of them on 5 November – when millions of pets cower in their own homes because the endless screeches and bangs have turned the outside world into a terrifying no-go area. Meanwhile, as Parliament passes numerous bills compelling us to protect the environment, we celebrate the survival of that same Parliament by filling the air with smoke and gunpowder.

David Cameron, instead of condemning the firefighters for striking on their busiest night of the year should ask if that night really needs to be so busy. Bob Neill, the fabulously named 'minister with responsibility for fire' took time out from his lengthy negotiations with King Louie from *The Jungle Book*, to say that the threat of a strike in London on Bonfire Night is 'disgraceful' and is 'made worse by the fact that, in this most diverse of cities, it is also Diwali'. So, the strike is not only ill-timed and irresponsible but also politically incorrect. I'm moved by Mr Neill's concern for those who celebrate the festival of lights but wish he'd show similar sympathy for the country's 5 million Roman Catholics who have to watch the effigy of Catholic activist Guy Fawkes ceremonially burned every year. At the famous celebrations in Lewes, East Sussex, they throw in an effigy of Pope Paul V – pontiff at the time of Fawkes' failed plot – just to make the proceedings a little less ambiguous. I know Fawkes was a terrorist but does that make it all right? I doubt it would go down that well if someone mooted a national festival at which effigies of the 7/7 bombers were ritually burned. Interestingly, the only time I've read complaints about the effigies at Lewes was when the revellers burned a likeness of Osama Bin Laden. Many local councils have famously banned Christian imagery at Christmas to avoid offending other religions but the nation-wide celebration of oppressed and embittered seventeenth-century Catholics being tortured and executed is embraced with open arms.

I know the kids enjoy Bonfire Night but the recent growth of Halloween celebrations in the UK should compensate for its loss. If you're going to have Catholic-burning hot on the heels of that obtaining-gifts-by-menaces extravaganza, trick-or-treat, don't be surprised when people talk about the nation's unruly youth. Fire-services stretched-to-breaking, children burned and blinded, pets under traumatic house-arrest, the air polluted by smoke, and citizens united in a show of sectarian hatred – let's dump Bonfire Night. Maybe we could broaden-out Valentine's Day as a replacement. It might be a nice change to celebrate love – romantic, parental, interfaith – instead of 400-year-old hate.

Lorraine Kelly and Emile Zola – their courageous fight for truth

5 NOVEMBER 2010

Some years back, I was asked, in an interview with *heat* magazine, why I, at that time, dated women much younger than myself. I could have said something squalid like 'celebrity gives you a 20-years-off voucher and it seems a shame not to cash it' but I chose, instead, to suggest that I was a victim of circumstance rather than a slimy opportunist. In my teens and twenties I dated people the same age as me but all those relationships failed and, with each new decade, the pool of available contemporaries dwindled. People left the dance floor for long-term relationships. Most of the women in my age group were taken. Those that weren't inevitably came with a question mark. If they were as nice as they seemed, how come they were still on the dance floor? I tried to avoid asking that same question of myself. We, the still-unspoken-for, just carried on dancing around our stuffed-to-bursting emotional baggage, determinedly avoiding the gaze of anyone who looked as old and lonely as we were.

However, this was a comedian being interviewed by *heat* magazine. They didn't want bleak introspection. They wanted gags. I forgot Rudyard Kipling's advice. I talked with crowds but didn't keep my virtue. I opted for squalid after all. I'm loath to repeat it but I said I went out with younger women because 'most single women over 30 are as rough as arseholes'. It was a flippant and deliberately outrageous remark and the interviewer seemed to take it as such. However, when

I read it in cold isolation, repeated in a dozen different newspapers, it seemed brutish, arrogant and unkind. As if the line wasn't already bad enough, in some cases, not only the 'most' but also the 'single' had been removed. Columnists condemned me. Cartoonists lampooned me. Even glamorous Olympian, Sharron Davies said I was out of step with the modern world. Only Lorraine Kelly, with her sturdy Scottish commonsense, fought my corner in the press. 'He's a comedian. I imagine he was joking,' she said. It wasn't exactly Emile Zola on the Dreyfus affair but, nevertheless, she was right. It's hard to be hated for something you are but even harder to be hated for something you aren't – something you despise in others. A throwaway remark had been interpreted, through misunderstanding or malice, as a firmly held belief and, of course, in that context, it was unjustifiable. But I wasn't in a job where I could stop making throwaway remarks. Unscripted public speaking is inevitably a dangerous business.

Consequently, when I read Stephen Fry's comments about women not liking sex in the press this week – comments he insists were misquoted – I was inclined to give him the benefit of the doubt. Every purveyor of *bon mots* occasionally comes up with a *bon no*. Maybe, when you're interviewed by *Attitude* magazine, a celebration of gay sex as the one true church is too-tempting a crowd-pleaser. When I'm reading back through this column, before sending it off, I may stop at a sentence and think, 'No, that's not what I meant' and delete it. In interviews, when you're trying to come up with spontaneous sound bites, you don't have that option. Perhaps I should say, at this stage, I've met Stephen Fry, briefly, on two or three occasions, and, while he seemed nice enough, this is not a case of trying to help out a friend. Indeed, he's one of those celebrities who've nailed their colours to the very fashionable New Atheism mast so my first instinct is to renounce him and all his works. Claiming to know how another person experiences sex is like claiming to know how another person experiences tomatoes. Suggesting that an entire gender experience it in the same way is equally foolish. But surely we've all, in the sizzle of conversation, said things that, in the car on the way home, have caused us to ask ourselves, 'Why did I say that? I don't believe it.' Those words, of course, don't generally get into print. They fade and disappear.

Incidentally, it's always seemed to me that gay sex must lack passion because the undressing process is so slowed-down by the need to put everything on hangers. No, I don't really think that. I was just trying to be comical. I suspect that Stephen Fry was trying hard to give a good interview and ended up chasing a bad idea over a cliff. Fry is loved by many. He has nearly two million followers on Twitter, for goodness' sake. I don't do Twitter, partly because I really don't need a social-network system. My circle of friends is so small it would be perfectly practical to communicate with them only by illuminated manuscript. A man with two million followers – let's keep Hitler out of this – must have redeeming qualities. All Fry's previous funniness and intelligence are heaped on one side of the scales. On the other side are a few dumb, possibly misquoted, remarks. I'm not saying his popularity gives him licence to say what he likes. I'm saying we should take his previous record into account. That evidence seems to suggest he's too warm and intelligent to be a misogynist. Until I'm proved wrong, I'll stick with that.

My idyllic life as a benefit cheat

12 NOVEMBER 2010

I'm sure a great many people claiming unemployment benefit are desperately seeking work. Life, for them, can be a grim, debilitating house arrest imposed by lack of both funds and purpose. However, when I was on the dole, for quite a large chunk of the 1980s, I was definitely not seeking work. Nor were the majority of my unemployed friends. I remember one of them causing quite a stir in Oldbury Supplementary Benefit Office when he first signed on. Emboldened by home brew, he strode past the shuffling jobless, placed both hands on the counter and said, in a loud and confident voice, 'Is this where you get the free money?' On another drunken visit to the same benefit office, he tried to lead the assembled jobless in a chorus of 'Bless This House'. He came to regret those inappropriate moments of candour. To stay on the dole for a long time, one needed to become a ghostlike figure. Turn up, sign on, and disappear – the art of remaining a silent statistic, not a provocative individual. Those behind the counter were generally content to leave us alone, it seemed, as long as we played the game, as long as we made some vague job-seeking gestures, as long as we didn't appear too joyous. No one wanted to be first on the list when the schemes were being filled or, worse still, when the Job Centre decided to get proactive. Sometimes you were just unlucky – a blindly groping hand drew you from the benefits tombola – but often the choosing seemed downright revengeful. Thus, it was wise, as Paper Lace once said, to 'keep your pretty head low'.

Some readers may think us wrong to have claimed benefit while deliberately avoiding work – may feel we were stealing from the state. That widely held view obviously informs the new welfare white paper. There even seems to be a rewriting of the current recession as something caused by widespread benefit fraud. Meanwhile, the bankers get a big forgiving cuddle in case they get all sulky and move abroad. Well, I'm sure I've taken more money from the state, in recent years, by completely legal tax avoidance, than I ever did by claiming benefits. We made a choice back then. Most of us had tried working in horrible factories, bored out of our skulls for eight hours at a time. We decided that, free of dependants and responsibilities, an impoverished freedom was preferable to a more affluent life on the treadmill. Most people chose to work and prosper but, for us, having a car, nice clothes, a place of our own or even a family was less enticing than the lure of the unset alarm clock. We took the minimum benefit, lived in grimy bedsits, wore second-hand clothes, stayed childless, drank cheap sherry and read books. We were a living manifesto of non-materialism, kept by the state just as wealthy aristocrats in the eighteenth century would sometimes, as a spiritual/philanthropic gesture, keep an ascetic hermit in a cave on their rambling estate. We were the inveterate but undemanding unemployed. We gratefully accepted our meagre allowance and hid our sweet freedom under a bushel. It was our enemies, the inveterate but demanding unemployed, who regularly upset the equilibrium of the arrangement. They felt they should be as materially well off as employed people – decent houses, as many kids as they fancied, and various other trappings rightly reserved for the working population. They were always a smaller group than ours but inevitably, due to our preferred anonymity, got a lot more column inches. Few journalists would have chosen me for a feature on the scrounging unemployed. I would have been dismissed, I accept, as a weirdo waster but few would have envied my lifestyle. My greedier co-scroungers, however, were perfect for Middle England incitement. They still are.

Eventually, after four happy years, I accepted a job, helping to run a course for the long-term unemployed. Stick with what you know. Our clients had to turn up for their week-long course or they supposedly lost their benefits. One guy was an interesting test case. He'd been married twice, each union producing two children. He worked hard during the first marriage, providing his wife and kids with a lovely home and many material comforts. The marriage failed. When he met his second wife, they were both unemployed. He told me they lived in a council flat and really struggled to make ends meet but he'd seen his kids' first steps, heard their first words – things he'd missed first time around because he was working. I always felt having children while deliberately avoiding work was an abuse of the state's benevolence – those eighteenth-century hermits never moved the family in – but the two marriages offered an interesting insight into life on and off the materialist merry-go-round. I'm happy for my tax to support some inveterate but undemanding unemployed. They are a tiny speck on the economic landscape and one I have empathy with. I'd like to see a policy that gets rid of the greedy opportunists but leaves the ascetics in place. After all, as job vacancies become ever-scarcer we should be glad we've got people who are happy to not fill them – and who charge very little for that service.

I haven't been happy since September 24 1986

19 NOVEMBER 2010

David Cameron has asked the Office for National Statistics (ONS) to gauge the nation's general happiness levels and construct a Happiness Index. The 'science of happiness' already carries great weight in France and Canada and Mr Cameron has said that measuring, evaluating and watching over a population's happiness is one of the 'central political issues of our time'. The semantics are already causing problems. Writers on the subject casually replace 'happiness' with words like 'pleasure' – which seems to cover everything from ketamine to crazy golf – or well-being – which suggests a less-vibrant but deeper contentment such as one gets from listening to Radio Four or wearing trousers with an elasticated-waist. I'd say pleasure isn't quite as sturdy as happiness and its superficiality makes it more dependent on external factors. I've never tried ketamine but crazy golf, played alone in poor weather, is almost always accompanied by crushing despair. Well-being is more of a light, watercolour wash on which happiness can be painted. Happiness, being the umbrella-term, contains both the sizzle of pleasure and the calmness of well-being – like sharing a Radox bath with a flirty podium-dancer.

It won't be enough for the ONS to ask, like well-drilled American shop assistants 'How are you today?' They'll need to identify the general factors necessary for happiness so that these can then be maintained or manufactured by specific policy decisions. I don't envy the researchers because, in truth, happiness is a dreadfully dull subject. Take, for example, when friends tell us about their relationships. What we want are harrowing tales of psychotic girlfriends and scream-filled nights, ideally seasoned with tears. We'll enthusiastically inform the whimpering wretch that, if they need to unload more horrific anecdotes, we'll always be there for them. When, however, we encounter a friend who wants to share the lyrical wonderland of their latest blissful romance, we do everything to get the subject back to X Factor. Other people's happiness can be intensely tedious and other people's unhappiness can be fabulously entertaining. A French writer, whose name I forget, wrote about that happiness we experience when watching a close friend fall off the roof of a house. It's hard to base social policy on such conflicting and contrary needs.

Are people honest about their happiness levels? Anyone who's worked with me over the last 20-odd years will know that, when asked if I'm happy with something, I always answer 'I haven't been happy since 24 September 1986.' When inevitably quizzed further on this date, I explain it's the day I stopped drinking. Now while it's true that I've never truly replaced the white heat of happiness produced by drunkenness, I'm being disingenuous when I suggest that sobriety has sentenced me to unceasing gloom. My girlfriend always maintains that I'm the happiest person she's ever met. She says I'm like that chap on a bike who rides, whistling a jolly tune, past smiling villagers in old black-and-white films. Being a trained psychologist, she firms up this general observation by proposing a scientific explanation. She reckons I have high levels of serotonin – a naturally produced happy-pill. She partly bases this on the fact that I, a 53-year-old man, physically jump up and down, clapping my hands in anticipation, when I watch sausages cooking. When happiness is truly upon me, I experience a tickly inner-warmth – the sort of glow one normally only associates with celestial beings or regular consumers of Ready Brek. Despite this evidence, I continue to repeat my 24 September 1986 mantra. I suspect this is because, when I was a teenager, I heard a morose jazz saxophonist say his intellect was too developed to allow him to be happy. Angst is so cool. Unfortunately, I'm totally unable to maintain my tortured artist pose in the presence of sausages.

Uncontaminated happiness is generally synthetic and short-lived. A football match is a good example. Fans leap in the air and hug each other when their team scores or, alternatively, hold their heads in their hands and even weep when their team does badly. These people don't respond so extremely to the normal ups and downs of life beyond the football ground. They allow themselves to do so at a match because they know – deep down – it doesn't matter. Their Aristotelian ecstasy and despair is all part of the game. Some people identify sex as their greatest source of happiness but I find it too significant – too marred by insecurity and looming consequence – to provide uncontaminated bliss. I once, in post-coital rapture, tried to compliment the woman responsible by telling her 'that was the second-best sex I've ever had'. A general sense of unease marred the rest of the evening.

Putting cynicism aside, I like the idea that the government is taking happiness seriously. It would make a nice change to see policies based on philosophical theory rather than tabloid outrage. As for the questionnaire, income, housing and health should be easy factors to chart but happiness is much more multifarious than that. For example, I shave every other day. When I wake up and realise the day is a no-shaver, I am truly happy. The questionnaire is going to have to be pretty flexible to measure that sort of happiness – the little things that matter so much.

My really brilliant idea

26 NOVEMBER 2010

2011 is the four-hundredth anniversary of the King James Bible. A Trust has been set up to promote this milestone and, this week, I went to their launch party at the Banqueting Hall in Whitehall. Incidentally, I was delighted by the entry my personal assistant made in my diary for that day. It said, simply, 'King James Bible Launch Party'. Any archaeologist reading that, a few hundred years hence, will be extremely confused.

Charles I was beheaded outside the Banqueting Hall. In those days, the violence on Whitehall had a lot more style. I couldn't quite grasp the symbolism when that young man stood proudly atop the semi-wrecked police van, on Wednesday, his raised right fist in a Union Jack oven glove. Anyway, I was invited to the King James event because I'm a so-called celebrity but the reason I had the confidence to walk unaccompanied into a magnificent room and talk to a lot of very bright and successful strangers, many of whom have a background worlds away from my own, isn't about fame, it's about Higher Education. It didn't matter that I spent the first 20-odd years of my life living in a council house, that I was expelled from school, or that I got my A levels at a College of FE. A few weeks into the English degree course I did in the late seventies, I felt my brain begin to stir, my confidence begin to blossom and a whole new life begin to unfold. Higher Education unchained me.

A few weeks ago, I wrote about my happy sojourn on supplementary benefit. My student life was very different. I was so grateful for the opportunity to explore my potential I worked obsessively hard. If you're fortunate enough to get into Higher Education you have a moral obligation to get educated. I got a 2.1 for my degree and went on to get an MA. Those four years changed my life. It wasn't free – my parents, though they were both factory workers, were means-tested and had to contribute to my upkeep – but there were no student loans or, indeed, tuition fees. The current debate about Higher Education seems to ignore the fact that it's what students do with the opportunity that really matters. I think the payment of tuition fees should be based on performance. Anyone who drops out or fails their degree should have to pay a maximum fee. A third class degree student would pay 75 per cent of that amount, a 2.2 would pay 50 per cent, a 2.1 would pay 25 per cent and a First would pay nothing. The introduction of such a policy would soon put a stop to civil unrest. How many would be prepared to march under the More Money for Not Very Bright Students banner?

In the USA, experiments have been carried out in which schoolchildren were paid for handing in assignments, getting good marks and so on and the results were impressive, especially for pupils from underprivileged backgrounds. Some middle-class parents dismissed the experiments as bribery. One said she wanted her children 'to love knowledge for itself'. This is a nice ideal but the children of less affluent and often less education-friendly parents need a more nuts-and-bolts motivation. I did three years of factory work before I returned to education. The memory of it – my desire never to go back – was my motivation. You need something to keep you focused. I think we'd find underprivileged students performing better under my swot-and-save system because that free First Class degree would be the carrot dangling just above their work desk. Deferred gratification is a bit more dynamic when it's converted into hard cash. Also, industriousness is often seen as uncool by one's student peers but any bookworm accusations would be overridden by the streetwise reasoning of 'swot-and-save'. Of course, the tuition fees are meant to help fund universities but there is something neat about that funding coming from idlers, fools and unmotivated rich kids – and perhaps the government would be prepared to contribute more in exchange for widespread higher grades. I suspect they'd also be keen, under the circumstances, to ensure exam papers were rigorously marked and, consequently, standards would generally rise.

The government says students should pay tuition fees because their degrees eventually get them better-paid jobs. However, it also says highly paid bankers should be allowed bonuses because their efforts ultimately benefit the nation. Swot-and-save would be the students' bonus scheme. Surely well-educated people with a hard-work habit benefit the nation too. Some people feel there are too many people applying for university places but that might also change when it became obvious that the whole enterprise would require a lot more commitment. Drop-outs would have none of the benefits of academic qualifications but should still have to pay their entire bill. The scheme would encourage them to stick with their course and not fold when the going gets tough. A degree would be like a showbiz marriage – if you wanted to escape, you'd have to pay. It can be financially tough being a student. You only have to look at Edward Woollard – the fire-extinguisher man – to realise that many still have to cut their own fringe. However, swot-and-save could help make Higher Education what it should always aspire to be – a meritocracy.

A nation grovels
3 DECEMBER 2010

So England's 2018 bid failed miserably. I must say, I'm already over it. Watching us lose World Cups on the pitch is infinitely more painful. I wonder if it might be the other way round for the FA. To be honest, I've avoided the 2018 hysteria this week, like Ebenezer Scrooge hurrying past a festive brass band. After watching England in South Africa last summer, I decided to totally Unback the Bid. This was partly because, in the dark frustration of a massive post-Bloemfontein downer, I felt any country whose team played that badly should abandon their World Cup bid out of sheer embarrassment. I also felt estranged from England 2018 because the whole bidding process seems so utterly distasteful. Watching the bid-presentations yesterday morning reminded me of that cringe-inducing section on *I'm a Celebrity, Get Me Out of Here* when the contestants desperately plead for viewers' votes. Our Prime Minister began his speech by thanking FIFA 'for the privilege of allowing me to present to you today.' One doesn't bid for the World Cup any more, one begs for it. The FIFA officials are like cynically influential courtiers. You'd better hang on their every word, laugh long and hard at their jokes, and make sure you refer to the tournament as the FIFA World Cup – otherwise things could get frostier than a Scottish side-road. This week, paying for all the drinks in the Last Chance saloon were David Cameron, Prince William and David Beckham – our three lions, as the tabloids called them. Now, William and Mr Cameron are used to creeping around foreign dignitaries but I really wish David Beckham hadn't been asked to kneel and kiss FIFA's World Cup ring. I was at Old Trafford when we drew with Greece to qualify for the 2002 tournament. Of course, Beckham hit a marvellous free kick, in injury-time, that guaranteed our place, but he did a lot more than that. I've rarely seen one player have so much influence over a game. England weren't playing well but Becks took the game by the scruff-of-the-neck and forced the team to qualify. He'd made up his mind he was going to the World Cup and he wasn't going to let a little thing like a qualifying game get in his way. He was truly heroic that day – an example of how human determination can manifest itself as a force of nature. I don't like seeing him in his current role, operating as some vague, mascot-like figure for the FA. They used him in a similar role in South Africa. I hope he now he takes a bow, acknowledges his well-earned applause and strides proudly offstage.

The bid is dead but it leaves a nasty aftertaste. I couldn't believe the FA criticised the media for the timing of their FIFA corruption allegations. Perhaps Prince Andrew should have gone to Zurich instead of Prince William. WikiLeaks has shown him to be a great champion of putting profit ahead of exposing corruption. Besides, the tabloids nearly always save their kiss-and-tells and other potentially disruptive England tittle-tattle until the eve of a big game or tournament but I can't recall the FA ever publicly condemning that as treasonable behaviour. The difference is that these recent revelations may have cost us more than just a football match; they may have cost us a sponsorship-fuelled fortune. I'm surprised the FA didn't turn to that indispensable modern-day footballing lifesaver – the super-injunction.

Anyway, look on the bright side. Now it's all over we can get back to the noble pursuit of slagging off FIFA. The tournament used to be called the World Cup because it belonged to the world. Now it's called the FIFA World Cup. What does that tell you? I know they do a lot for charity but so did the Krays. Speaking of charity, I'm not sure England's pledge to equal, through its Football United project, the amount of money FIFA puts into social schemes was a good idea. President Blatter, as he was called throughout the presentations, doesn't like to be equalled in anything. You know that block of perfect-view corporate seating that remains empty at most Wembley games because it can't be resold to ordinary fans? Well, if you gaze deeply into it and allow your eyes to defocus, eventually, like a magic-eye picture, you'll see a clear image of the future of football if FIFA gets its way. They dream of turning grounds into a sea of suits and laminates. It's no coincidence that FIFA President, Sepp Blatter was regularly booed by the fans in South Africa. He is Darth Vader, FIFA is the evil Empire and the World Cup is their Death Star. I wish there'd been an Internet campaign to derail the bidding process like the one that derailed *The X Factor*'s Christmas number one last year. I'd love to have led a rage against FIFA's machine, maybe fixing it so that the 2018 World Cup was awarded to North Korea. Still, at least our bidding-team left the stage with a special FIFA certificate for having taken part in the bid, personally presented by President Blatter. I trust that now lies in a Zurich skip, its wooden frame warped by the combined urine of the entire English delegation.

Privacy is dead.
I never liked it
much anyway
10 DECEMBER 2010

The battle-lines are well and truly drawn. WikiLeaks, representing an alternative society of geeks and visionaries that constantly questions the world-view handed down to it from above, is at war with the elite who inhabit and maintain that mysterious above. It's like when, in those years before the Reformation, a few brave seekers of truth printed and distributed bibles in the vernacular so that the people might read and judge for themselves rather than mutely accept the possibly jaundiced interpretations of their supposed betters – betters who stood to gain much from retaining the status quo. The very name, WikiLeaks, reflects their brutal straightforwardness. They're completely upfront that the operation is about leaks and plenty of them. It's a classic case of doing what it says on the tin. Even Wookieepedia feels the need to add 'the *Star Wars* wiki' as an explanatory subtitle. Likewise, Chickipedia employs the by-line 'the wiki of hot women'. WikiLeaks speaks for itself.

Even if Julian Assange turns out to be guilty as charged, it should not distract from the frightening beauty of his creation. WikiLeaks, on one level, tunes into our worst nightmare. That sudden, dreadful fear we experience when we're criticising a friend, and it occurs to us that we might have accidentally pocket-dialled them, that they might be listening to all our muffled bitterness – that fear is why we shudder at WikiLeaks' revelations. On the other hand, the nagging suspicion that the stuff we're fed about wars, foreign policy and general political decision-making is all sleight-of-hand makes WikiLeaks utterly compulsive. Some of us, of course, don't want to know how the trick's done, or even if there is a trick but WikiLeaks takes us by the hair and forces us to peer into the mirrored cabinet.

They're not the first. They're part of a continuing movement. An Irish friend of mine told me that, when the very first tampon advert was shown on Irish television, his mother, avoiding the eyes of her family, stood up and left the room muttering 'Ah, there's no secrets any more.' She had recognised the trend – the slow but unavoidable death of privacy. But privacy is overrated. We may associate it with peace, with being left alone, but privacy also gave us sexed-up dossiers, bomb-making in Yorkshire bedsits and Josef Fritzl. There would have been no MPs' expenses revelations if privacy had been fit and well. I went to a comedy show a while back and it said on Twitter that I 'never laughed once'. It was true but, by the time it became cyber-gossip, I'd diplomatically told the comedians how brilliant they'd been. I recently arrived home on a snowy night and told my girlfriend I'd had to get the tube. 'I know,' she said, 'it was on Twitter.' Thank goodness I'm not sleeping around. I got three points on my licence because CCTV saw me going through a red light. The BBC is being pressured to publish artists' fees. In short it's getting harder and harder for people, especially those in public life, to be unkind, deceitful, irresponsible or greedy. People used to behave well because they thought God was watching. Now the secular world has come up with its own hidden observers. I wasn't terribly happy that Twitter caught me not laughing or that CCTV caught me breaking the law but I took a breath, set my jaw, and nodded respectfully to the truth – thus acknowledging the time-honoured concept of the fair cop. The enigmatic elite, behind their smoke and mirrors, never pay homage to an intrusive truth. They rail at it and seek angry retribution. Let's face it: international diplomacy is just a type of lying. It's ridiculous that extremely important relationships between countries are conducted like a schoolyard romance – the fear of being oneself, the worry they'll dump you on the basis of a trifling misunderstanding and the terrible anxiety about what your friends think. If diplomats and statesman refuse to embrace honesty it's time it was roughly imposed upon them.

WikiLeaks seems to honour a Reithian obligation to educate, inform and entertain. We may learn much about French foreign policy when reading that President Sarkozy's plane was rerouted in case seeing the Eiffel Tower lit in Turkish colours made him angry. But also, don't you just love the *Dr. Strangelove* nature of it all? We've learned from reality TV – another manifestation of the death of privacy – that, as with the Phantom of the Opera, the really interesting stuff comes when the mask falls off.

It's true that the dispersal of significant information is a dangerous business but isn't it time that, like those sixteenth-century Reformers, we stopped letting a secretive elite decide what's good for us. WikiLeaks is scary. That which brings liberation can also bring bloodshed but, at the moment, I trust their motives slightly more than I trust those of this or any other government. WikiLeaks' aim is to illuminate, with a secondary recreational desire to embarrass. The aims of the world's governments are considerably less apparent – but not for much longer. The truth has been released from captivity and is running wild and free. Our fear of its sharp teeth competes with our desire to look it straight in the eye.

Shouting, pushing and trying to look hard

17 DECEMBER 2010

I was walking down Whitehall, this week, when I heard a middle-aged lady say to a policeman 'Excuse me, is it a riot-day today?' The officer explained that there was 'nothing planned'. I like the fact that the tuition-fee protests have already been absorbed into normal London life. It's like the sign I pass in a spray-paint-covered subway near Waterloo that lists elements – like racist language or graphic depictions of sexual acts – that should not feature in the graffiti, or the menacing-looking punk rocker, with a bright orange Mohican, who's photographed with tourists in Leicester Square for a pound a time. We like a little bit of rebellion in this country. We don't quash it; we domesticate it. If the regular student-protests continue they'll soon morph into a cosy cross between a Sealed Knot re-enactment and Children in Need night.

A lot of bus routes weren't operating after the last riot so I decided to walk home from the West End. I asked a policeman if Whitehall was still closed off. He said 'I'm not sure. The officers there are on a different wavelength.' I don't normally sidestep an opportunity for a smart-arse remark but his heavily scuffed riot gear somehow sapped my confidence. As it turned out, Whitehall was open, but only to pedestrians. This made for a surreal midnight stroll through a near-silent post-demonstration Westminster. Police vans and officers were on every corner but they remained a shadowy presence. It was the calm after the storm. You could have heard a fire-extinguisher drop. Just a few hours before it had been like a scene from Dante. If you saw those bits on the *X Factor* final where Stacey Solomon was in the centre of Colchester, struggling to be heard amidst a near-hysterical Essex mob – cast adrift on a Primark ocean – you'll know how terrifying a big, chaotic crowd can be, even when their mood is celebratory. You'll also know that Stacey Solomon can reach a level of excitement where she sounds like Roland Rat being strangled.

In the eerie post-riot hush, I walked past the Winston Churchill statue on Parliament Square, its base still scrawled with swearwords and anti-police invective. Churchill, however, was unmarked. I suppose the students saw the stick-wielding figure swamped by an enormous army greatcoat and assumed he was one of their own. I have to say I'm not too worried about the dismantling of the occasional police van, or even a *Bugsy Malone*-style attack on the royal Rolls-Royce, but I don't like people messing with the Churchill statue. In a game of anti-fascist Top Trumps, Sir Winston would beat any NUS member, no matter how many BNP marches they've thrown stones at. I think, the night before Westminster-based protests, the Churchill statue should be removed and replaced by one of those human-statue street performers, painted-up in thick grey paint so no one would know the difference. If he could bear to keep still long enough, Charles Bronson, the man sometimes described as 'the most violent prisoner in Britain', would be an ideal stand-in. He's about the same size as the statue, he's already bald, numerous rooftop protests have given him a good head for heights and, should anyone get the urge to go climbing on him, they would soon come to understand the meaning of blood, sweat and tears.

Speaking of crowd-control, the police seem to be currently considering the much-less-inventive option of the power-hose. This might seem hardcore but the rebel-domestication process will soon lighten things up and before we know it we'll be watching footage of a student standing with his foot on the hose until there's an enormous bulge. As soon as an unsuspecting officer gazes down the nozzle to see what's wrong, the student will raise his foot and the ensuing surge of water will, of course, knock the officer's helmet off. Then they'll cut to that same student, begging for mercy as he bounces high and out-of-control atop a jet of water coming from the now-smiling officer's skyward-pointing hose. If things don't turn out quite so affable and the power-hose becomes a terrifying deterrent, couldn't the students just switch their protests to coincide with the regular summer hosepipe ban?

Anyway, I continued past Churchill, on my still-tranquil journey, and reached the Peace Camp opposite the Houses of Parliament. A handful of peace protesters stood gazing at passers-by. They usually fix strangers with an accusatory stare but on this unusual night, they seemed strangely melancholic. I wondered if they felt slightly outdone or superseded, like the IRA after 9/11. They'd been the hotshot protesters in these parts but now, having witnessed a day of facemasks, fence throwing and fires, they'd been forced to look at themselves in the dissenters' mirror and accept that their own protest consisted mainly of, well, camping.

I have a lot of sympathy with the protesting students but also with the police. When this little marching season is over I imagine they'll both look back with some pride and embarrassment. With time, I suspect we'll all come to realise that the great bulk of the conflict centred on those three great mainstays of all English street-confrontation – shouting, pushing and trying to look hard. I find that oddly comforting.

The Queen's Christmas message – a Dadaist, free-form experiment

31 DECEMBER 2010

Just when I thought nothing could overtake woman-puts-cat-in-bin as my highlight of 2010, Her Majesty the Queen steps in with a late entry that turns everything upside-down. The joy of woman-puts-cat-in-bin was the unlikely nature of the protagonist. We're perfectly aware that children do unkind things to domestic pets on a regular basis. It's a distressing fact but we're stuck with it. However, the sight of a respectable-looking middle-aged woman indulging in such evil practices was somehow, once we knew the cat was saved, fabulously exciting. It was the joy of the unexpected, the strangely out-of-context. Likewise, the Queen's Christmas Message – that most straight-laced and resolutely non-controversial of all TV programmes – turned out to be a sort of Dadaist, free-form experiment – wilfully random and unfathomable. It began with the Queen at Hampton Court, choirboys in the background – the sort of stuff one expects from this seasonal filler. Her Majesty pointed out that 2011 is the four-hundredth anniversary of the King James Bible. Good subject for a Christmas Message – very British, very royal, very Church of England. I settled back on the sofa, anticipating the message's usual mix of unchallenging banality, multicultural tokenism and horses. Her Majesty talked about the King James Bible's 'glorious language' its harmonising effect on the Christian Church, and then, with no warning, there was a discernible jolt, like one experiences with a clunking edit in an old silent movie, and suddenly she was talking about sport. Was this two Christmas messages roughly spliced together? Had I dozed-off and slept exactly one year? I felt destabilised. I assume the nation felt destabilised. Soon there was footage of people in dinghies, competing in some sort of event and being watched by the Princess Royal. Where was the court of King James, the great achievement of Lancelot Andrewes, or the Queen's explanation of Ezekiel 13:18? Of course, Her Majesty mentioned the Commonwealth Games because they've got the word 'Commonwealth' in them and she never misses an opportunity to say 'Commonwealth'. Then suddenly the earth moved again. 'King James may not have anticipated quite how important sport and games were to become in promoting harmony' she said, without, one imagines, too much fear of contradiction. This was the only point where she didn't quite carry off the 'Yes, I'm jumping from the King James Bible to sport and back again – what of it?' motif. As she acknowledged King James's lack of foresight as far as the harmonising effect of sport was concerned, I spotted a slight grimace, as if she could hear the violent scraping of a square peg being forced into a round hole. Then she quoted the bit from Matthew's gospel about doing unto others, wished us Happy Christmas and was gone.

Perhaps it was a wager. Perhaps, as they sat munching toast one morning, the Duke of Edinburgh bet her she couldn't make a Christmas Message out of two unconnected subjects chosen by him. She probably baulked at the idea when his first choices were racism and harness racing but when he, keen to rescue the wager, switched to the King James Bible and sport the bet was on. Maybe there's a simpler explanation. I remember that my granny, as she moved into her nineties, took to having shepherd's pie and Guinness for breakfast. She'd decided that the normal social constraints shouldn't apply to a woman of her age. Perhaps King James and sport for Christmas lunch was the Queen's version of this old-age-liberation. At 84, she's decided she'll say whatever she likes – a policy Prince Philip adopted when he was about 45.

Of course, when the Queen says 'sport' that twinkle in her eye has nothing to do with Bobby Moore holding up the World Cup or even Virginia Wade winning Wimbledon. Her Majesty will be reliving some golden memory of a Scottish stag being brought to its knees by snarling hounds or a hare being pulled apart by lurchers. Maybe that's where the Christmas broadcast fell down. The Queen's original plan was to combine bloodsports with the Bible. Perhaps the passion of the Christ and other such gory Biblical episodes were to be intertwined with various bloodsporting images. But, when the producer politely suggested that the illustrative footage the Queen had chosen was somewhat inappropriate – 'perhaps it's a bit too Frankie Boyle for Christmas Day, ma'am' – she lost her bottle and they replaced the disembowelling with dinghies.

Then again, I may underestimate Her Majesty. Perhaps the Christmas broadcast was so carefully constructed that the message was in the very form of the piece. The Bible and sport roughly grated against each other. That jagged juxtaposition cannot have escaped the Queen's attention. I think she was making the point – surreptitiously so as to pay lip-service to the modern, secular nation she leads – that the spiritual, represented by the Bible, and the physical, represented by sport, are incompatible and eternally in conflict. It's too big a concept for a nation in paper hats to take on board so she wrapped up her golden wisdom in a sugary Christmas message like coins secreted in a Christmas pudding. Massive respect to her and a Happy New Year to all our readers. Next week – hair-extensions and Hobbes' *Leviathan*.

Hey, Baldy! Here comes the stem-cell cavalry

7 JANUARY 2011

An old friend of mine, who was inclined to become melancholy when drunk, would often tell me he only had death and baldness to look forward to, and he prayed they came in that order. He got his wish. Another friend recounted the horror of suddenly discovering he had a bald patch. The grim fact had evaded him whilst washing or combing. Then, one day, he was leaning backwards on his chair, the front two legs off the ground, when his head came into contact with the wall behind him. He felt its smooth coldness against his scalp. He knew. The awfulness of this story comes, I think, from the juxtaposition of the boyish balancing on the chair with the sudden awareness of ageing and decay. Another bald friend admitted to me that he had stared enviously at a man sat on the pavement, clutching a cardboard 'hungry and homeless' sign, because he had a full head of hair. 'It was wasted on him,' he told me with a mixture of frustration and shame.

Britain has 7.4 million balding men. However, 2011 starts with great news for them all. Some clever scientist-types have discovered that male pattern baldness is all to do with stem cells and, armed with that knowledge, the baldness-boffins reckon they can rethatch the world's baldies within ten years.

I have a slightly receding hairline. I've always had a high forehead but nowadays I have to stand on a chair to cut my fringe. Generally, however, my hair's held on pretty well. This is tremendous news because, to be honest, I always had a certain sympathy with that friend who said he'd rather die than live with male-pattern baldness. I'm totally happy with grey hair as long as it lingers. I don't buy this theory that baldness is a sign of virility. That has to have come from a bald scientist. Besides, what's the point of being virile if no one wants to have sex with you because you're bald? Surely, it's a slur on men with hair to say that baldness is connected to virility. However, because we're the lucky ones, we have to let the poor baldies get away with it. One sees a similar 'let's attack the fortunate' philosophy in the current advert for Kerry Katona's workout video. The slightly chunky Kerry is described as a 'real woman'. Of course, if this was a Keira Knightley – same initials, different body-shape – workout video, the voice-over person wouldn't dare say such a thing. Are we to deduce from this that Keira Knightley is not a real woman? I have several bright, funny, caring, down-to-earth, thin female friends. They seem pretty real to me – perhaps even more real than Kerry Katona, if such a thing is possible. The bald and the chunky are completely deserving of love and respect, of course, but they must allow similar rights to the unbald and unchunky. This is especially true if they're trying to sell a video that promises to help people look more like the skinnies they're subtly slagging off. Anyway, if baldness is a sign of virility, why are there so many bald football referees?

Before the stem-cell cavalry turned up, men used old-fashioned subterfuge to deal with baldness. One has to look no further than a nineties' shot of the Bee Gees to see that both surgical weaves and trilbies can be employed. I imagine the third, noticeably hairy, Bee Gee was only there as a control. The comb-over is probably the most sneered-at method for hiding the truth. I once followed the broadcaster, Robert Robinson, down some stairs. He had grown his remaining hair very long and then coiled it into a mesmerising spiral atop his bald dome. It was not so much a comb-over as a Brylcreem vortex. It looked like his hairdresser was Bridget Riley. But is this any worse than the current method of shaving the whole head in the forlorn hope that people will think 'Ah, what we have here is a man with a lustrous head of hair who has decided to deliberately simulate baldness because it's such a great look'? Hooray for the BBC's Nick Robinson – same surname, similar follicles – who's gone bald the way men used to go bald – just a bit round the sides and back. He is so delightfully

Larkinesque, I can imagine him walking into the BBC newsroom, wearing bicycle-clips and carrying sandwiches wrapped in greaseproof paper. He bears his baldness like Christ bore the cross – not with pride but with tight-lipped acceptance.

Some psychologists believe that women are attracted to bald men because their baldness suggests reassuring maturity – bald psychologists, obviously. If male pattern baldness has a purpose, I reckon it's to keep men loyal. The hirsute youth marries his sweetheart and, by the time that love has worn thin, so has his hair. He stays because he cannot imagine another woman being interested in his now-bald self. Baldness brings the sort of humility that keeps marriages together. The boffins should accept that they may, with their stem-cell cure, bring about a level of infidelity that will destroy family life forever.

PART TWO
OTHER WRITINGS

YOUR CUT-OUT-AND-KEEP
MARGARET THATCHER OBITUARY

When Michael Jackson died, people gathered in the streets in the USA, unsure of how to mark the event. They just milled around, shaking their heads, wiping away tears and then, as if the appropriate response suddenly became obvious, they danced. I always imagined that when Margaret Thatcher died I'd just cut straight to the dancing.

On the night she stood down as Prime Minister, back in November 1990, I was hosting a comedy gig in Birmingham. I began by leading the audience in an exuberant version of 'Ding, dong, the witch is dead'. Just like the newly liberated Munchkins, we truly felt that, at last, freedom from grim oppression had come. When the song was over I explained to the crowd that I was glad she'd gone (more raucous cheering and applause) but I was sad she'd gone in that fashion, shabbily betrayed by her former colleagues. The crowd was confused by my misplaced compassion. 'No,' I said, 'I didn't want her to go like that. I was hoping for an assassination.' Even louder cheering ensued.

It was absolutely the norm to hate Margaret Thatcher in those days. At least it was if you travelled in the circles I did. Anti-Thatcher jokes were a mainstay of what was then called 'alternative comedy'. She was the living, breathing representation of what we were the alternative to. She was middle England – stiff, humourless and narrow-minded. Worse still, she was a cold-hearted headmistress who was cruel to the weak and needy children whilst making favourites of the toffee-nosed, arrogant, head boys. She created the yuppies: smartly dressed, madly ambitious, materialistic monsters with fast cars and, worst of all, mobile phones. Alternative comedians – usually unshaven, always broke, neurotic intellectuals, dressed in Oxfam suits and Green Flash trainers – were everything that yuppies weren't and passionately proud of that fact. It was our duty to hate Thatcher and all she stood for. She and her yuppie army were an easy way to define exactly who we were – NOT THEM.

Anyway, she stepped down and less combative figures succeeded her as party leader. From John Major to David Cameron, they seemed and seem like pencil sketches compared to the vivid oil painting that was Thatcher. I've struggled to properly hate any of them. Maybe that's because they're too bland to evoke such full-on emotion or maybe I've just mellowed. During Thatcher's years in power I was firstly a student, then on the dole for three years, then an alternative comedian. With each of these, hating Thatcher came as standard. Now I'm older, and indeed richer, does that hatred endure? Well, I hadn't really thought about it much until, in 2005, I interviewed the newly crowned Queen of the Jungle, Carol Thatcher, on my ITV chat show. I'd really enjoyed watching her on *I'm a Celebrity* and felt her to be a worthy winner. The interview started well but five minutes in she referred to her mother. I suddenly felt myself becoming indignant. Somehow, I'd forgotten she was Margaret Thatcher's daughter. All the pleasure Carol had given me as I'd watched her in the jungle faded away and I found myself growling about how her mother had ruined people's lives. It seemed the old malice was still there.

So, when I heard that Margaret Thatcher really was dead – how did I feel? Well, I didn't dance but I did think about the railway journey I used to regularly make from Langley Green to Birmingham, New Street. In the seventies, that train passed factory after factory, belching out smoke, busily producing metal things that fitted onto other metal things that duly took their place in the massive machinery of national productivity. By the mid-eighties all I could see from that train were empty buildings, broken windows and rust. The people who'd worked in those now silent shells were the people I saw when I signed on at Smethwick Benefit Office – a place where some wag had written on the wall 'Margaret Thatcher says "beggars can't be choosers".' I remember one guy, probably in his late fifties, who always wore a suit and tie when he came to sign on – an attempt, I guess, to retain a bit of dignity though he knew he'd probably never work again. I haven't forgotten but the truth is Margaret Thatcher outlived my hatred. If she had been assassinated in 1990, I'd have conducted that comedy crowd's singing with even greater gusto but, instead, she grew old and frail. There were stories of her telling people they had to 'wait for Dennis' years after her husband had died. That tragedy made her human. She became just another frightened old lady trying to cope with loneliness, ill-health and looming mortality.

Margaret Thatcher is dead and I feel I should say something positive about her. Well, I admired her work ethic – I always suspected she'd deliberately had twins in order to save time. It's just a pity that someone who clearly needed a focused purpose in her life robbed so many other people of theirs. She gave me one good line that I reeled off to anyone who accused me, usually correctly, of being drunk. 'As Margaret Thatcher said,' I'd reply 'there is no such thing as sobriety.' I suppose that's my positive note. Like Michael Jackson she was a great gift to comedians. The pencil-sketch men who followed her have less character and thus less to caricature. That, I'd say, is a tribute of sorts.

THE NEW GOING OUT –
WRITTEN FOR *PORT* MAGAZINE

A few years ago, I spoke to two guys who'd just got back from a holiday in Italy. I can't remember exactly where they'd been, just that they'd shared a cheap room in a cheap hotel and found a nearby cinema that showed a different old American movie every day. For two weeks, they got drunk every night in the hotel bar and spent their afternoons ignoring subtitles. Aside from the alcohol, they existed on takeaway pizza and strawberry-flavoured milk. They slept till midday. The film started at two. They did no sightseeing, they didn't even sunbathe. I was genuinely appalled to hear about their wasted trip. The idea of them sitting in darkness, while Italy was right there outside the cinema, actually unnerved me. I never looked at a guidebook after I'd left a holiday destination in case I came across something I'd missed. I knew such an omission would torment me. I was upset for these two guys – I anticipated their deep remorse at some future date – but they were completely confused by my reaction. They argued that holidays were all about doing exactly what you wanted to do, with no alarm clocks, must-sees or itineraries. I trotted out that old line about people on their deathbeds regretting what they didn't do rather than what they did. They shrugged, smiled and started talking to someone else.

The conversation had a profound effect on me. I think it's important that all our opinions are disposable otherwise we cling to wrongness simply because it feels like part of us. On reflection, their want-to-do seemed much more authentic than my ought-to-do. Should I really be on my deathbed, wishing I'd found time for the Leprosy Museum in Bergen? If God had meant us to have deathbed regrets he wouldn't have given us dementia. I felt the ripple effect of this freshly forming opinion. I wasn't just thinking about holidays any more. I was applying these revelations to life in general. Had I been trying too hard? Maybe I didn't have to see every talked-about new movie or hot band. Maybe I could experience a new thrill – the thrill of not-being-there. Why queue for tickets when I could just stay-in and drink strawberry-flavoured milk?

I asked myself what I wanted to do that I hadn't been doing. Surprisingly, it was staying-in that came to symbolise my new freedom. In those days I never stayed in. I always felt like the best party ever was happening just over there, wherever over there was. I needed to be out-and-about, looking for it. Now I asked myself if the party-quest was a want-to or an ought-to. Clearly it was the latter. At some parties I'd stand there and literally no one would speak to me. Those were the only ones I enjoyed. The abstract idea of a party is exhilarating. The practical reality isn't. Crisps tend to snap when you use them to scoop guacamole and most people are a poor substitute for Google. Staying in is the opposite of a party and the opposite of a party was exactly what I was looking for. I realised that staying in, for me, was now definitely a want-to. To be fair, I often enjoy dinner parties nowadays but that's just because they're like staying-in at someone else's house.

Those who still desperately seek that elusive party cannot conceive of the joy of staying in – cannot imagine its unexpected delights. Take, for example, the glory of cancellation – that night when, steeling oneself to go out, one receives a last-minute reprieve. My terribly sorry friends are always impressed by how understanding I am, how sympathetic to their unforeseen situation. I hold the phone in my left hand; my right hand punches the air. It feels like a moderately sized lottery-win. Then there's the gift of minor illness – a licence to stay-in, indeed an obligation to do so. Such sickness wraps around me like a soft, warm blanket. I noticed, recently, that while reading an article about a prison-riot, I pronounced the words 'solitary confinement' just to feel them on my lips. Pronounced them with that same slippery sensuality one usually reserves for a phrase like 'chocolate éclair'.

I'm not championing misanthropy. It's merely a question of distance. I love people watching, but mainly from the window of my eleventh-floor apartment, like Harry Lime looking down from the Ferris wheel in *The Third Man*. However, I'm no recluse. I live with the woman I love. Sometimes we stay in together and that's beautiful but staying in alone, of course, is the purer discipline. The German poet, Rainer Maria Rilke, felt strongly that lovers should embrace their separateness. He felt they should be 'the guardians of each other's solitude'. Some people really wouldn't like that. I once went out with a woman who'd get upset if I rolled-over during the night and, in so doing, turned my back on her. In retrospect, we were ill matched.

Staying in alone, for me, has developed some central themes. What I wear is important. Ideally, my outfit should be twice my size, have no zips or buttons, and be only slightly interrupted by elastication. In such clothes, I seem to revert to liquid form. The very idea of sitting upright seems ridiculous. Of course, I also ditch my contact lenses and wear spectacles. This fits in with the need to look as unsexy as possible, a key policy in my opposite-of-party manifesto. Also, I feel my eyes are having a night-in too so I cut them a little slack. I had my eyes tested recently and part of the examination required me placing the weight of my head on a metal chin-rest. I imagine it's to keep the head completely still but it was very relaxing and I did wonder if such rests were commercially available. I like the idea of a night in with my neck muscles completely disengaged.

For food, I generally cook steak. This is partly to do with the eating of it but mainly to do with the cooking. Because my nights in alone feel strangely masculine, I like the whole flat to smell of meat. I guess it's how the cave smelled when the sabre-tooth tiger was on the griddle. The masculine-thing needs some explanation. I don't regard myself as particularly male. In fact, I'd say, generally speaking, I'm testosterone-intolerant. I think my solitary nights in only assume an air of maleness in response to the fact that my girlfriend is out. Even then, it's not horribly male. I'm not drinking beer and watching pornography. I'm eating steak and watching a 1950s science-fiction movie. Don't get me wrong. I'm sure there are women who love *It Came from Outer Space* but I'm guessing they stay in on their own a lot too.

I hear staying in is the new going out. Well, I'm living the dream. There will be readers who feel I'm wasting my life but one of my favourite things is learning. I don't necessarily mean doing a course in something, I mean just acquiring ideas and stuff. I can learn more from watching *Forbidden Planet* than I ever did from someone shouting small talk at me in a fashionable bar. I've given up cool for cosy. I've stopped worrying about that deathbed checklist too. Just don't bury me in anything tight. And get me a coffin with Blu-ray. I hear death is the new life.

OPHELIA REDEFINED
A short story for the *Sunday Times*
15 NOVEMBER 2009

Horatio whispers louder than most men speak. This bed, scented with sweet flowers, cannot ease me into sleep while the roar of his servant-shushing, at intervals irregular, jerks at my lashes and lips. His booming voice bids them be quiet, lest they wake me. His clumsy concern is like his sword-calloused hand on my naked arm as we lie in darkness. This manly love suits me well. I watch him, sometimes, gloriously out-of-place amidst the fawning and finery of court. His impatience and inattentiveness thwarts the oily sycophants and gives me licence to laugh at their spineless folly. How joyous when great Fortinbras himself leaves their scraping unacknowledged to stride on and shake Horatio's honest hand. But when our golden-armoured king dips to kiss my gentle fingers, what taste finds he there? Does his royal palate discern the blood and greasepaint intertwined? Sometimes, when the kissing's done, his raised eyes grip me in an interrogatory stare and cold shivers prick my neck and shoulders. Perhaps he feels those tinglings in my still-held hand and ponders my mysterious agitation.

When I, emerging from my secret place – my corridor of shadows whence I witnessed dreadful truths – first met good Fortinbras he looked at me in puzzlement and awe. He, newly arrived and bent on occupation, had found the power he planned to seize already at his feet. The corpses, dribbling and split-apart like windfall-fruit, lay all around him as he picked his way across the sticky floor. I watched in dark anticipation, like a palpitating player about to join the vivid scene.

Fortinbras hailed Horatio, a standing man who might put name to all this breathless brood and shape the seeping chaos into order with some brief, explanatory tale. The lifeless lay upon the chequered floor as Fortinbras attended every detail of their moves and motivations and scratched his head to find himself the winner of a game he had not played. My own part in the story was, I felt, too rushed and undersold. Horatio knew but little of my central role and crucial contributions. What he knew he squandered in his whirl.

'Old King Hamlet died,' he said to Fortinbras as they, the teller and the told, now sat, each in his animation. 'Claudius, his brother, took the Queen, with movement hasty and all lawfulness in doubt and so King Claudius became. He filled his brother's place between the lion-headed armrests of the throne, all keen, by new decree to reinvent the kingdom as his own. Between Queen Gertrude's full-round thighs he likewise forged a new regime and made that place deny all previous rule, and kneel and bend according to his whim.' Despite his partial narrative, with waving hand and sad expression, Horatio began his story well. When, in previous times, I had been near him and he knew it, his manner was most proper and restrained. I liked him better in this passion. The resurrected king and queen were puppets in his drama and Fortinbras, himself no stranger to ambitious bloodshed and deceit, gasped and gape-mouthed at Horatio's torrid tale.

But then the story's sprightly pace declined into an elegiac crawl: too much young Hamlet and his noble rage – his fearless frankness and his broken heart – and dull, repetitive laudation of the seeming wondrous prince. Here my recollection fails. Prince Hamlet's praise released Horatio's grasp on my attention. I picked at masonry and stretched and squirmed and fidgeted in my narrow lair. My thoughts were drawn to poor Queen Gertrude but I could not let them linger there. When I had watched her fall I swung my focus all around, avoiding detail of her tortured end. But everywhere I looked she lay, a squirming backdrop to the centre-stage. Even there in darkness, eyes shut tight, essential patterns of her agony seemed imprinted on my disobedient mind. On hearing shreds of ghost-talk, I turned a tearful eye once more to observation. 'It was old Hamlet's spirit,' said Horatio. The words hung in the air like clotted smoke. 'I asked its purpose, but no answer gave it to my questioning.' I smiled as wide-eyed Fortinbras looked to his left then right, studying each shadow for a spectre, though all around him lay the undisputed dead. Fearless Fortinbras, unmanned by superstition – wan-faced, shallow-breathed and all a-tremble – as never seen amidst the battle's storm, clutched Horatio's hand and made him swear his story was no after dinner turn, more often told with candle at his chest to cloak his face in shadowy effect. How the warrior faltered at the unseen foe – the murky malevolence of the vaporous realm. It was good sport but still I stood impatient for my own part in the tale. When it came, Horatio scarcely left me time to bow. He laboured long upon my father's part, as if to echo that same parent's windbag way. Though, unlike me, Horatio was no witness to the murder, he told in detail, how poor Hamlet unaware did take the life of my secreted sire. He spoke as advocate, intent to clear his Prince's name and wipe the accusing gore from Hamlet's blade.

Then suddenly, 'Polonius had a daughter, who ached in vain desire for Hamlet's love. On hearing of her father's awful accident, she drowned herself and left her brother, brave Laertes, twice bereaved, twice fervent in revenge. That same misled Laertes lying lifeless now, beside poor Hamlet's corpse.'

This last scene, though brief, had much to criticise. In parts he lied, in others was deceived. I ached for Hamlet but only ached for him to end his whining suit. My eyes did ache but only from the notes and tedious poetry he slid beneath my bolted door or pressed, with feverish urgency, into my incomplicit hand. But here Horatio played the loyal friend and rendered me a foolish girl. He never told of powdered lies and much-repeated promises. He never said, 'They spoke of crowns and carriages. He called her "Princess" and "my future wife".' I stood veiled at my own uncovered grave and watched Lord Hamlet weep and moan. His motivation was not grief for me but only that he might out-mourn my tear-smeared brother, discomposed by his unpunctual guilt. Those two jousted for the agony-rights and Hamlet, desperate to be recognised as the most tortured soul, screamed like a frustrated child determined none would match his towering desolation. An instant later he stood separate from the throng and, with Horatio, shared seafaring yarns that painted him adventurous and brave. No slight or subtle reddening of the eye suggested he had sobbed so soon before. I see from here only Hamlet's feet and have no yearning to see more.

On hearing this inaccurate account – my own part shrunk to mere adornment – I rolled my neck and shoulders, took deep breaths and set myself to make my glorious entrance. I rattled at the heavy latch and watched them startled to their feet. They waved their swords and called aloud to hide their fear of what might issue forth. I shoved against the secret door with such force it swung open to the full. The accompanying thud and dust near drew their eyes out from their heads. They stared silent in alert anticipation. I counted three then stepped into the room. Fortinbras, though shaken by the sudden noise, seemed much relieved to see me standing there. He was confused and curious but not afraid. He did not take me for a walking ghost. But poor Horatio, at his side, gurgled in jaw-dropped disbelief at sweet Ophelia, risen from the levelled ground. His trembling wonder made me smile in secret reminiscence of a previous performance that had set his hair on end. I coyly bowed my head to hide my smirking. I had, by then, an overflowing basket deep in actorly tricks which I selected with great care to suit my various ends. I told my tale, reluctant, blushing and with tears. 'It was not me the soil was thrown upon,' I said, 'but my poor father, killed by Hamlet.' This detail's sudden bluntness shook Horatio as I knew it would. I had no special urge to damn Lord Hamlet, but yearned to make his old friend twitch and twist. Now, shaken by this rival voice, this differing stress, this contradictory air, and eager to defend both Hamlet and the trueness of the tale, Horatio made to interrupt me but I would not yield so early in my speech. 'My sweet prince,' I continued, loud enough to quash all interjection, 'who loved my father like he loved his own dead sire but who, with actions well intended, was moved by trembling tapestry to reckless thrusting that sent poor Polonius heavenward.' Now, I enjoyed my tale too much. To name my father for alliteration's sake seemed to make me not myself. And playing me was still my strongest skill – all stories wrapped in delicate maiden-silk. I doused my wordiness with tears and my still-attentive audience, aching for explanations, bid me continue if I could. I spoke of vile King Claudius who nuzzled and nudged me like a straining beast, eager to pin me 'neath his heated guts. 'At all times opportune, he pulled me to a doorway or pressed me to a wall and whispered crude suggestions through lips made reckless by that same wine that gathered into slime-strands and globules at the bubbling corners of his hot, lascivious mouth.' For this last speech I approached the corpse of Claudius and pointed at that gaping mouth now red, with blood not wine. In my authentic rage I spat upon the dead king's carcass, unaware the impact till I heard my audience gasp. I hurried to conclusion, distracting them from my unguarded act – my angry desecration.

'In endless repetition I wept and swore my only love was Hamlet but this rebuttal only fuelled great rage and, with a rhythmic pounding of the wall, his fat fist growing red and swollen with each stroke, Claudius vowed to bring about the death of my sweet prince, that he might take me as his own. "But your good wife, the mother ..." I protested. "I would kill them both," he said, examining his bloody hand, "to free this fretful and restricted passion." I had them again. They barely moved. They barely breathed; determined no intrusive sound should mask a syllable of my tale.

'So to his wife, Prince Hamlet's mother, I did in desperation turn. She had harboured dark suspicion which my words now shone bright light upon. Our plot, conceived hugger-mugger in this palace of whispers, required me to be no more. Then, all motive for sweet Hamlet's murder gone, I would to a nunnery, with good Gertrude's help, where I'd become invisible to men, hidden by the veil and left in peace. I heard, from my dark hiding place, loyal Gertrude paint me, in the glassy stream, a poor wretch in garments heavy with their drink. The portrait was so pitiful, I wept at my own drowning. But women such as we were poorly formed for counterfeits and scheming. Events we meant to mould have spun into misshapen form. Poor Gertrude and my sweet, sweet prince ...'

At this point, I allowed some time for them to chew this furious feast. Released from speech I fell to weeping, gazing on dead Hamlet, prematurely robed in funeral garb. I thought to throw myself upon his body, to show some desperation at his loss, but my yearning for Horatio already scratched within the shell. A falling on the corpse might hint that I could love no other and the nunnery gates would swing ajar once more. I took my listeners' hands in mine. 'Royal Fortinbras, wise Horatio, I beg you, help me. I am all alone. My father and my brother killed . . .' Here, I, stuttering, sensed a shortfall in my scene. I had not mourned my lately murdered brother. I turned to his vacated corpse, already greening at the gills. 'Sweet Laertes gone,' I groaned, as if recalling happy times. It tasted of an afterthought – some geegaw added, at departure, to the garment of my grief – but my audience, once won, would not, in haste, desert me. They took my tale as wholly true and blessed me for my bravery and candour.

Breakfast herrings and hot bread creep in scented tendrils all around me. Soon, reluctant knocking and a barely whispered 'mistress' will test my slumber's depth. I sleep so well my easy sleep uneases me. Should I not lie in guilt-chilled alertness, staring into endless night? Am I so lost no phantom nags or dares to raise a reprimanding finger in the gloom? Instead, sunk in silken pillows I join the rhythm of my husband's breathing and melt into dreamless peace. I am more disturbed by this scent of sizzling onions than by my previous deceptions and sinister designs.

The ghost was my great triumph. Mighty Hamlet thought himself so brave to approach the spectre, but to *be* the spectre was to cast the dice with all possession placed at stake. In the old king's armour did I walk but my talent was my true defence. My great grey beard and greasepaint-darkened brow were not a compensation for my skills but rather served as supplement to artistry. Interior workings steered the transformation and gave the king more life than God had ever granted. The dead king was the living king enhanced. I took his voice but gave that sound more substance. Finer thought, more eloquently, did the ghost express than any speech old Hamlet spluttered forth. My king, no blustering braggart, told not tedious tales of boar-hunts and battle-fields. His words made 'each particular hair to stand on end, like quills upon the fretful porcupine'. The memory of it rouses not my conscience but my pride. What painted player could do what I did then, my audi-ence inches from my face and their displeasure darker threat than catcalls and decaying fruit? I was the king and he the better for my being him.

I grow now self-absorbed and arrogant. Could I have played my role so well without direction and external eye? Fair Gertrude knew each nod and sniffle of old Hamlet's way. She tutored me in every vowel and gesture, robed me in his garments and regalia and, at my mirror, trimmed and glued and smoothed me into him. I shed no tear for my good father and my brother dead. Nor for dithering Hamlet do I weep. The life of Claudius was an insult to Heaven, his death a meagre recompense for vile misdeeds. But, when I think of Gertrude's gentle hand upon my face, her patience and instruction, her courage and her love, then do I cry for secret moments and mourn our common time.

He chose me first, the serpent Claudius, but I did never tell her that. I was still journeying to womanhood, between the schoolroom and the lady's chamber, when he first lingered upon me. Soon he took to tracing his fat finger down my soft white neck and stroking those exposed parts of my barely swollen breasts. With that same finger he would ease apart my trembling lips and stroke my tongue until I gagged – part at his probing, part at the sourness of his all-intrusive breath. He wanted more. I always fled in terror and he never called me back. Instead he sought my father and together they discussed the deal. Old Hamlet's grave was still yet fresh when Claudius and my goodly father spoke. The dark and narrow passageway within the wall, found by chance amidst a hiding-game, did serve me well and keep me safe. I never feared its spider webs and scurry-sounds. It soon became my second home, or should I say my first, for as the web of my contrivance grew, that passage was the only place I truly was myself.

'Take Gertrude first,' my loyal father said. 'King Hamlet's death has loosed the foothold of our state. Your own rights are much questioned, young Hamlet's much advanced. To kill the king tore down the sails of our great galleon. New canvas must be well secured or we may be becalmed and free to plunder. Ophelia is young, better ripened than rushed. Take Gertrude first for she has still the people's love. When all's settled, she too may sleep and, by thy leperous distilment meet her end.'

Tears did agitate my cheeks, I will admit, when I still-hidden, heard my father's words. My love for him fell off me like a cloak. My hatred of fat Claudius grew keener as they spoke but, looking back, I'll this confession make. His deferment of me – his ability to wait – angered me more than murder of our king. His wild-horse lust soon bowed to take the bridle when ambition cracked its domineering whip. I thought he lived for me. I thought he wrung his knuckle-gnawed hands and mouthed my silent name. He did not. My cold curse condemned them both. A few days later, I observed Laertes laugh to hear the deal outlined. 'She is our future guaranteed,' my father said, and rubbed his hands together with the thrill. I joined my brother to the list of my impatient threefold curse.

This herring's good and I sit, pillow-propped, left to eat in peace. This morning I'll take honeyed wine. Since my resurrection, simple has sufficed. Wild wassail can loosen lips and I must only speak with utmost care. Today, I'm keen to tell the chilling tale, to lay myself and my behaviour bare. I planned, with Gertrude as my guide, that I'd return to tasks well done before. I'd recreate my spectral role but this time greybeard kingship would not walk. Pale, piteous Ophelia would, in Hamlet's chamber, suddenly appear. My goading ghost to old King Hamlet's would have reinforcement been, in hope the cowering prince would be more frightened of these doubled dark petitioners than of the raging consequence of striking Claudius down. Relieved of heavy armour and constraining paste, that held my beard and rat-tail strands secure – with my own voice, allowing me more nuance and affect – what wondrous magic I'd have weaved. Hamlet, guilt-filled and aghast would surely at my word have ventured forth, with manful strides towards the sacred throne, and sliced the head of Claudius from its trunk, despite the attendant court's full-vantaged view. I like cruel Salome would have laughed to hold the dripping dome and stare into its fear-expanded eyes and tug the dribbling offal at its base. I would have said 'You used me badly, Claudius. Your only caring gesture came when I was, you supposed, no more and on some unread document you scrawled that I might be entombed within the consecrated ground.'

How Queen Gertrude sighed when I, in my naivety, suggested we ask Hamlet straight to be the right arm of our rightful and revenging quest. 'We must instead,' she said, 'raise our inferno high, a blazing heap of terrifying ire, that by its stature it might drive the prince toward the lesser flames.' If only we two could have dealt the blow and freed the task from conscience-care and yellow-backed meandering debate. There would have been no reticence or ritual – no last-word graces or respectful air – but rather simple severance of the undeserving life – a bloody and yet businesslike dispatch. But minstrel-songs that rose above the tankard-clamour, the mongrel's yapping and the strumpet's mock-delight, whispered of a politic ambition and the godless gloom of regicidal night. To kill the killer-king, albeit amputation of a cankerous limb, would seem, to many, further crime against the consecrated crown. Only Hamlet, cleansed by right revenge could gain forgiveness from the rabble roused and take his place unchallenged at the helm. And then the Queen and I might, on each arm and at each ear, have steered him wisely through the storms of state.

But all that's gone. The Queen, my sweet confederate, lies in the ground where worms eschew her poisoned flesh. And Hamlet, our blunt blade, is slaughtered by an all too sharper sword. For him I care little – the others less – but Gertrude lingers in my mournful mind. By relentless and perceptive observation, I could have grasped the plot and by corrective measures, redesigned its end. I could have saved sweet Gertrude from that dance of death, and by a predetermined antidote preserved Prince Hamlet, our convenient heir. In truth, my immature thrill at choosing my own funeral dress distracted and intoxicated me and in my shrill excitement I released the reins. So much studied scheming, then to stumble at a sable-silken gown.

That's all. I've spoken full. Come out now, husband. Your noisy subterfuge below did not divert my mandatory watchfulness. I know you have, for weeks unnumbered, hidden in my former shade and watched me in my private time. Did you anticipate some secret suitor or an unshared peccadillo you might furtively observe? Come out, Horatio. I know the lure of that sequestered place. All I said I said because I knew your shadowed presence. I chose to end my play-making but found it hard to empty all while you were in my eye. This morning, eased by honeyed wine and your unseen attentions, I've removed my cold and unresponsive mask that you might kiss or spit upon my true, untutored face. Step out now – push aside the wall – and let your touch, caressful or unkind, be real and unrestricted, your Ophelia redefined.

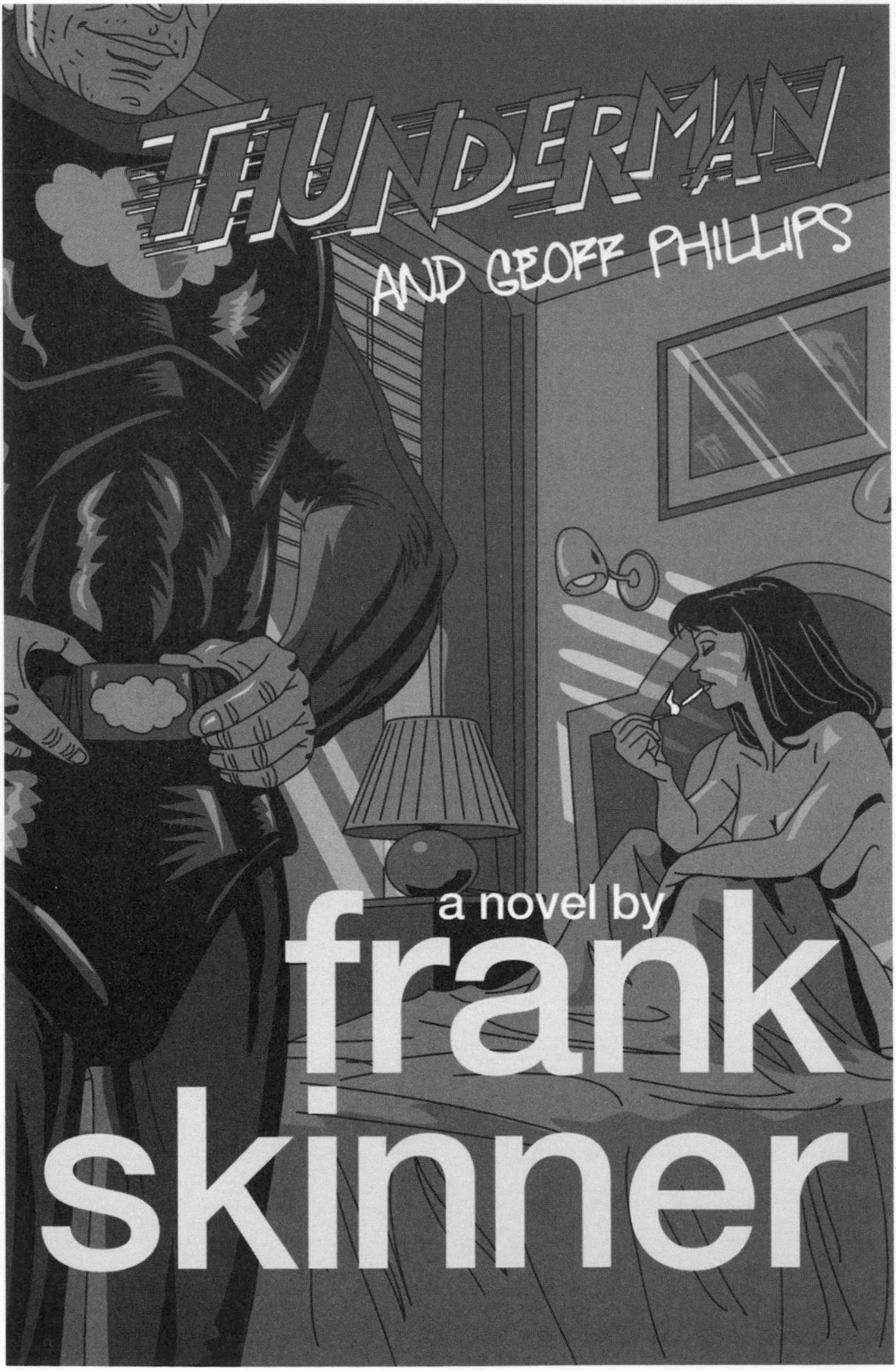
THUNDERMAN
AND GEOFF PHILLIPS
a novel by
frank
skinner

MY GREAT UNFINISHED NOVEL
(WELL, THE FIRST TWO CHAPTERS)

Thunderman and Geoff Phillips by Frank Skinner

CHAPTER ONE

As he stood in the crowded function room at the Majestica Hotel, Geoff let the long, thin strip of beef jerky lay across his upturned palms and stared at it as if it contained vital information; as if he were reading it; as if the greedy paper-barons had finally flattened all the world's beautiful forests and mankind, now completely devoid of paper, was having to print on beef; as if Geoff now stood beside a hastily constructed beef teleprinter machine and read the latest news from beef ticker tape which, as it jerkily, yes, jerkily emerged from the steadily overheating contraption, filled his nostrils with the smell of the slaughterhouse. Oh, we took paper for granted but, without it, the world had become a grotesque pantomime where books, leather bound with beefy pages, were now scientifically classified as: cattle (inanimate). Thus, the once pure, cleansing flame of the foot-and-mouth bonfire now brought to mind old footage of brownshirts, twirling literature into the inferno. One publisher had gone so far as to include, with each volume, a complete cow's tail, connected to the spine of the book just as, in life, it had been connected to the spine of the cow. Each of these tailed volumes bore a sticker that said, 'With organic bookmark'. The tail was a hit, combining, as it did, both novelty value and practicality, but some sensitive readers were disturbed, as they moved the bookmark into position, by the sound of crackling cartilage.

Publishers were, one might say, having a field day, with regular books and talking books now classified, simply as 'herd' and 'heard'.

Of course, none of this had actually happened. It was just something that sprang to mind when you saw how he held that jerky.

Geoff, not being party to the authorial voice, was off on his own flight of fancy. This was the first time he had held beef jerky; indeed, the first time he had seen it. But he liked the name, 'beef jerky'. He thought it sounded like some desperate phase a cow might pass through when coming off drugs the hard way. He could picture the poor beast, twitching and snorting as it thudded its head against the wall of a clinical, white-tiled room, pathetically mooing for one more fix, whilst, in an adjoining office, a bespectacled man in a lab coat, gazed in through a two-way mirror, making the occasional note on his report sheet: '17.06 – Some frothing at the mouth. 17.40 – Lies down. 17.51 – Starting to rain. A connection?'

'Is everything OK?' The voice of an American male popped Geoff's cow-in-rehab bubble and, suddenly, with the jerky still laid on his upturned palms, he was back in the real world. As he refocused, there remained a faint whiff of disinfectant left over from the imaginary clinic, and also, confusingly, a vague smell of slaughterhouse that he couldn't quite place.

He turned towards the voice. A tall, clumsily large man, in an unfortunate bright-blue suit, stood smiling at him. I mean, really smiling. Geoff had read somewhere that it took 43 muscles to frown but only 17 to smile. This smile seemed to be using a lot more than that. This smile, though Geoff didn't realise it at the time, was an American corporate smile. It sent out the usual smile-signals like 'I'm happy' and 'I'm friendly' but the more discerning recipient sensed that these only served as an attractive outer-coating for a core-message that said 'I'll kill you if I have to'.

Liberace smiled like this. His teeth were like unblemished ivory panelling, reflecting the rainbow-flashes from his bejewelled fingers as they scampered across the keyboard. But behind the swirling mists of breath-freshener, he lay bald, spread-eagled, and braced for sodomy, whimpering under the brutal assault of a cynical young football player, just as the respectable old ladies whimpered when he signed their souvenir programmes. But, hey, that was Liberace. What secrets lay behind this capped and straightened façade?

'You look puzzled,' said the man, widening his eyes and raising his eyebrows as he spoke, as if he knew the physical practicalities of forming words would interfere with the perfectness of his smile, so was using other parts of his face as a sort of temporary decoy.

Geoff wondered how many muscles this extra-curricular smile-work brought into play. Clearly, estimating muscle-usage in this way was a tricky business. On the surface, a frown seemed much less exacting than a smile, yet, according to statistics, it used two and a half times as many muscles. Maybe the American's upper-face shenanigans were actually using fewer muscles than Geoff's puzzled look. Geoff smiled, thus moving his muscle-usage back into charted territory. On the lapel of the bright-blue suit was a badge that said 'Billiam Moore. Morton's Beef Jerky'.

'This is my first time,' Geoff said, raising the jerky a little higher, like he was offering it up as a sacrifice. Of course, the real sacrificial offering was Geoff's confession that, when it came to jerky, he was a stranger in a strange land. He was saying to this man: 'I have no experience whatsoever in an area where you are clearly an expert so, for the next few minutes, I am happy to play the part of your slightly awestruck acolyte, dazzled and delighted as you weave your beefy spell. I stand at your altar, with my jerky slightly raised, and wait passively for you to initiate me into its mysteries.'

'Well, enjoy,' said the man and walked away. Maybe it was just as well. Geoff had already begun to worry that he might, instinctively, spit in the face of the American if, during the course of his jerky sermon, he should happen to use the word 'math'.

Geoff looked around the room. There were probably three hundred people; a lot of them journalists but Geoff also recognised a few fan-club people, and Keith Hell, the comic-book artist. All had laminated passes that bore the symbol of a grey cloud with a bright red '50' across it. Each pass was a collectors' item. High above the hotel, eBay hovered, vulture-like. Geoff took the jerky in his left hand, allowing his right to check that his own pass was still there. It was, and that knowledge brought a warm tingle. 'Here I stand,' he thought, 'in the very midst of the laminatti. Entitled to be here; entitled to be, eventually, in his presence; to hear him speak and maybe, even, to speak to him.'

'Would you like a drink?' said an approaching hotel employee in a slightly-too-tight red acrylic uniform. She too smiled a corporate smile, but hers was British corporate: professional but with humanity leaking out at the edges. This smile could hide maybe a hangover or PMT but there was no sense of sequestered menace, no sugarcoated threat or distant shriek of sodomy stringendo. This smile, whilst paid for by the Majestica Hotel, was not big enough, nor opaque enough, to completely obscure the human being behind it. British corporate smiles never are. Oh, it said, in large block capitals, 'Welcome to the Majestica Hotel' but it also said, in letters only slightly smaller 'I'm just a woman with big ankles, trying to make a living.'

As she poured white wine into his glass, Geoff eyed the rectangular name badge on her red acrylic jacket: 'Karen. Events assistant'. He was beginning to enjoy the easy accessibility of these pin-on potted biographies. Would the world not be a better place if everyone wore a badge with his or her name and profession on it? There'd be no more office juniors sobbing into their alcopops because the manager called them Jane instead of Julie, no more internationally acclaimed soul divas outraged at being told, as they arrived at the stage door, that the other cleaners were already in the auditorium. Life would be simpler and less painful and, having passed a carefree hour in an all-night amusement arcade, the corpulent businessman would not, in all innocence, offer a lift home to that feverish youth in the 'Kyle. Rent Boy' badge.

'Can I ask you a question, Karen?' Geoff said, as if addressing an old friend. She suddenly became visibly alarmed. Her muscle-usage must have been nearing three figures.

'How do you know my name? Who are you?' she said. Both these lines of questioning betrayed a lack of badge-awareness that Geoff found unacceptable in an events assistant. Then it occurred to him that she might be about to scream. 'It's on your badge,' he blurted out. She looked down at her lapel. She couldn't quite make it out from this angle, but there was a badge there, with words on it, and sometimes you just had to trust people.

The truth is she didn't even try to read the badge, knowing from past experience that reading upside down was not one of her gifts. She had once found herself, during an illicit affair with an optician, sprawled across his desk, in an act of full sexual intercourse. Flat on her back, legs in the air, she lay, gazing upward, as, with each forward thrust, his face drew closer to hers and then, on the corresponding backstroke, drew further away again. She slowly became aware that, each time the optician's face retreated; it went slightly out of focus. 'Oh, dear,' she had thought to herself, 'I think my eyesight might be deteriorating,' at which point, she decided to take advantage of her surroundings and squeeze in an impromptu, mid-coital eye-test. Leaning her head back over the edge of the desk, she located a chart and began the examination. She chuckled to herself when she noticed that, as a freak side effect of her particular situation, the bottom line was clearer than the top one. This led her to consider, in a down-to-earth, events assistant kind of a way, how different people viewed the same thing from different perspectives, different points of view, and how much trouble this had brought into the world. At the same time, however, she couldn't help thinking how refreshing it was to view a familiar thing in a completely new way.

Then, drawing back from the bigger picture, she switched her concentration once more to the eye chart. She was surprised to see that, though some of the letters were perfectly clear, she was unable to identify them, not because of faulty vision but because she simply couldn't, it became apparent, read upside down.

Anyway, she resolved to check her name badge in the mirror later because, whilst upside-down reading was beyond her, she knew for sure she could read backwards.

She had discovered this whilst having an illicit affair with an office executive at her previous place of employment. As she, pinioned across his desk, facedown this time, having learnt her lesson at the optician's, hastened towards climax, she realised that she had completely forgotten the executive's name and therefore had nothing to call out during her special moment. Luckily, he had a Perspex name-plaque on his desk, but there was a complication. She lay looking out towards the now-locked office door but the plaque was for the benefit of people entering through that door and thus was turned away from her. She was concerned that the executive might notice if she suddenly, mid-groan, spun the plaque around to face her. True, he hadn't objected to her turning around the two or three framed photographs of his wife and children that were about eight inches from her nose, but that, she reasoned, was because he had genuine respect for her feelings. He might not be quite so understanding when he realised she was using his office name-plaque as an aide-memoire. That, she felt, might cause genuine offence. So, ever resourceful, she cleverly read the words through the back of the Perspex sign, undeterred by the fact that they appeared in reverse. As it turned out, her diplomacy was somewhat undone when, contorted with ecstasy, she finally screamed out 'Chief Executive Officer'.

The awkwardness of the moment increased further when her flailing arm sent a picture frame crashing to the floor, the suddenly cracked glass fracturing the joyous expressions of a loving couple and their two handsome sons, on a sunny day out at a popular theme park.

Geoff could see that Karen, having checked her badge, had calmed somewhat. The smile was back, and it looked like she'd called a few extra muscles into the fray, or was it a few less? 'Anyway, what is your question, Geoff?' she said. She was a quick learner. 'If you want me to pose topless in the *Daily Star*, I'm afraid you're out of luck.' It was a conversational bombshell and, as the smoke cleared, Geoff could see that her smile had taken a good deal of the blast.

The remark had caused him discomfort on two counts. Firstly, even before she'd finished the sentence, somewhere between 'Daily' and 'afraid', he'd looked at her breasts. They were, of course, completely covered, by her red acrylic jacket and pink acrylic blouse, but Geoff's look had suggested that this was no obstacle to his all-seeing glare. He had looked at them the way a dog looks at a tin of dog food, unable, of course, to see the contents but absolutely certain that his feverish anticipation, based not just on experience but on some sort of mystical intuition, would not be in vain. Geoff knew she had seen his look and she knew that he knew. It was her own fault. She had been deliberately frivolous because she felt guilty, was trying to compensate, for having thought, when he called her Karen, that she had recognised in his manner the tell-tale overfamiliarity of the habitual sex offender. She was trying to make up for this irrational slur. She was trying to say, 'I trust you so much, I will give you the thrill of hearing me say "topless", because we both know it's just a bit of harmless fun, and you are, I now realise, not the kind of man who would make that moment sordid by looking at my admittedly ample breasts.' But she had overcompensated, she had given too much, and he had repaid her trust with a leering disrespect.

The second source of discomfort for Geoff was that, despite what it said on his laminate, he did not actually work for the *Daily Star*. It was a ruse. He would have done anything to be at this reception and so he had lied, and now he would probably have to lie again, but not, this time, with a phone call or a letter on mocked-up *Daily Star* headed notepaper. No, this time he would have to tell his lie face-to-face, to Karen, the events assistant. He was already blushing about the breast glance. If he was forced into a period of sustained dishonesty, his face would generate such heat that someone would have to open a window. Then he saw Karen gaze at his crotch, for about four seconds. Oh no, his zip must be undone but, with a wineglass in one hand and jerky in the other, he was helpless. She would think that, having looked at her breasts, he was unable to restrain his great brute of a penis and it was now, even as they spoke, battling to get at her. He felt his blush increase in intensity. He couldn't think straight. Before he could stop himself, he had mopped his brow with the beef jerky. Again, that faint smell of the slaughterhouse.

In fact, his zip was not undone. She had stared at his crotch by way of retaliation for him staring at her breasts. She was raised on Girl Power and, though she may have suffered past humiliations – like when she realised her Chief Executive Officer spent most of their desk-time trying to exactly match the rhythm of his Newton's Cradle – she had vowed that no man would ever misuse her again. Especially one who dabbed himself with processed meat in a four-star hotel.

As Geoff used the stiff edge of the beef jerky to slowly squeegee-out his sweat-sodden eyebrows, flicking the debris into the air as he completed the action, he could not help but notice Karen's disapproving look. 'Maybe she's Hindu,' he thought. He felt sure there must be white Hindus. And while they might arouse suspicion and accusations of insincerity from their co-religionists on the Asian sub-continent, they were certainly capable of being offended by the sight of someone using a section of sacred animal as a makeshift sweat extruder. What else could have caused a disapproving look of such intensity? Then it occurred to him that to look directly at the breasts of a Hindu woman was also probably a great blasphemy. Inevitably, this thought caused him to look at them again. His face was generating such heat now that, had he a selection of herbs and spices, he could have, by cradling the glass against his cheek, mulled the wine she had just poured for him. She was looking at him expectantly. Was she waiting for an apology? Or was she waiting for his response to her *Daily Star* remark? His throat tightened as he considered the latter task. He knew she didn't *really* think he was about to offer her a glamour model career but, despite that, any comeback was still a diplomatic minefield. If he suggested her appearance in the *Star* was out of the question, she might take it as a slur on her physical appearance, if he apparently warmed to the idea, he might offend her Hindu sensibilities. He looked at the small stage, halfway down the room. Would *he* really stand there?

She couldn't believe he had looked at her breasts a second time. She would have slapped his face if she'd had easy access to an oven glove. Or would she? To her surprise, that rage she had anticipated, that rage she would use to fuel her verbal onslaught on this all-too-typical representative of the gutter press, this paparazzi, who thought he could treat her like a prostitute, just because she was curvy, that rage did not manifest itself. But something was happening. At first, she was unsure but then, all at once, she recognised the warm, invigorating glow of pride. She was flattered. Oh, he knew she'd caught him looking at her breasts. That's why he'd blushed. But, despite his embarrassment, and her revenging crotch-stare, he just couldn't stop himself from looking again. The need was too strong. OK, it might have been purely professional. He might have been imagining how she'd look in the *Daily Star*, wearing tiny briefs and a Liberty's bracelet, sharing the page with a story about a woman from Maidstone who'd found half a rat in a bag of crisps, but so what? It was too early for him to know how he really felt about her.

She would take it easy, not make the same mistakes she'd made in the past. She was glad she'd done her roots last night, glad she'd lipsticked just before the reception, glad, even, that she was wearing a matching bra and pants. Room 410 was empty. She knew that for a fact. She'd been on top form just lately: new job, new regime – gym twice a week, regular sun beds, regular wax. It was as if she knew, instinctively, that opportunity was about to knock. She'd often thought she might be psychic. There was that time Auntie Marge had stood on a three-pin plug and had to go to hospital. Just a few days before, Karen had dreamt about Auntie Marge. OK, there was no plug involved; in fact, the 16-stone, middle-aged Marge had been weeing into a box of chocolates and then turned into some sort of chair but still, it was quite a coincidence. Karen imagined Auntie Marge, sometime in the near-distant future, making snotty remarks about her doing topless and immediately resolved not to send her a Christmas card this year. Karen smiled, in an extremely non-corporate way, as she visualised the fat bitch stepping out into the wintry street, wearing only her nightdress, calling after the postman, asking him to check that Karen's card had not become wedged in one of the post bag's internal folds, and then, as the postman shook his head, the now-disappointed Marge trudging mournfully back into her house, leaving three-pin plug marks in the morning snow.

Why shouldn't she be a topless model? It would be a whole new lifestyle for her; the eye chart viewed from another angle. OK, there was the ankle thing, but maybe her signature, not-quite-nude accessory, could be eighties-style leg warmers. Other tabloids might take the Mickey but she would rather be called 'the saddo *Kids from Fame* wannabe', by a rival paper, than 'the busty, elephant-ankled stunner' by her own. And as for the unsightly brown birthmark on her left inner thigh, that never stopped John-Boy Walton and his was on his face.

'I just want you to know,' said Geoff. 'I have massive respect for the Eastern religions. I cried when George Harrison died.' As he said this, an image of Karen rose up in his mind. She wore a red acrylic sari, a name badge inscribed with Eastern-style squiggly writing, and an ankle-bracelet that would serve most women as a belt. Around and around she spun, her twirling torso creating a whirlpool in the joss-stick mist, as a tiny band of Indian musicians banged out a frantic instrumental version of 'Got My Mind Set On You'.

'Now, who's overcompensating?' she thought to herself. It was a rhetorical question but that's internal dialogue for you. This young man, she was guessing about 25, disenchanted by long days spent door-stepping the parents of missing children and picking used condoms out of soap stars' dustbins, had become ashamed of his own profession. He ached for her but knew she couldn't be won over by the tabloid trappings of champagne and jacuzzis. So, now, desperate to win her love, he was painting a picture of himself as a sensitive, spiritual soul, a man untarnished by the squalid tittle-tattle he peddled, a man who washed his inky fingers in tears the day that bloke who played Han Solo died. She didn't even know he *had* died. No wonder he wasn't in the later ones. Or were they earlier ones? She could never work that out.

She looked at Geoff's crotch again but not, this time, as an act of retribution. Now, she was saying, quite deliberately, 'I too am unable to resist a second look.'

Oh, no. His fly was definitely undone and he had to act fast. He put the jerky in his mouth, reached downward with his now free hand, and began probing at his genital area, his fingers searching the full length of his zip for gaps.

She smiled another un-corporate smile. Oh, he could cry the bitter tears of bereavement, and talk about Eastern religions till the sacred cows came home, but his body language told a very different story: he had swollen to the point of discomfort and was hungry for sweat-smeared meat.

His zip was not undone. 'Maybe she has a lazy eye,' he thought. He tried to remember whether she had looked crotchward with one eye or two. Was it possible that both eyes could be lazy? What was a lazy eye? It seemed to be one of those medical problems that had become unfashionable, like flat feet. 'They should make a programme about it: a sort of medical "Where are they now?"' he thought. Karen must be some sort of throwback. He noticed a plaster on her heel, previously obscured by a Brobdingnagian ankle. There was some redness there. The skin was broken. 'Probably trench foot,' he concluded. He bit into the jerky and tore the remainder from his clenched teeth. She winced.

For the seventeenth time since his arrival, he looked nervously towards the opening door. But it was just another laminatti, with shoulder bag and Che Guevara T-shirt, looking around, recognising someone, melting into the crowd.

'I don't work for that bit of the *Star*,' he replied. 'I do the writing, not the pictures.' She was a little disappointed by his elitist tone. Was he really suggesting that her semi-nakedness was somehow inferior to the tale of the half-rat, her full-breasts and Liberty's bracelet the poor cousin of the ready-salted rodent? He'd let her down like they all let her down. Her new love, her new career, lay, like that snapshot of a once happy family, fractured and forlorn. She had really tried this time. She'd said 'topless' and gone back for crotch-stare seconds but the fitted-sheet in Room 410 would remain unsullied.

Geoff now remembered his original question, the thing that had been nagging at him, the reason he had spoken to Karen in the first place. He had not been in many four-star hotels, didn't know the ropes, couldn't speak the lingo, but it seemed odd to him that anyone would call a function room, 'The Jack the Ripper Suite'.

'I was wondering about the room,' he said. She gasped. Once again, it seemed, the fitted-sheet was up for grabs.

'It's empty,' she said, deliberately taking the edge off her South London accent in order to give the words more weight. He looked around the room, certainly three hundred people, possibly four. Perhaps her statement was informed by some branch of Hindu metaphysics that dismissed modern materialism and the ensuing spiritual vacuum as a sort of emptiness. This was a daunting, indeed damning, view of the world, but it presented him with an opportunity to show her that he respected her beliefs and her intellect and was not, in any way, trying to imagine her naked breasts. 'So, if the room's empty, where does that leave us?' he said.

The pulses in her neck caused her dangly earrings to vibrate slightly. Was this man, with his straggly ginger hair and the shaving-cuts on his neck, to be her destiny? Oh, he was ginger, very ginger. In fact, he had such a high level of gingerness that even his teeth seemed slightly ginger. Suddenly, it was her and Geoff at the theme park with their two handsome sons. She smiled to herself. Her naturally dark hair had won the genetic arm-wrestle that decides these things and both boys were brunette, if boys can be brunette. There was a slight hint of ginger in the younger son, but Karen reassured herself that this was just the sunlight bouncing off the artificially created rapids that splashed and sparkled their way around the park's white-water rafting ride. But wait. Her genetic dominance may have lain waste the ginger hordes but this victory brought with it a terrible consequence.

She focused now on the boys' grinning faces. Childhood's grin rarely comprises the purity we impose upon it. We want to see a freshness unpolluted by experience, a suggestion that they still hear, albeit faintly, the angelic music which filled that mystical place from which their tiny souls so recently emerged. But experience starts early and the seemingly innocent grin that warms our heart is often triggered, not by celestial flashbacks, but by the pained expression of another. Maybe the snivel-ling grimace of a more timid classmate, rabbit-punched into a fun-free zone of exhausted isolation by a daily dosage of whispered threat and undercover violence; or perhaps the wide-eyed terror of a tiny, tremu-lous mouse, sticky-taped, on a sweet summer's day, to a jam jar filled with tiddlers, and then burnt and blistered by the bright light of a carefully aimed magnifying glass, the twisted alchemy slowly turning sunshine into suffering, the creatures trapped within darting and diving as they sense the anguish of the creature trapped without.

Now, in the grins of her own children, Karen could see anguish. But not the reflected anguish of a smouldering rodent or a cowering contem-porary, not some dark suggestion of their cruelty to others. No, what she saw was the heart-breaking evidence of fate's cruelty to them, clouding every sunny day, undermining every grin. And despite the fact that these children were, as yet, imaginary, she could not construct and reconstruct them according to her design, she could not edit out the grim ingredient that cast its dark shadow across them; she could not, try as she might, erase the unsightly brown birthmark that marred their not-quite-happy faces. Somehow, she seemed to have cracked the protective glass on another happy family.

Well, she would not put those innocent boys through that ordeal. She would sooner sacrifice her own happiness. It was obvious that Geoff ached for her, and equally obvious that that passion would soon turn to love, but how long would that love last when their children came out piebald? It would be her fault and Geoff would never forgive her, and the children, when they weren't being kept awake at night by the fact they looked like Jack Russells, would be kept awake, instead, by the resentful recriminations of their parents' early hours screaming. At least John-Boy was surrounded by love, by people who didn't care if he was, in some areas, slightly chestnut. Her children would find no refuge from the dramas of discoloration. She could not be so selfish. With hardly a backward glance, she gave up her dream so that her children might be saved from pain. Truly, her heart was as big as her ankles.

'Anyway,' Geoff said, 'isn't it sort of bad taste to name a room after a serial killer?'

Quickly recovering from her recent loss, Karen answered him with a distinct tone of don't-be-so-ridiculous, and even a slight chuckle. 'Oh, no,' she explained, 'it's not *that* Jack the Ripper.' She noticed the new arrival in the Che Guevara T-shirt making 'I need a drink' hand-gestures and moved off towards him, leaving the man who was once her future, desperately trying to think of another Jack the Ripper, wondering how this other chap had qualified for such a nickname and, of course, how he'd coped with the endless jokes and misunderstandings that must have ensued.

Geoff would never know it but he had been only an unsightly brown birthmark away from full intercourse in Room 410. Karen had planned to show him the breasts he seemed so eager to explore but instead she showed him only a clean pair of heels, well, one clean heel and one slightly scabby one. 'While my trench foot gently weeps,' Geoff muttered to himself, as he watched her walk away.

Karen approached the thirsty newcomer, looked at his T-shirt and said, 'Oh, I love Enrique Iglesias.' The man smiled and then looked at her breasts. And the world continued to turn.

Geoff felt a sizzle of adrenalin. Four men in black News Channel T-shirts, who had been leaning against a wall, drinking wine and making slightly-too-loud defamatory remarks about a well-known sports reporter, suddenly moved towards their respective cameras and effects mics, put on headsets, and, as was ever their way, adopted a steely resolve to be unimpressed by whatever events were about to unfold. The overture was moving towards its crescendo.

Karen wittered on in the background – 'Che Guevara? Is that that French restaurant in Hoxton?' – giving no hint of the profound dialogues that bubbled within her. She had so nearly been the mother of Geoff's children but now, for him, she had ceased to exist. He didn't even notice her smile, now coloured by a maternal ache for what might have been, as she walked past him, empty bottle in hand, heading for the exit. He looked at the stage, at the door, at the cameramen, at the door, but not at her.

When he turned back to the stage, it was no longer empty. The American man had stepped up and moved towards the clear-plastic lectern. He slightly adjusted the attached microphone with his big, awkward hands and, after a presidential-bodyguard-style look around the room which, though brief, seemed to not only headcount the whole assembly but also to individually check their laminates, he switched his smile on to full-beam.

'Ladies and gentlemen, welcome, all 311 of you, to this very special event, sponsored, of course, by Morton's Beef Jerky. I'm Billiam Moore.'

Geoff gulped. When seeing the American's name badge earlier, he had assumed it was a misprint, an accidental hybrid of the informal and formal options, Bill and William. Geoff had imagined a late-night meeting to decide exactly what the badge should say; black coffee and cigarette smoke, voices raised and desks thumped, in an office high above the ragged splendour of the old city. Arguments, for and against, run and rerun till mayhem became mantra, and 'Will-Bill-Willie-Billy-William-Wills' bounced around the room like a children's skipping song. Then, the combatants, having stood together at the window watching a London sunrise, muttered their nothing-personals and departed. Only one remained, and he, with cigarette in one hand and short straw in the other, typed the name badge and tried to remember which conventions of lapel literature he was supposed to be adhering to.

But no, there was no amalgam. His name really was Billiam. Geoff felt suddenly elated. This man, who he had previously viewed with some suspicion, perhaps, after his bodyguard-stare, even a little fear, was called Billiam. The ridiculousness of the name enveloped Geoff in a contented glow. He loved this man, now. OK, he seemed very guarded, sinister even, but none of that mattered. Billiam might not have worn his heart on his sleeve but he wore his name on his lapel, and his name was Billiam, and for that Geoff could forgive him almost anything, including the fact that Morton's Beef Jerky tasted like it should only be sold in pet shops. His instinct now was to warmly applaud, whoop even, but, alas, he felt he had missed the moment.

Billiam, yes Billiam, continued. 'I believe it was Captain James T. Kirk who said, "If we wait any longer, the whole thing could blow to pieces."' He stared at the crowd like a teacher divining for guilt in a group of schoolboys. Suddenly, there was an uneasy tension in the room as 311 people tried to work out whether or not Billiam had just made a joke. There were few clues. He did not deliver the line as if it were a joke. In fact, he seemed to deliberately imbue it with gravitas, but, given that it was a quote from *Star Trek*, some felt he might be cleverly adopting this elevated tone in order to exploit the absurdity of his source.

He wasn't. The truth was misfortune had struck Billiam as he sat in his hotel room the previous evening; misfortune of the technological type, leaving him gently prodding at his laptop like a bitch nuzzling a dead puppy. The Internet was down and, as a direct consequence, so was Billiam. He needed some cyberspace. He was 48, had married aged 20, and was finding it more and more difficult to masturbate from memory. There was that girl at college but she had since died in an automobile accident. Calling to mind the curvature of her firm bottom now seemed disrespectful; the once-reliable erotic reminiscence made forever flaccid by the smell of embalming fluid.

Worse still, for it was always professional rather than personal pain he felt most keenly, he had yet to write his introductory speech for the Majestica event and the Famous Quotation websites, from which he filched almost all of his public-speaker wisdom, were now inaccessible.

He had phoned Reception and been told that the hotel's Internet room was closed for refurbishment. He had told the receptionist that he would be happy to work among paint pots and panelling but she just giggled and said, in a jolly tone, 'Sorry for any inconvenience caused, sir. Have a good evening,' and put the phone down. He was about to phone back and be less friendly but his dealing-with-people-who-work-in-hotels instinct told him the process would be like pushing a very large boulder up a very steep hill.

Of course, he was in a big city and Internet access was never far away. But he felt so comfortable, showered and scented, in his hotel robe and slippers. He really didn't fancy an early hours adventure among the tramps and travellers at the local cyber café. Besides, a communal computer could only solve the professional half of his problem. Then again, it was Thursday night in London's West End. He'd be sure to pass a drunken English girl, lying in her own vomit, skirt upturned to frame an ample thigh. He could freeze the image in his head, scamper back to his room and press playback. Or maybe he could stay out, find a bar, meet a girl with black hair ringletting down her forehead and a cigarette waiting to be lit. But no, he had hit the barrier that stops so many men from diving headlong into a film-noir nocturne of lipstick, tango and tequila. He was snug. He would turn on the TV and trawl for hotel porn, the pay-per-view pastime of so many businessmen away from home. As for the speech, he would break with his normal practice and deliver it sans quotation. It was only a brief preamble, after all.

The first channel was CNN. There was a coup somewhere in Africa. Billiam yawned. He hated so-called World News. It was always hurricanes or ethnics with automatic weapons. He flicked. A blonde girl with an Australian accent was stepping up and down on a gym machine specifically designed; it seemed, for stepping up and down on. Billiam wondered if this little lady might save him a pay-per-view fee but she was just too sporty. Dead or sporty, embalming fluid or embrocation, it was a bad night for dream-girls. He flicked. MTV. Some young men were on fire, and some other young men, who giggled a lot, were urinating on them in order to extinguish it. He flicked. National Geographic. He flicked. *Star Trek*. Captain Kirk, young and handsome, yet so wise. Billiam had an idea. They were always saying profound things in *Star Trek*. It was like an enjoyable version of Shakespeare. It was, well, quotable. Billiam picked up the hotel notepad and pencil from his bedside table. Usually his speech writing was a fusion of the old and the new; the recycled rationality of yesteryear, revamped and reinterpreted onto his state-of-the-art laptop. Tonight the roles were reversed. He would write freehand, like the scribes of old, but his second-hand sagacity would be poached, not from the past, but from the future.

It was a mistake. Deep down, he had known the quote was not altogether suitable. He'd tried to help it out with a Kirk-style dramatic delivery but . . . Oh well, at least his ride on the Starship *Enterprise* had not been completely wasted, his problems not completely unsolved. His mind flashed back to Lenore, the daughter of Kodos the Executioner.

'Greatness,' he went on, emerging apparently unscathed from the smouldering wreckage of his sci-fi allusion, 'true greatness, is a rare thing. Most people never even come into contact with it. But you will. You will come into contact with greatness, tonight.' As these words were leaving Billiam's mouth, a little man was racing around, inside his head, hastily constructing a speech that did not include the other *Star Trek* references he had lined up. He was particularly sorry to lose his little digression on Morton's unique recipe for jerky. All day long he'd looked forward to the laugh he would surely get with 'Spice, the final frontier', but now he had lost his nerve.

The little man, however, had found a couple of quotes in the back of a brain-cell filing cabinet and perhaps Billiam could weave them into his now slightly faltering address. Admittedly, there was no obvious tie-in with 'The longest journey starts with a single step' or 'The living are merely the dead on holiday' but he was determined to include these pearls of wisdom if he could.

During this internal deliberation, his mouth was operating almost independently: 'Of course, we over-use the word, "great". I mean, the Great Wall of China, is it really "great"? Or is it just long? Clearly, it's just long, but no one's going to fly all that way to see the Long Wall of China. Not that length is a bad thing, of course.' Here, he got his first laugh, but didn't know why. 'I mean, Morton's beef jerky is long. Most jerkys come in bite-sized chunks but Morton's comes in a nine-inch strip. So it's long, but it's also great. The so-called Great Wall is just, well, long.' He suddenly brightened. 'Still, you know what they say; "The longest jerky begins with a single bite."'

The blank expressions of the crowd could do nothing to dampen Billiam's euphoria. He had set up the specialness of the occasion, sung the praises of Morton's jerky, and not only incorporated a quote he had just, this second, called to mind, but tailored it to his specific needs. James T. Kirk's lame remark was a distant memory. The crowd, of course, would never know the public speaker juggling act he had just pulled off, but he knew, and he felt good. OK, he had clearly offended the two Chinese guys in the corner but, if you're going to make an omelette ... Anyway, back, with new-found confidence, to the main event.

'Remember this moment, ladies and gentlemen. Remember this sense of anticipation. In fact, I would advise you to remember as much as you can about tonight. It'll be a story you tell for the rest of your life.' He pointed to the door that Geoff had been watching all evening. 'Greatness lies just the other side of that door. And soon it will be amongst us.' Billiam lowered his hand. He waited, sure now that he had 311 people hanging on his every word.

Geoff was completely still, eyeing the door handle, unable to move before it did. Even the TV crew, despite their career-long battle against the forces of enthusiasm, were beginning to look slightly less bored. Karen, however, remained oblivious to the electricity of anticipation as it crackled in the air. She, opening wine bottles in an adjoining room, was too busy weighing up the pros and cons of slipping the word 'topless' into her conversation with the Enrique fan.

Billiam savoured the silence, let it hang there, let it take the air from the room. Then he went on, 'Ladies and gentlemen ...' Fingers flexed, anticipating applause but Billiam could not resist one last moment of silence, one last pull on the emotional reins, one last showcase for his suspense-management skills. He briefly closed his eyes – perhaps an anti-gremlin incantation – then opened them again, and spoke the name that 311 people were aching to hear: 'Thunderman'.

Applause ensued, flesh against flesh, the sharp violence of the individual clap repeated, multiplied and thus transformed into a rich, interwoven network of sounds. A bearded technician in a 'Hendrix Lives' sweat-top pressed a button and the tiny pockets of silence, which aerated that applause, were filled by the oily orchestration of 'The

Thunderman March'. Sounds became sound and only then did the door handle begin to turn and, as it turned, it seemed, like a dial on a radio, to turn up the volume of the whole room. Louder, still louder and then, as the turn reached maximum, the door opened. And there stood Karen, with a new bottle of wine, a new smile and new sticking plaster on her ankle. The applause faltered and might have collapsed altogether, were it not for the booming buoyancy of the music, urging it to stagger on.

Karen stood in the doorway, glowing as if she had walked into a surprise party of family and friends. Then, suddenly, she flinched; not the near invisible flutter of an upper lip or the delicate tremble of an eye. It was a silent movie flinch, big enough to reach the cheap seats but real enough to make you care. It would be hard to estimate how many facial muscles were employed, but most of them seemed to be in spasm. When Geoff looked back at Billiam, he half-expected him to be holding a smouldering firearm. But all Billiam held was his smile; well, not so much 'held' as 'clung to', like a shipwrecked man clung to a bobbing chest of drawers. It was not what you'd call 'seaworthy' but it was all he had. Yet, still, he mechanically clapped his chubby hands, knowing that, if he stopped, the already teetering applause construct might crumble, leaving the Thunderman March plaintive and unpercussed.

The gremlins had snubbed his supplication. Oh, the music was right on cue, the door did not stick or stutter, but why was this fat-ankled girl in the doorway, and why had Thunderman just squeezed her bottom?

CHAPTER TWO

From his onstage vantage point, Billiam was the only person in the room who could accurately deconstruct Karen's flinch into its shock-fear-pain components. Now, the acid-anticipation of her post-grope response was making his stomach swirl. He considered the facts, as he saw them. If modern America, excluding those citizens who had 'The South will rise again' etched across their gunstocks, had a league table of socially unacceptable behaviour, worst at the top, working downward to the not so bad, squeezing a woman's bottom without her permission would be below rape but several places above mass murder. An Arkansas teenager walks into his local hardware store, takes out a samurai sword, and turns half a dozen citizens into steak tartare: this would probably be seen, certainly by the liberals, lesbians and left-wing millionaire film stars who constitute the political correctness policy control unit, as an inevitable and completely justifiable response to a childhood of beatings and Beastie Boy songs. If, however, on the way out of the store, he squeezes a woman's bottom, let that low-life fry.

Nowadays, even in Italy, a country where, in a black-and-white *dolce vita* past, the tight, mysterious bottoms of haughty, young Loren-look-alikes were squeezed by sweaty, unshaven pasta chefs, taking cigarette breaks outside restaurants, and the massive near-equine haunches of middle-aged housewives were treated similarly, at bus stops, by tooth-less old men whose greying moustaches rose upward with their ensuing smiles, squeezing women's bottoms is an absolute no-no. How then was such behaviour regarded in the United Kingdom? Billiam was about to find out. He considered a joke about being 'touched by greatness' but felt it might make matters worse.

Karen turned to Thunderman. Within the whoops and whistles and booming brass, she heard a high-pitched scream, like that of a terrified child. She knew at once the scream could only be hers, a spontaneous, indignant shriek, rising up from the epicentre of her femininity, no, from the Mother Earthly core of all femininity, a cry not just for herself but for every violated women.

Thunderman towered above her in a black catsuit, black body-armour and black leather 15-hole assault boots. You had to say he was themed. He was dressed for elegant enforcement – a sort of Armani riot cop. In the old days he had been masked, but now he stood broad-shouldered and bareheaded, hair cropped, teeth capped, and dark, dark eyes that you hoped, for his sake, were not the windows of his soul. On his chest, was the grey cloud logo that had, in blood-stained alleyways and hypodermic-strewn apartments, in hugger-mugger boardrooms and too-scared-to-scream bordellos, caused the most ruthless, amoral wrongdoers to pause, to reconsider, and often to run. The same logo that now graced the packaging on Morton's Beef Jerky.

In the panoply of smiles that we have, thus far, considered, his was perhaps the most surprising, the most mysterious. It seemed profoundly inappropriate on the face of a man who'd just closed his steel-strong fingers on the tender butt-flesh of a woman he did not know, a man who now stood looking into the eyes of that woman, as they slowly filled with tears. His smile suggested great warmth, great humanity. If it was false, it was a masterpiece of supra-corporate guile, contrasting with Billiam's grin as Method does with melodrama. It completely threw Karen. Of course, having been applauded by a large group of strangers, unexpectedly grabbed in a sexual way, and then forced to accept that the probing fingers belonged to a man who, despite trauma and tragedy, had given his life, almost exclusively, to the righting of wrong, Karen was already a little thrown, but it was that inappropriate smile that sat teardrops on her lower lids. Even his dark, dark eyes, eyes that suggested a mournful memory of Hell glimpsed, seemed to soften, seemed almost illuminated by that smile.

It made her uneasy, it mocked her world-view, each one of her definitelys became a perhaps. It said that vice mingled with virtue, that brutish misogyny could dwell alongside compassionate humanitarianism. She knew famous men became cruel and corrupt, like Roman emperors. Star-struck girls hung from them, almost unnoticed, as they indulged their evil celebrity-opportunities. They were sucked as they snorted, rimmed as they raged, begged for kind caresses as they popcorned their way through snuff movies and horse sex videos, where crack-slave women looked accusingly to camera as once-noble beasts emptied themselves into their sad mouths. That was fame. She knew because her cousin had been out with a guy from *Emmerdale*. And she knew such men grabbed at young girls, young girls who were just trying to do their job, keeping the guests topped up and cheerful. Grabbed not even their buttocks but just below, feverishly searching for unprompted intimacy, for private places, for licence without love. Karen knew all that, but what she did not know was that they could smile such goodness.

For a half second of that smile, she scratched around for a scenario that would explain this contradiction. Had he stumbled, reached out to save himself and then, by sheer mischance, grasped support just a few millimetres from her anus. Had months of scientific study, a module, she imagined, on some super-hero degree course, enabled him to recognise a rare and dangerous insect on her skirt that he had then, putting his own safety to one side, lunged at, his probing fingers like a lizard-tongue taking out the unsuspecting bug.

Now it was her doing the clutching, at straws that snapped and splintered at her grasp. Then, amidst the stubble, she gripped a firm and sinuous stem that gave her purchase to rise up above her confusion, to taste the fresh air of reason. 'Maybe it wasn't him. Yeah, that's it. But if it wasn't him, who was it?'

Just beyond the doorway, just beyond the righter of wrong, stood an elderly man, slim and moustachioed, wearing the compulsory greys and beiges of senior citizen chic. He was avoiding her stare, peering into the room as if seeking a friend. Karen decided that he would soon be seeking a general practitioner. She slid past the celebrated crime fighter, closing the door behind her. Thunderman stood inside the room, raising a hand to punch the air, and Karen stood outside the room, raising a hand to punch the old-age pensioner. Incidentally, the old man was only there to ask if anyone owned the silver-grey Ford Focus that was blocking him in.

Billiam was still attempting to decipher all he had witnessed. A few seconds earlier, Thunderman had self-destructed. His reputation, his career, his deal with Morton's beef jerky, the newly released paperback edition of his best-selling autobiography, *It's a Thunderful World*, all lay in ruins, just because he couldn't keep his hands to himself. What then of Billiam? Though he wore the sponsor's logo, he did not work for them. He worked for Thunderman: business manager, personal assistant, confidante, friend. His career was inextricably tied to the man in black; they were going down together. That prurient prod had finished them both. Billiam imagined how the *Wall Street Journal* would celebrate the ghastly incident and their resulting ruin. He could see the banner headline: 'The goose that cracked the golden egg'. It was too much. For one brief but remarkable moment, he ceased to clap and to smile and, cloaked by the martial music and roaring crowd, he released a high-pitched scream, like that of a terrified child. A scream that only the fat-ankled girl seemed to hear. A scream that, though he would never know it, she had claimed as the plaintive howl of woman-hood.

But now Billiam's scream seemed premature. There had been no face-slap, no loud declamation, but wait. Where was she heading now, with such intensity of purpose? He had to follow her, to bribe, to beg, to browbeat, whatever it took. He had to save himself. He had to save Thunderman.

As the hero's handshaking, aw-shucks sideshow slowly moved towards the stage, Billiam passed in the opposite direction, his heart sinking as he smelled alcohol on Thunderman's breath. Trouble, it seemed, lay within and without. In a moment of spine-twisting in-decision, he turned with trepidation towards the conquering hero, but his feet dragged him doorward, to the chequebook charm-offensive that lay without.

Geoff had not moved towards the main attraction. Geoff had not moved at all. He was taking Billiam's advice. Remembering. Savouring every second and actively, almost physically, slotting it into his memory banks like a supermarket assistant dextrously packing a grocery bag. Many cameras flashed but not Geoff's. He was capturing images that would be developed, not for wallet-sized souvenirs but for inspirational retablos. Geoff wanted to carry these moments in his heart, not in his pocket.

Karen's flinch, however, had not made the cut. He had not thought it relevant, unconnected, as it clearly was, to the great man's arrival. It was probably part and parcel of her indolent eye; some sort of uncorrected post-war squint that her yogi put down to the misdeeds of a previous life.

Of course, this night's collectable memories were not all visual. The current one, for example – the sound of black leather 15-hole assault boots against a 10 mm hardboard stage.

Karen was not a violent person. She'd once dragged her fingernails down the face of a chap who'd tried to kiss her at a Christmas party but she'd been shopping all day and made herself tense. The would-be kisser had stopped in his tracks, taken aback by the extremity of her rebuttal. She'd stared at the four wounds – the dribbling blood made Christmassy by traces of her glitter nail varnish – then walked away to check her lipstick, almost certainly smudged in the assault. Night-clubbers stared. His wounds bloomed into even clearer definition. Boys thought of Bruce Lee in *Enter the Dragon*, girls thought of Adam Ant.

Despite that single lapse which, after all, had only happened because they'd sold out of singing fishes and she'd eased her resulting anguish with too much Tia Maria, Karen was essentially anti-violence. However, her new regime of non-exploitation by men, in order to be practical, required a muscular deterrent. In the corridor outside the Jack the Ripper Suite, a cowering, moustachioed pensioner was becoming her Hiroshima and Nagasaki.

As Thunderman stood, now visible to the whole room, the roar increased, palms reddened. Hendrix Lives, more professional than his pothead demeanour suggested, eased down the music lest timpani thundered louder than love. The hero stood there. There were no 'simmer down' gestures, no raised-voice interruptions, he just stood. He savoured their applause; he warm-showered in their whooping; he had no desire to cut them short. Billiam, though outside the room trying to negotiate an out-of-court settlement, and considerably distracted by a senior citizen hugging his leg and screaming 'Help me!' timed the ovation at two minutes, 27 seconds. Eventually, Thunderman spoke.

'Thank you very much. I worked out that I haven't been in England for nearly five years. I thought you might have forgotten me.' It was a remark calculated to provoke more applause and even a few cries of 'no' and 'never'. It worked. Thunderman gripped the edges of the lectern. Geoff looked at his left hand. It was another snapshot for the memory book. The third finger was missing. Web-lore said that Thunderman had deliberately severed it, wedding ring and all, when his wife was murdered. He vowed he would never marry again, never put anyone else in that kind of danger, so the finger became superfluous. Its absence symbolised hers, reminded him that that kind of closeness would always end in loss, and in agony. If the finger wasn't there, he couldn't be tempted to put another ring on it.

This was speculation. Thunderman had never spoken of the missing finger, no interviewer had dared to ask the question, it did not feature in *It's a Thunderful World*, but still the chat rooms prattled, the forums held forth. Of course, the FAQ to end all FAQs was 'Where's the finger now?' Endless cyber-spiel ensued. Chuggy claimed to have seen it in the aftermath of a fan convention in Amsterdam. As they rolled up the posters and put the unsold plastic body armour back in the crates he was, he claimed, approached by a 'weedy guy in specks' who had the finger in a knotted condom. Thundo said a man phoned his comic shop in Idaho and offered him the digit for $10,000. Bernard said he actually had the finger in his possession and would give it back to 'it's originnal owner' [sic] if he contacted the website. So the misspelled speculation and ungrammatical gossip mongering went on.

Having established that England had not forgotten him, Thunderman continued to manipulate the crowd. 'Obviously, I would have been back sooner but, honestly, I've been rushed off my feet. I've had to spend a lot of time in Hollywood.' More applause but not from Geoff, who hated *Thunderman: The Movie*, hated hunky Mel Miller, who played the title role, hated 'The Thunderman March', that was its main theme. He also hated *It's a Thunderful World*, be it in paperback, hardback or in audiobook form. He would also have hated it on processed beef, had the idea occurred to him. Geoff hated the whole 'Thunderman as celebrity' thing. Why didn't the crime-fighter just fight crime, like in the old days? What happened to that English kid who read American comic books and then decided to do it for real, and who *did* do it for real, to the point where he would actually shout 'Let the storm begin' as he sprang into action, delivering his battle cry with no irony, no archness, with none of the Roger-Moore-as-James-Bond-I-know-this-is-silly-but-it's-in-the-script self-awareness that Mel Miller felt compelled to employ? When Thunderman said 'Let the storm begin' there was no post-modernist wink to camera. He meant it. And the storm he spoke of was the old-fashioned battle between good and evil, a storm that ripped and roared at those bold enough to brave it but a storm that was followed by skies bluer and brighter than any seen by the legions of look-the-other-way, gutless skulkers who populated modern society. Their undignified don't-want-to-get-involved wretchedness left them to walk in endless, spirit-sapping drizzle.

But that was the old Thunderman, who said, live on CBS news 'We have come to believe that evil cannot be defeated. We cower, we look at our feet, and few bad men spoil the lives of millions because millions allow them to do so. (Now turning to camera, very much sans wink) 'Well, if there's any bad men out there watching, you'd better come and get me because, if you don't, I'm going to come and get you.' Geoff smiled as he remembered how the wilful simplicity of the phrase, 'bad men' had given the threat an Old Testament-like power.

But that was the old Thunderman, who fought a seemingly one-man battle against badness, without macho posturing or Dirty Harry right-wing radicalism and, at the same time, had the courage to tell the well-intentioned would-be liberal reformers why, sometimes, you needed an iron fist in a socially conscientious glove; who championed addict help centres and literacy programmes but could still sleep easy, 40 minutes after throwing a paedophile off a skyscraper.

This Thunderman, plugging his paperback on the beef jerky sponsored 'Thunderman at 50' personal appearances tour; this Thunderman, who sold a range of 'all-action thermal clothing' with the slogan 'Let the warm begin'; this Thunderman was different. Or was he? Geoff felt, in his heart, that if he could just talk to the man in black; if he could just remind him of what he meant to those who cherished the legend; he could bring the real Thunderman back, not from the dead, but from this cold storage of soul-emptying celebrity.

In the corridor, Karen, her own iron fist slightly blooded, was confused. If someone had said to her, a few minutes earlier, 'What do you think would happen if you hit a senior citizen?' she would have offered a few, quite obvious, suggestions: 'I'd be overwhelmed by a terrible sense of guilt; I'd be restrained by passers-by; I'd be arrested by the police.' All these would have sprung to mind. What, almost certainly, would not have not sprung to mind is 'A man in a bright blue suit would hand me a cheque for ten thousand pounds.' Such was the unpredictability of life.

She had stopped punching the old man now and was, instead, tugging viciously at his moustache as if trying to unmask a man-of-a-thousand-faces master criminal, her grip made easier by the clotted nose-blood that gave a new graspability to the once silky 'tache.

The pensioner, his top lip pulled upward to reveal that tell-tale ridge where denture meets gum, was considering an old adage about how 'for the want of a nail, the shoe was lost', a repetitive incantation he remembered from a David Niven movie that illustrated how one small event could have disastrous consequences. It had been three days since he had gawped at this young woman's breasts in the hotel lift, and he'd been sure she hadn't noticed. Furthermore, because, on returning, invigorated, to his room, he'd had sex with his wife for the first time in three and a half months, he'd since come to feel that his elevator ogle was morally justified, a sort of 'white leer'; he had, after all, turned his base instinct into the gold of marital love. But no! He was paying now for committing adultery in his heart – no mean feat when you've got a pacemaker. Clearly, God was just and quick to punish and, the old man reasoned, if this beating was payback for a casual breastward stare, he had best abandon his recently hatched plan to murder his wife and take a teenage Filipina bride, or things could get completely out of hand.

Thus, an old lady sat knitting, in the passenger seat of a car on the

Majestica car park, not knowing that, in the corridor outside the Jack the Ripper Suite, her fragile but not unhappy life was being extended for a few more years. Thanks to a lecherous lawman, a confused events assistant and a misplaced Ford Focus she would indeed finish that cardigan.

'There's an old Hollywood saying,' Thunderman continued, '"Always get a part of the action", but I have my own version: "Always get a part of the action figures!"' As he said this he produced, from behind his body armour, action figures of himself and Ed Berry, the serial killer he had wrestled with on a rickety fifth-floor Brooklyn balcony whilst crowds oohed and aahed in the street below. During the film-version of this tussle, Mel Miller called down to the awestruck spectators, 'Sorry to do this on the balcony but the air-con's broken.' In the non-film version Thunderman was too busy completely gouging out Berry's left eye to indulge in such badinage. The 'action figures' line, however, was a smash. The anxious uncertainty that gripped the crowd, post-*Star Trek* quote, was now, finally, exorcised. They had regained their joke-recognition confidence and celebrated the fact with a chorus of guffaws. They say a cameraman smiled. In fact, laughter and applause exploded so loudly that the Jack the Ripper Suite could not contain the sound.

In the corridor, the noise hit like a laughter bomb, shocking the combatants into silence. Karen let go of the old man's moustache, the old man let go of Billiam's leg, Billiam let go of the cheque for ten thousand pounds and the two Chinese men let go of Billiam's throat. What's more, the Orientals stopped repeatedly saying 'Why not great? Why not great?' and suddenly stood motionless, like terracotta soldiers, their duty done, waiting for the next command.

Geoff, of course, did not laugh, but he was still packing that grocery bag. He had noticed that TM, as they called him on the websites, had flashed a couple of winning smiles to a rock-chick type, with a red streak running through her jet black hair, who stood on a chair at the back of the room. Since the death of his wife, Thunderman had decided it was too dangerous to enter into a long-term relationship with any woman. He had sat in a lonely hotel room, one night, considering his emotional future. Finally, he saw that there were only two possible options: a life of celibacy, or a never-ending string of meaningless one-night stands. He resolved to sleep on it. His eyelids were about one-third of the way down his eyeballs before he'd made his decision. Twenty minutes later, he was speaking to a well-dressed blonde in the hotel bar. Twenty minutes after that he was autographing the condom.

Since then, the thunderstorm had been replaced by several hundred scattered showers. TM flashed another winning smile and now the red-streak rock-chick was smiling back. Geoff, however, was using more muscles than the two of them put together. He saw the whole groupie thing as another example of Thunderman's decline. In the old days, the only time TM held a stranger's ankles was when he dangled stubbornly secretive miscreants from high buildings, Ed Berry had had that treatment, dripping both vitreous and aqueous humour on the crowds below, now Thunderman was becoming that most unpleasant of all creatures, a ladies' man. He was becoming Mel Miller. Life was imitating bad art.

Geoff had nothing against the red-streaked lady, he told himself. He was against their apparently imminent union only because the strength she would sap from Thunderman, the time she would take away, wasn't rightly hers. It belonged to the people, the good people who, fear-stricken by grim foreboding, needed a champion to hold back the dark tide, a warrior to watch over them. If he was going to mount anything, it should be an endless vigil, not a woman in a Def Leppard T-shirt. It was that forsaken responsibility that made Geoff frown. That was why he disapproved of Thunderman's flirtation with this lady. Geoff, very definitely, had no problem whatsoever with her dwarfism.

Index

Acknowledgements

Special thanks to Anne Spackman and Robbie Millen at *The Times*, Cathy Galvin at the *Sunday Times*, Katherine Minnis, Alice Russell and Hannah Wilkinson at Avalon, my personal assistant, Jenny Canty, and especially to my manager, Jon Thoday, on our twentieth anniversary.